The Park Builders

*A History of State Parks
in the Pacific Northwest*

The Park Builders

*A History of State Parks
in the Pacific Northwest*

Thomas R. Cox

UNIVERSITY OF WASHINGTON PRESS

Seattle and London

Library of Congress Cataloging-in-Publication Data

Cox, Thomas R., 1933–
  The park builders.

  Includes index.
  1. Parks—Northwest, Pacific—History. I. Title.
II. Title: State parks in the Pacific northwest.
SB482.N94C69   1988   333.78'3'0975   88-5462

ISBN 0-295-96613-0

An earlier version of Chapter 3 appeared as "The Crusade to Save
Oregon's Scenery," *Pacific Historical Review* 37 (1968): 179–200, and of
Chapter 4 as "Conservation by Subterfuge: Robert W. Sawyer and the
Birth of the Oregon State Parks," in *Pacific Northwest Quarterly* 64 (1973):
21–29. Part of Chapter 2 appeared in "Weldon Heyburn, Lake Chatcolet,
and the Evolving Concept of Public Parks," *Idaho Yesterdays* 24 (1980): 2–16.
All are used here with permission of their respective publishers.

Text design by Judy Petry

Contents

Illustrations

Governor Albert Rosellini with daughters
Governor Tom McCall fly fishing
Robert Straub with aerial photographs of Oregon Coast
Glenn Jackson's swearing in as chair of Oregon Highway
    Commission

Maps

Preface

State parks are far more important than is generally recognized. They are visited by more people each year than are national parks, even though their collective budgets are far smaller. They play a major role in the tourist trade, which is a key element in the economy of many states. Their history tells much about changing patterns of recreation and much else in American society.

But that history is brief. Few state parks existed prior to the twentieth century; then they came with a rush. In the 1920s park building became a virtual crusade, and the National Conference on State Parks emerged to coordinate and encourage it. However haltingly, Oregon and Washington were swept along by events. By the 1950s the development and management of parks had become a generally accepted function of state governments across the land; even Idaho, the regional laggard, joined its western neighbors in building them. What had started as a campaign of dedicated private individuals had come to be dominated by parks professionals, bureaucrats, and politicians. This change hardly comes as a surprise, for it reflects transformations in American society as a whole. The story of state parks thus has ramifications that extend far beyond the confines of conservation, recreation, and scenery preservation.

Long ignored in scholarly literature, state parks have in recent years begun to receive the attention their importance warrants. Ronald J. Fahl's comprehensive *Bibliography of North American Forest and Conservation History*, published in 1976, lists some seventy-six articles dealing with state parks. The vast majority came out during the preceding two decades; many more have appeared since. But much remains to be done. Existing works, although numerous, have tended to be narrowly focused geographically, usually dealing with a single park or state. Few try to place their subjects within their changing social, political, and economic milieu, let alone to evaluate their contributions to these changes.

This volume attempts to cast a broader net. It traces the development of state parks systems in Oregon, Washington, and Idaho, places events in these states in a national context, and compares them with one another. More than a study of state parks, it is a study of the evolution of recreation, conservation, and government. It demonstrates that, for all the importance of the larger forces of class and group, individuals have played a key role in shaping America's parks—and, by implication, policies and government in other areas as well. Finally, however indirectly, it shows the internal differences that have served to make the Pacific Northwest more a label of geographic convenience than a region in the truer sense of the term.

This work began with far more modest aims. Some thirty years ago, when I was a beginning graduate student, Earl Pomeroy suggested that a history of Oregon's state parks would make a good master's thesis. The University of Oregon library, he said, had just acquired the papers of Robert W. Sawyer, which were rich with materials on the subject. I took on the task, encouraged by Edwin R. Bingham, who helped me to see the value of a semi-biographical approach to the contributions of Sawyer, Ben Olcott, and others who played central roles in the events I was tracing. As I pursued the story of Oregon's parks, I found myself continually being led beyond the state's borders. To understand what was going on inside the state, it seemed necessary to study events outside—especially in neighboring states. After years of false starts, delays, and detours, this book has emerged. It bears small resemblance to the study originally planned, but it is the product of that undertaking nonetheless.

The debts owed to Earl Pomeroy and Ed Bingham are immense, but others in the scholarly world contributed to this work in major ways too. Ronald J. Fahl and Raymond Starr, good friends as well as professional colleagues, provided more help than they realized by their continued interest and encouragement. When it came into penultimate form, Fahl, Richard T. Ruetten, and Douglas H. Strong read the entire manuscript and made many useful suggestions. Starr, Merle Wells, and Judith Austin read individual chapters. Lawrence Rakestraw, drawing upon his own vast knowledge of conservation in the Pacific Northwest, supplied materials as well as suggestions.

Elisabeth Walton, Richard Berner, and the late Martin Schmitt provided guidance and encouragement—as well as vital documents.

Also invaluable was the help and cooperation of principals. Governors Robert E. Smylie and Robert Straub, and parks superintendents John Emmert, Chester Armstrong, David G. Talbot, Clayton Anderson, and Charles Odegaard provided materials, support, and remarkably candid interviews. Informants could hardly be more helpful than these men were. I hope that the end result merits the trust in me and in the value of historical research that each of them showed. Research grants from the San Diego State University Foundation and a travel grant from the National Endowment for the Humanities helped to bring the study to fruition.

To all of these and to the many others who aided me, I express my gratitude. I am delighted to have this work done at last, not only because it feels good to be finished, but also because completion is the only way I have of paying the debt I owe to all those who have lent their support. Small though the repayment is, I hope that they all realize with how much gratitude it is made.

Thomas R. Cox
San Diego, California
January 1988

The Park Builders

*A History of State Parks
in the Pacific Northwest*

Chapter 1

The Northwest and the Nation
A Parks Movement in the Making

In January 1921 some two hundred people met in Des Moines, Iowa, at the invitation of Governor W. L. Harding. The gathering was the first in a long series of annual meetings of the National Conference on State Parks, a group resulting from apparent need and the encouragement—including financial aid—of Stephen T. Mather, director of the National Park Service. In spite of short advance notice, representatives from twenty-eight states attended. A major movement for state parks was already under way, as the large turnout and crowded program showed, but creation of the NCSP encouraged, focused, and drew attention to it as never before.[1]

Mather had mixed motives in fostering the NCSP. On the one hand, he was a dedicated preservationist eager to protect America's scenery from destruction. On the other, as director of the National Park Service, he knew well the continual pressure to extend national park status to new sites, many not up to the standards he was striving to maintain. State parks offered a way to protect sites of local or regional significance while reducing pressures on the NPS. Mather had been working to encourage state parks even before the gathering in Des Moines; creating the NCSP represented a continuation of the effort.[2]

But state parks existed long before there was a state parks movement, let alone an association to foster it. Some suggest that Massachusetts Bay Colony took the first action leading to state parks (or the equivalent) in 1641, when it set aside the colony's "Great

Ponds"—bodies of fresh water of ten or more acres, a total of some 90,000 acres—as reserves for hunting and fishing. Actually, the purpose behind this action was more utilitarian than recreational; and, while the act assured the public of access to major waters, it was largely forgotten until 1923. Massachusetts did not acquire Mount Greylock, its first real park, until 1898. The Great Ponds Act did have a lasting impact, however, for in Maine—a part of Massachusetts until 1820—it has remained in force to the present, providing the basis for public access to fishing and hunting on privately owned riverfronts and shorelands. But even in Maine, it did nothing to bring parks into existence; when parks appeared in that state, they arrived by a different route.[3]

The real vanguard of state parks did not appear until after the Civil War. True, in 1820 Governor DeWitt Clinton, wanting to protect sources of water for the Erie Canal, did urge New York's legislature to halt the sale of state land in the Adirondack Mountains. But not until 1872—the year Congress established Yellowstone National Park— was a bill to create Adirondack Park actually introduced into the state legislature. Not until 1885 did legislators finally act, stopping land sales in the area and authorizing Adirondack State Forest, which was to evolve into the nation's largest state park (embracing over 2.5 million acres of public land). In 1885 New York also established a "state reservation" at the falls of the Niagara River; it was a full-fledged park from the outset.[4]

Some of the early state parks later changed status. In 1864 Congress authorized Yosemite Valley and the nearby Mariposa Grove of giant sequoias as a state park. California accepted the land two years later. After prolonged controversy and charges of mismanagement, this land was returned to the federal government in 1906 and incorporated into Yosemite National Park. Reversing the process, in 1875 federal authorities created Mackinac National Park on Mackinac Island, Michigan, and then in 1895 ceded it to Michigan to become Mackinac Island State Park. Wisconsin also acted early, setting aside several tracts of state-owned timberland as a "park" in 1878. Wisconsin's primary purpose appears to have been watershed protection for flood control. The land was never administered as a park—indeed, it was simply ignored until it was disposed of beginning in 1897.[5]

Out of all of this has come a welter of claims for the first state park. Sites in Massachusetts, California, and New York have all been accorded the honor. Others probably could be added to the list. Of them all, Niagara Falls has the best case for primacy. No state park still in existence was established earlier; none of the great ponds of Massachusetts were actually treated as parks until long after Niagara was created.

Around the turn of the century, increasing numbers of states began setting aside scenic, historic, and recreational sites as parks. In 1893 Minnesota established two: Birch Coulee, the location of a battle between whites and Sioux, and Itasca, located around the headwaters of the Mississippi. In 1895 New York and New Jersey created the nucleus of Palisades Interstate Park, located along the Hudson; in 1902 California launched Big Basin Redwoods State Park in response to a campaign by citizens of nearby communities; and in 1909 Wisconsin became the first state to develop a plan for a statewide system of parks. By 1919, when Mather began traveling widely to encourage the preservation of scenery at the state and local levels, some twenty states already owned parks.[6]

Appreciation of the outdoors had long been in evidence in the Pacific Northwest, but no real parks movement emerged in the region until the second decade of the twentieth century. Idaho's first state park came into being in 1911, Washington's in 1915; Oregon trailed, not obtaining its first state park until 1920. Pacific Northwest states occasionally pioneered developments—as Oregon did behind the leadership of Samuel H. Boardman—but for the most part they represented the solid mainstream of the movement.[7]

Far from the nation's main centers of population, wealth, and intellectual activity, Northwesterners approached park building slowly. The first American settlers in Oregon's Willamette Valley wrote glowing accounts of its fertile soil and equable climate, but seldom of its scenic beauties. Still, with limited capital and few cultural outlets, they, like early settlers in Washington and Idaho, frequently took their entertainment out of doors. By the 1860s Oregonians were going to the mountains during the summer and fall for hunting, fishing, berry picking, and relaxation. Residents in the Palouse country of eastern Washington and Idaho often took refuge from summer heat by retreating to the cool forests around Coeur d'Alene, Chatcolet, and Hayden lakes.[8]

Mount Hood, the most accessible of the Northwest's major peaks, was first scaled in the 1850s and with increasing frequency thereafter. Climbers did not attain the top of Mount Rainier until 1870, but as early as 1834 Dr. William Fraser Tolmie, a young Scot employed by the Hudson's Bay Company, was drawn to Rainier, the most massive of the region's peaks, and ascended to well above timberline. In 1887 a group of Portland-area residents joined to form the Oregon Alpine Club, the first mountaineering club in the West. It engaged in far more than mountain climbing, serving to advertise the region's scenery and to encourage its appreciation. Anyone interested could join. In 1894 a group of purists, insisting that only real mountain climbers belonged in an alpine club, withdrew to form the Mazamas. The new organization proved even more active than its forerunner in championing the scenic beauties of the alpine Northwest.[9]

The seashore drew people too. By the 1870s Northwesterners had taken to vacationing in coastal towns like Seaside, Gearhart, and Newport, and clambakes on the beach had become favorite social occasions in Coos Bay and other communities.[10]

Recreation developed appreciation. Residents of the Pacific Northwest gradually came to cherish the scenic beauty that most of the first settlers seem to have taken for granted. One early manifestation was Oregon's—and the region's—first public park. After a long legal battle, Thomas S. Summers, a Willamette Valley settler, established his claim to a tract of land east of the town of Lebanon. In 1871 he platted a townsite around a mineral spring on the property and named it "Sodaville." In his plat he designated the block that included the spring for public use; "nature's special gifts," he explained, "are not intended for private exploitation."[11]

Summers was ahead of his time. Few were ready to tackle the problems of preserving "nature's special gifts," but many were at least becoming conscious of them. In time this led to action. William A. Goulder wrote a long article in the Boise *Idaho Statesman* in 1876, lauding the glories of Shoshone Falls on the Snake River. By 1898 Senator George Shoup was working to have the public land around the falls withdrawn from entry so that it would not be taken up by private claimants under the Carey Act and its beauty ruined in order to bring water to thirsty land nearby.[12] In 1899, responding to other local spokesmen, President William McKinley signed a bill creating Mount Rainier National Park. Similarly, when explorers discovered a magnificent crater-rimmed lake in the southern Cascades, the region's press helped spread the news, extolling the beauties of "Lake Majesty." Concerted local pressure—led by William Gladstone Steel, first president of the Mazamas—resulted in the establishment of Crater Lake National Park in 1902.[13] By 1911 a less successful campaign was under way to get Idaho's Sawtooth Mountains set aside as a national park too.[14]

Others were also at work. In Portland Leo Samuel turned out promotional pieces publicizing the beauties of the Northwest. His *Columbia River Illustrated*, published in 1886, was one of the first indicators of the growing affection of Portlanders for the gorge created by the Columbia as it ground its way through the Cascade Range toward the sea. Simpler sights moved Frances Fuller Victor, later to gain minor fame as an historian. In 1876 she published "An Oregon Spring," a poem voicing her appreciation of the natural beauty of the region. Similar works, most with little if any literary merit, flowed from the pens of other Northwestern writers. Bit by bit, the groundwork for scenery preservation was being laid, and here and there action was beginning.[15]

More than the passage of time lay behind this growing interest in the out-of-doors. The Pacific Northwest was changing in ways that encouraged appreciation of nature. The population was growing; life was becoming more urban and complex.

The 1880s were pivotal. After suffering through depression during much of the preceding decade, the region witnessed the return of prosperity, spurred on by the completion of transcontinental rail connections. With prosperity came renewed confidence, and with the railroads came a flood of outside investment capital and new residents. Washington, though its white settlements came later than Oregon's, and it did not become a state until 1889, forged ahead, thanks largely to its superior harbors. Washington's population grew some 380 percent during the decade; Oregon's only 80 percent. Tacoma changed from a minor village to a city that some thought was destined soon to pass Portland in size; east of the Cascades, Spokane's growth was almost as dramatic. New businesses sprang up everywhere. In the forefront were a number of large sawmill firms erected by lumbermen from Minnesota, Wisconsin, and Michigan who moved to the Pacific Northwest in anticipation of the day when the commercial stands of timber in the Lake States would be gone. Most of these firms, like most of the new residents, located in

Washington rather than Oregon. Idaho lagged in population, as it always had, but its rate of growth was also more spectacular than Oregon's. Between 1880 and 1890, Idaho's population showed a net gain of 171 percent.[16]

Oregon's topography partly accounted for its slower growth. Much of western Washington's timber was accessible to early logging technology. Vast stands in Oregon remained locked behind mountain and canyon barriers until the logging truck and railroad construction up the Deschutes River canyon opened extensive new timberlands in the twentieth century.[17]

But Oregon's deliberate pace may have resulted from social factors too. Samuel Bowles, the influential editor of the *Springfield* (Massachusetts) *Republican*, once described Portland as more like a New England city than any other he had seen in the West. The outlook Bowles detected seems to have been reflected in Portland's business world as well as in other matters. Leo Samuel, looking at the way Washington was outstripping Oregon during the eighties, decried in his magazine *West Shore* the "mossback" conservatism of his city's business leaders. On other occasions, when boom turned to bust north of the Columbia, he was smugly satisfied. Oregonians, he noted, had not gotten carried away with speculative, get-rich-quick schemes, but had moved at their own deliberate pace to lay a solid foundation for lasting prosperity.[18]

There was a seed of truth in Samuel's assessment. Portland's business leaders came from within the state and built with internally generated capital to a greater degree than was the case in Washington and Idaho. The economy of the area around Puget Sound had developed quickly during California's Gold Rush in response to sudden demand for building materials. Most early sawmills were erected with capital from San Francisco and were controlled by Bay Area entrepreneurs. Residents often complained that their area was an economic colony, exploited by investors in California who drained wealth from Washington while contributing little. The pattern was modified as timber magnates moved into Washington from the upper Great Lakes states during the 1880s, but leadership continued to be distinctly different than in Oregon—and more frequently external. Perhaps this, as much as anything, explains the subsequent differences in state and local conservation—and much else—in Oregon and Washington.[19]

Idaho—without any cities worthy of the name, tied more to mining and irrigation agriculture than either Oregon or Washington, and
with a political conservatism influenced initially by a large contingent
of ex-Confederates—followed a path of its own. The politically volatile
Mormon question and rivalries between the northern and southern
parts of the state helped set Idaho apart, but in its speculative, booster-
oriented approach to growth it probably was more similar to Washington than to the business conservatism in Oregon. As in Washington, most of Idaho's business leaders and investment capital came
from outside. With less opportunity apparent in Idaho, they came in
smaller numbers and perhaps with smaller dreams.[20]

By the beginning of the twentieth century urban pressures were
beginning to mount in all three states, leading more and more people
to look to the outdoors for relief. And with major irrigation systems
coming on line, with new railroads about to open up central Oregon,
and with truck logging and the automobile revolution in the offing,
scenery seemed endangered as never before. The voices calling for
the protection of the region's natural beauty began to gain in numbers
and in stridency, especially near the urban centers where the threat
was most apparent.

Programs to provide recreational facilities and protect natural
beauty began to appear. Seattle had an embryonic city parks program
in 1900. Soon thereafter it added a system of tree-lined boulevards
and hired John C. Olmsted, of the noted Olmsted Brothers firm of
landscape architects, to lay them out and plan for further park
development. Portland and Spokane proceeded in the same direction, the latter thanks largely to the work of A. L. White. Both cities
followed Seattle's example and hired Olmsted to aid in planning.
Setbacks occurred, but by 1911 Portland's parks program had become
a major undertaking, an integrated system with major plans for the
future.[21] In 1907 Thomas Davis, a prominent local citizen, donated
forty acres along the Boise River to Idaho's capital city for use as a
public park. The *Idaho Statesman* was enthusiastic; the gift, it proclaimed, would help make Boise "truly a city beautiful." In Oregon,
Salem, Ashland, and various other smaller cities were beginning to
move in the same direction.[22]

Construction of a highway through the Columbia River Gorge
began in 1913 and was completed in 1916. Engineer Samuel Christopher Lancaster laid out the roadway to protect the scenery of the

gorge. His work and ample press coverage combined to fire local interest in saving the beauty of the route. One means to that end was Portland's system of city parks. Osmon Royal donated the scenic vista at Crown Point to the city; Simon Benson and George Shepard donated land around Multnomah and neighboring waterfalls. Both locations were far to the east of Portland's city limits, but there was nothing in Oregon law to prevent the city from accepting the gifts; it did so and promptly made both into parks. Jacob Kanzler and others took a different tack, persuading Forest Service officials to set aside 14,000 acres of national forest in the gorge as a recreational and scenic preserve.[23]

Even more far-reaching was the proclamation by Oregon's Governor Oswald West in 1911 preserving the state's beaches for public use. Lacking a better means, West simply declared them public highways (stretches actually having been used for some time as vehicular routes). It was a bold stroke that received national attention. Ex-President Theodore Roosevelt, after visiting the young governor, lauded West as "a man more intelligently alive to the beauty of nature and of harmless wildlife, more eagerly desirous to avoid the wanton and brutal defacement and destruction of wild nature and more keenly appreciative of how much this natural beauty should mean to civilized mankind, than almost any other man I have ever met holding high political position."[24]

Not until the 1960s did it prove necessary to move beyond West's proclamation in order to protect Oregon's beaches. In the meantime, the state built a string of seashore parks to provide access to what West had set aside.

These examples of preservation were not coordinated. Some sprang from widespread conditions, some from strictly local circumstances. The parks in Seattle, Spokane, Portland, Boise, and elsewhere reflected both the City Beautiful movement, which was gaining momentum across the land, and the boosterism that had long permeated the West. City parks movements also reflected working-class concern over worsening urban living and working conditions, but this was less of a factor in the Northwest than in some other parts of the country.[25]

The building of the Columbia Gorge Highway, and the steps to protect the scenery along it, came from the Good Roads movement and the associated automobile revolution which promised ultimately to bring hordes of tourists to the region. At the same time, improved roads and efficient internal-combustion engines led to truck logging, which threatened the very scenery that the Columbia Gorge and other new highways traversed and which tourists were expected to come to see.

In its own way, the automobile revolution contributed to a gradual change in what was deemed "scenery"—and thus worth saving. In the days of railroad palace cars, tastemakers had deemed only those places that made grand destinations for the wealthy as being worthy of admiration. Preservation efforts had been aimed almost entirely at the awe-inspiring monuments of nature—"nature's special gifts," to use Thomas Summers's phrase. But in the early 1900s the automobile became more than just a rich man's toy—by 1909 there were over 3,000,000 registered in the United States. As the number of autos rose with increasing rapidity, more and more people, including many of relatively modest means, came to use them for family outings. As they did, they came to value pleasant vistas and roadside rest stops, places that would have gone largely unnoticed and unappreciated earlier. Scenic tastes were being simplified—and democratized.[26]

Less clearly, but no less certainly, some activities of the period came from the back-to-nature movement that developed in the late nineteenth and early twentieth centuries as cities and their problems burgeoned. Across the country, well-to-do people were fleeing cities not in search of new homes or of grand resorts, but of temporary retreats, however modest, where they could restore themselves before returning to urban centers to earn a living and enjoy their cultural benefits. As they did, efforts to save what they left the cities to find grew apace.[27]

This mixture of attitudes, motives, and efforts carried overtones of transcendentalism and romanticism, which lauded the beauties of nature and saw communion with it as a means of spiritual uplift. But a distinct new element was coming to the fore, spurred on by the rise of progressivism: the active use of government as the major means of protecting scenery. The individualism at the heart of transcendentalism was giving way to a sense of duty to the whole of society and to a recognition that such duty could be better fulfilled by using the powers of government than by individual action. The creation of Yellowstone National Park in 1872 and of scattered other parks in the years that followed had been harbingers of this change, but not until the Progressive Era did such activity become more than occasional among those who would preserve scenery. The drive which culminated in the creation of a National Park Service in 1916 and the rise of state parks programs in Wisconsin and elsewhere were evidence of the new approach. Stephen Mather and the delegates gathered in Des Moines were among its spokesmen.[28]

The movement that the NCSP represented had begun during the Progressive Era and was, in its own way, typical of progressivism. At heart, it involved active use of government to improve society—in this case by providing non-urban facilities for the recreation, relaxation, and spiritual renewal of an increasingly urban populace. Those involved in the movement had backgrounds common among progressive reformers: they were well-educated, upper- and middle-class urban professionals from Protestant, northern and western European backgrounds. When they came together in Des Moines, they were acting in a manner familiar among progessives, seeking through group action and improved planning to further the particular reform they championed.[29]

Surely, not all those present in Des Moines considered themselves progressives. The state parks movement included archconservatives such as Madison Grant, who fought vigorously both to protect scenic beauty and to save American culture from immigrant hordes, and it embraced others who were liberals dedicated to increasing social and economic justice in American society. But regardless of their views on other issues, parks advocates shared a conviction that scenery preservation represented a legitimate use of government power. In short, the common denominator unifying them was not just a love of nature, but a belief that government should be used to protect it.

Under the circumstances, it is hardly surprising that the efforts to create state parks were most successful in those areas where progressivism was strong—that is, from New England across the upper Midwest to South Dakota and in the tier of states on the Pacific Coast. By contrast, little headway was made in the South or in the Rocky Mountain-Intermountain Basin states. In the South, poverty, traditions of limited government, the weakness of transcendentalism (thanks in part to its ties to abolition), and the pastoral-plantation ideal that extolled the country estate rather than unsullied nature, combined to discourage participation in the state parks movement. In the Rocky Mountain–Intermountain West, an overriding concern with economic development and the presence of large federally owned tracts in relatively pristine condition made state parks appear less than desirable, for they promised to "lock up" additional resources in a region where too much seemed locked up already.[30]

The advocates of state parks in the Northwest never argued, as champions of national parks sometimes did, that the lands they sought to preserve were worthless for commercial purposes. The economic value of roadside stands of timber, which many state parks embraced, was self-evident, and many other parklands were suitable for business establishments, grazing, or other purposes. When the states did not already own lands wanted for parks, advocates usually argued that the lands they sought were bargains and that, as time passed and they went up in price, they would soon be out of reach given the limited funds available. Park lands were, in short, investments that would in time yield good returns not just in aesthetic values, but also in tourist dollars.[31]

Whatever their successes locally, the champions of state parks were largely unknown outside their home states. Sometimes they were not well known in them, either. Most often they depended upon personal persuasion and individual effort to gain their ends. At times they worked through various middle-class civic organizations, automobile clubs, and the like, but on the whole they did little to build mass bases of support. While they frequently spoke of working for the good of "the people," their movement was far more elitist than they seem to have realized. Still, what they wrought came in time to serve the very masses that had been so little involved in its building.

However removed from the mainstream, the champions of state parks labored on in the Pacific Northwest, especially in Oregon and Washington, where progressivism flourished. As they pushed forward—winning converts, establishing precedents, and ensuring the preservation of a variety of tracts—they provided a support network on which national leaders and other local conservationists depended. Conservation was not something that Mather, Roosevelt, and Gifford Pinchot imposed from the national capital, but a movement with strong roots at the state and local levels. The story of state parks in Oregon, Washington, and Idaho thus has ramifications far beyond the Pacific Northwest, and their builders deserve to be more widely known.[32]

Chapter 2

Weldon B. Heyburn and Robert Moran
Two Men and Two Parks

In the first decades of the twentieth century, appreciation of scenery in the Pacific Northwest had not yet been translated into a widespread desire for state parks. The cases of Weldon B. Heyburn and Robert Moran make this clear.

Heyburn and Moran differed in many ways. Heyburn, a United States senator, held conservative, state's rights views; Moran, a wealthy retired industrialist, greatly admired Henry George. Although both were Republicans, Heyburn was a solid standpatter while Moran, who attended the GOP national convention as a Roosevelt delegate in 1912, was a dedicated insurgent.[1] But the two shared an appreciation of scenic beauty and a conviction that something ought to be done to save the best of it. Heyburn set out to create a park around Lake Chatcolet in Idaho's northern panhandle, Moran to have a premier tract in Washington's San Juan Islands set aside as a state park. The frustration each encountered made it clear that there was a long way to go before major programs of acquisition for state parks were apt to become a reality in the Northwest.

Heyburn's efforts came to fruition first. On 14 July 1911, Idaho purchased land around Lake Chatcolet that the senator had been championing since 1907. With that action, the first major state park in the Pacific Northwest came into being.[2] Beautiful though the site was, its acquisition hardly represented an auspicious beginning for state parks, either in Idaho or in the region as a whole. Heyburn himself told his fellow senators, "I do not believe in creating a park that shall

be the property of the state. We have all had some experience . . .
with [state] parks and enterprises of that kind. . . . They are always
a subject of political embarrassment." State parks required regular
appropriations for their support, which led to legislative battles, and
they contributed to patronage struggles by creating positions for
spoilsmen to contend for. Instead of such problems, the senator
explained, "I want in Idaho one national park."[3] Local boosterism
(and perhaps a desire for a share from the national pork barrel) had
overcome his distrust of federal interference in Idaho.

Heyburn may have wanted a national park, but circumstances
dictated otherwise. The Coeur d'Alene Indian reservation was being
terminated as a result of policies instituted under the General
Allotment Act of 1887. Each Coeur d'Alene was to select and receive
160 acres of reservation land in severalty. The land left over after all
Coeur d'Alenes had filed for their allotments was to be opened to
homestead entry by whites. Since there were only 638 Coeur d'A-
lenes, this meant that some three-fourths of the reservation would
soon be available to homesteaders.[4] Afraid that selection of key tracts
in the area near Lake Chatcolet by either Indians or whites would
result in barring the public from the area or the destruction of its
beauty, Senator Heyburn sought to have it withdrawn from entry
before the Indians were to make their selections in the spring of 1908.[5]

Toward this end, Heyburn introduced a bill in Congress on 5
February 1907 to set the area aside as a park to be administered by the
Secretary of the Interior. The Senate Committee on Indian Affairs
recommended passage, but, apparently at the request of the Department of Interior and Bureau of Indian Affairs, called for payment to
the Coeur d'Alene Indians for the land. Heyburn and the Senate
accepted the amendment and quickly passed the bill. Sent to the
House, it was referred to the Committee on Indian Affairs and never
heard from again.[6]

Three days after the Senate passed Heyburn's bill, the Idahoan
arranged for the introduction of an amendment to the Sundry Civil
Appropriations bill, then under consideration, to provide funds to
pay the Indians the appraised value of land taken for the park.[7] Some
such tack was necessary since appropriations bills must originate in
the House, and the amendment to Heyburn's original bill meant that
an appropriation would be needed for the park to come into being. To
protect against the possibility of his earlier bill not passing, and to

avoid the appearance of proposing funding for a park not yet authorized by Congress, Heyburn included in his amendment a section restating the wording creating the park.

The House and Senate versions of the Sundry Civil Appropriations bill differed on a number of points. Only the Senate's version contained Heyburn's amendment creating the Coeur d'Alene park and appropriating funds for it. Although the House conferees recommended against it, Congressman Burton L. French of Moscow, Idaho, not far from the park site, tried to persuade his fellow representatives to accept the amendment. The site, he explained, was "rugged land lying at the junction of the beautiful St. Jo [sic] river with Lake Chatcolet, . . . one of the most beautiful spots in Idaho, . . . [and] would have splendid value for park purposes, because it would be preserved as a beauty spot to which visitors could come from all the Northwest and, in fact, the whole country." Representatives asked the cost of purchasing the land, but French was unable to furnish a figure. He could only assure them that it would not be much.[8]

Though laudatory, French's description failed to do justice to the site. Lake Chatcolet lay at the foot of steep bluffs covered with dense, old-growth stands of pine and fir. Behind the bluffs, uplands of open pine forest stretched to the rolling wheatfields and grasslands of the Palouse country. In front, beyond Lake Chatcolet, the alder- and willow-lined St. Joe River meandered. Beyond that lay Round Lake. The whole was a sunken valley across which the river flowed, its silt-raised banks barely above water.

Until 1906, when the Washington Water Power Company built a dam at Post Falls on the Spokane River (outlet to Lake Coeur d'Alene), the site had only been flooded seasonally. During the dry months, cattle grazed on natural meadows where Round and Chatcolet lakes later lay. With completion of the dam, water levels were stabilized, and the lakes became permanent.

Even before stabilization the site had drawn tourists. An interurban electric railroad carried excursionists from Spokane to the town of Coeur d'Alene, located at the north end of the lake of the same name. Steamboats took them down Lake Coeur d'Alene and up what publicists called "the shadowy St. Joe" to the town of St. Maries. Many stayed on, renting houseboats on Lake Chatcolet to escape the summer heat of the Palouse.[9]

But the merits of the site were largely unknown outside the

immediate vicinity, and Republican Congressman James A. Tawney of Minnesota, chairman of the House Committee of Indian Affairs, was cautious. He noted that although Heyburn's amendment did not include the term, "this simply means starting up another national-park proposition." Such parks, he added, not only required appropriations for the original purchase, but also regular appropriations thereafter. Under the circumstances, he argued, Congress should not act until the feasibility of the site for use as a park and the cost of maintaining and operating it as one had been established.[10]

Tawney's warning no doubt had its effect. Previous Congresses had set aside some parks with little thought to their quality or national significance, apparently viewing them as matters of only local importance. Once created, however, parks, no matter how marginal, generated repeated demands for federal funds. Among the national parks then in existence were Wind Cave in South Dakota, Sully's Hill in North Dakota, Platt in Oklahoma, and Hot Springs in Arkansas, all of such questionable quality that when Stephen Mather was made director of the newly created National Park Service in 1916 he quickly mounted a campaign to eliminate them from the system and head off the addition of similar ones. Only the best scenic sites deserved national park status, he maintained; others should be saved by different means.[11] The Coeur d'Alene site was of premier quality and might well have met even Mather's exacting standards, but that was not clear to the assembled House.

Republican Congressman Wesley L. Jones of Washington, apparently a supporter of the proposed park, reminded the House that the chance to preserve the land might well be lost if immediate action were not taken, for the Coeur d'Alenes would soon be selecting their tracts. The park was feasible only if the site were set aside before parts of it passed into private hands. Jones asked if the land could be temporarily withdrawn from entry while Congress investigated its potential. It was late in the session, however, and investigation of potential parks was beyond the ken of the House Conference Committee, the group which would have had to handle the matter. The House rejected the amendment, and, for the moment, the matter was dead.[12]

Heyburn tried again in the next Congress. On 4 December 1907 he introduced a bill declaring the area "a public park or pleasuring ground for the benefit and enjoyment of the people." The park was to be under the Secretary of the Interior who would issue regulations "for the preservation from injury or spoliation of all timber, mineral deposits, natural curiosities, or wonders within the park, and their retention in their natural condition."[13]

The bill, given a "do pass" recommendation by the Committee of Indian Affairs, sailed through the Senate without debate.[14] The Secretary of the Interior and the Bureau of Indian Affairs also supported Heyburn's proposal. So did the Coeur d'Alene tribal council, which seems to have recognized that after termination this, one of the tribe's favorite fishing and hunting sites, was more apt to be preserved and protected if in a national park than if opened for individual settlement.[15]

Once again, however, Heyburn's bill stalled in the House Committee on Indian Affairs. Whether the committee was busy with the annual Indian Appropriations bill or whether opposition in the House continued is not clear.[16]

As before, Heyburn offered an appropriations amendment to provide the necessary funds, this time to the pending Indian Appropriations bill.[17] Once more, the Senate accepted Heyburn's amendment, and the House balked. When the bill went to conference committee, Heyburn's amendment was one of several that almost caused a stalemate. Attempting to eliminate differences over the Coeur d'Alene park site, yet provide for its preservation, the Senate conferees proposed that the wording be changed to allow the state of Idaho to buy the tract for use as a park. The House committee members agreed.[18] The conferees tried to reach Heyburn to clear it with him, but the senator was out of town. Pressed for time, they went ahead with the change.[19]

When the conference report reached the floor of the Senate, Heyburn protested the substitution, but he had little room left to maneuver. The Coeur d'Alenes were to begin selecting allotments in about two weeks. Unless the tract were withdrawn before then, members of the tribe might choose land within the park site and its preservation would be made impracticable.[20] Apparently still hoping that the area might be made a national park in the near future, Heyburn accepted the substitute. His lack of enthusiasm for state parks, plus his conviction that the state of Idaho had no constitutional authority to purchase park lands, suggest that he viewed the amendment as a stopgap to provide protection until the site could be made a national park. There is no indication that he expected Idaho actually to buy the land, let alone name the park after him once it did.[21]

The House and Senate both accepted the conference committee's report, and on 30 April 1908 President Theodore Roosevelt signed the amended bill into law.[22] Contrary to Heyburn's expectations, Idaho's legislature was quick to respond.

Heyburn had reason to be surprised. While his park legislation had been before Congress, Idahoans had shown little interest in it. The state's leading paper, the *Idaho Daily Statesman* of Boise, reported the bill's progress without comment; most of the state's press did not do even that. Heyburn received significant expressions of support only from Coeur d'Alene and St. Maries, both towns located near the park site.[23]

Still, some of Idaho's citizenry was more interested in parks than Heyburn believed. In November 1907 Thomas Davis, a prominent local citizen, donated forty acres along the Boise River to the city of Boise for use as a park. The *Statesman* was effusive, not only in its praise of Davis's philanthrophy, but also of the site's potential for helping to make Boise "truly a city beautiful."[24] At about the same time various newspapermen, moved by the natural beauty they had seen when the state press association met by Payette Lake in 1906, were calling for a state park in that area. Responding, two legislators introduced a resolution in 1907 directing the State Land Board to withdraw from sale all state-owned forest land within two miles of the Payette lakes "for pleasure resort and park purposes." The legislature balked at so sweeping a preserve, but authorized the land board to set aside land "bordering or in the vicinity of any lake, waterfall, spring, or other natural curiosity." The following legislature specified lands on the south shore of Payette Lake for "a public park." No money was appropriated for the "park" and the withdrawal was only for twelve years. Still, this legislation, like Davis's donation, showed that Senator Heyburn was not the only Idahoan interested in preserving the state's scenic and recreational resources.[25]

Soon after Congress had opened the way, the Idaho legislature authorized the expenditure of $15,000 "or so much thereof as may be necessary" from the state's fish and game fund to purchase the tract around Lake Chatcolet, established a commission to administer it, and named it Heyburn State Park. The fund, however, did not contain enough money to make the purchase. The next session of the legislature tried again. This time it authorized spending $12,000 out of the state's general fund, to be reimbursed from the fish and game fund when the amount in it was sufficient.[26] The State Game Warden was outraged. "I believe it is unjust to place the burden of a state park, which is of no benefit except to the community in which it is located, upon any department and especially upon the Fish and Game Department." The warden argued "there is [in the park] 5,000,000 feet of timber that is fully matured . . . [which] should be sold while at its best; . . . cutting . . . would be a protection from fire and would not mar the beauty of the park in the least. If the timber were sold, the park could be paid for and still have a balance of $10,000 for improvements which are badly needed." The proposal, which had more financial than aesthetic merit, was soon implemented.[27]

Heyburn himself was not yet out of the picture. For years he had carried on a running battle with Gifford Pinchot and the U. S. Forest Service. Heyburn was opposed to federal interference in Idaho's affairs and convinced that the policies of Pinchot's Forest Service were blocking the development of the state. The creation of forest reserves in Idaho especially galled him. Under the act admitting Idaho to the Union, the state could select land for schools and other endowments from the public domain. To Heyburn, the withdrawal of prime forest lands to create federal forest reserves was, at best, a breach of faith that robbed Idaho of its right to select from those lands. So much land was being withdrawn, he and other Idahoans came to fear, that only desert would be left for the state.[28] The wording of the deed to the Heyburn park site that was issued to the state by federal authorities brought these attitudes to the forefront. In the deed, as in the Forest Service and timber withdrawals, the senator thought he detected intolerable infringements on Idaho's rights.[29]

According to the amendment that had allowed Idaho to purchase the tract around Lake Chatcolet, the transfer was to be made "for such consideration and upon such terms and conditions as the Secretary of the Interior shall prescribe."[30] Attorney though he was, Heyburn had seen nothing ominous in the wording. He soon discovered his error. When Idaho purchased the land in 1911, Secretary of the Interior Walter L. Fisher drew up a deed that not only required that the land be used in perpetuity as a park, a proviso

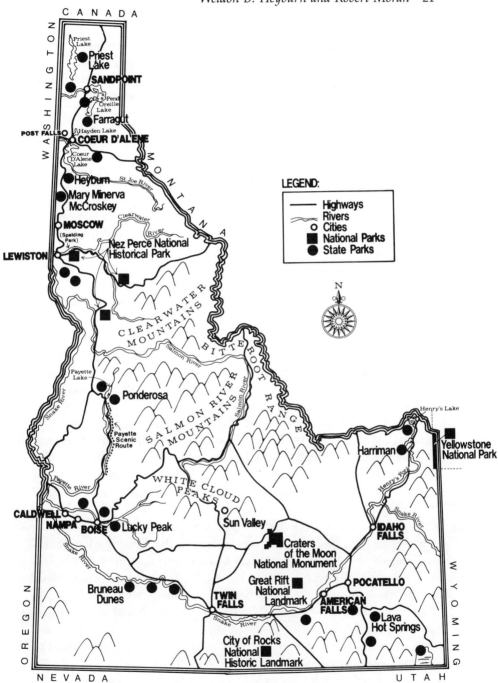

Parks of Idaho

Heyburn had included in his own bill, but which included other restrictions as well. Mineral rights on the land were reserved to the United States as was the right to "flood or overflow the said lands, and to permit, license or authorize the same for domestic, irrigation and power purposes."[31]

Heyburn was outraged. In June 1912, with the support of Governor James H. Hawley, he introduced Senate Joint Resolution 114 directing the Secretary of the Interior to issue "a good and sufficient conveyance by patent, in lieu of the conditional patent heretofore issued." The senator's statements in support of his resolution indicate that his reaction to the deed was as much emotional as legal. Secretary Fisher, he argued, had not acted in conformity with the law in placing the restrictions in the deed. The argument was not well taken. Congress may not have expected such restrictions, but the wording of the enabling legislation clearly gave the secretary the right to include them. Having begun on this untenable ground, Heyburn went on to lash out once more at the penchant of federal bureaucrats for interfering in Idaho's affairs. The Interior Department, he said, wants "to give the State a plaything, they want to make some offices up there, they want uniformed [federal] inspectors and special agents up there, and we do not want them in the park. We will probably make provision by which the local constable will arrest them if they go there." Heyburn contended that he had offered to forget the whole idea of a park if the secretary would refund Idaho's money, but that the secretary had refused. Heyburn was transfering to the Department of the Interior and Secretary Fisher his pent-up hatred of Pinchot and the Forest Service. If there was a logical basis for his hysterical charges, it is not apparent.[32]

In October 1912 Weldon B. Heyburn died. By then, Senate Joint Resolution 114, like so much of the rest of the senator's legislation dealing with the park around Lake Chatcolet, had run into opposition—or lack of interest—in the House. Without the senator to push it, the resolution and the issue that it represented dropped from sight. Heyburn State Park continued on under the conditional deed granted to Idaho in 1911. Not until the 1970s, and then for very different reasons than Heyburn had imagined, was the wording of the deed to prove a real source of concern to the state.[33]

Heyburn State Park was Idaho's first. In many ways it is also, to this day, the state's best—indeed, one of the finest state parks anywhere. But its creation did not demonstrate the presence of a nascent state parks movement in Idaho. It was the product of the growing interest in national parks, of local boosterism, and of a desire for funds from the federal purse. It became an issue only because of opportunities provided by the termination of the Coeur d'Alene Reservation. There was little other than local interest in or support for Heyburn's efforts. In the end, the creation of the park led to nothing larger, and probably would not have even if the senator had lived beyond 1912.[34]

If Weldon Heyburn was frustrated during his attempt at park building, Robert Moran must have been even more so. Some four years after Heyburn began his efforts, Idaho purchased the tract he championed; by contrast, it took Moran over a decade to persuade the state of Washington to accept a magnificent park that he offered to donate outright.

Robert Moran first came to public attention as a shipbuilder. He arrived in Seattle in 1875 with only ten cents in his pockets, but gradually saved enough to open a machine shop and, eventually, a shipyard. The latter, known as Moran Bros. & Co., pioneered in building steel-hulled ships in the Northwest. The firm turned out a host of vessels, including the torpedoboat *Rowan*, the battleship *Nebraska*, and a dozen sternwheel steamboats used to meet the demand caused by the gold rush to Alaska and the Yukon. In addition, Moran served as mayor of Seattle from 1888 to 1890. Then in 1905, suffering from ill health and mistakenly given but six months to live, he sold his business for $3,500,000 and retired to Orcas Island in the San Juan chain north of Puget Sound.[35]

Orcas Island was no spur-of-the-moment choice. Moran recalled that when he had first visited the San Juans in the 1870s, he had been so taken with them that he resolved to settle there if he could ever retire from city life. Thirty years later, failing health provided the opportunity to do so.[36]

Moran built Rosario, a magnificent large estate, by the protected waters of East Sound. Rising sharply behind his new home was Mount Constitution, a peak whose summit offered an impressive view of the San Juans, Puget Sound, and the distant Cascade and Olympic ranges. Below the rock outcroppings of Mount Constitution's upper reaches stretched a forest of fir, hemlock, spruce, and cedar; nestled in the forest were two clear, blue lakes. Moran not only laid out spacious grounds around his house and acquired nearby orchards, he also purchased land around the lakes and much of Mount Constitution itself. Visitors like historian Edmond S. Meany of the University of Washington were enchanted both by the setting and by Moran's openhandedness in sharing it. The Mountaineers, a Seattle-based organization of alpinists of which Meany was a leader, soon started annual trips to the island. The combination of outstanding scenery, magnificient facilities for evening gatherings, and Moran's talent as a host drew the group again and again.[37]

It was apparently at one of these gatherings, probably in 1910, that Moran mentioned the idea of making Mount Constitution, the lakes, and the surrounding forest into a state park. He offered to donate his own holdings if the state would acquire the rest and provide for the site's permanent preservation. At the moment, Moran believed, the state could round out his holdings via condemnation at a small cost, for the land involved had little value for agriculture or lumbering. If the state did not act quickly, however, Moran feared that private parties would establish summer resorts there, thus despoiling the site and driving up the cost of the land. Perhaps in a bid to win the support of Meany and other influential figures at the University of Washington, Moran suggested that the summit of Mount Constitution, having more clear weather than most places in western Washington, would make an ideal location for the university to establish an astronomical observatory.[38]

Nothing seems to have come of the proposal, so, a year and a half later, Moran tried again. He reiterated his plan to Meany and proposed that a group from the University of Washington come to the island "so they would be in a position to advise understandingly, either for or against, from the University point of view." Moran believed that the site would be useful not only to the university's astronomers, but also for field work in botany, forestry, geology, and zoology.[39]

Meany laid the plan before university president Emanuel Kane and set about arranging for a contingent to travel to Orcas Island. He told Moran, "I look forward . . . to a consummation of the park plan with joyful enthusiasm."[40] When the group finally travelled to the San Juans in the fall of 1912, it included a large contingent from the campus as well as state Senator Ralph D. Nichols and members of the Mountaineers. They were impressed with what they saw and heard.[41]

But when Moran prepared the papers to facilitate the donation and forwarded them to Senator Nichols for introduction into the legislature, his hopes for prompt action were quickly dashed. Nichols told Meany that there was little interest in the legislature in the project and that he doubted it could be persuaded to buy as much land as would be needed to round out Moran's gift. Part of the problem was that there was no agency in the state government responsible for investigating such proposals or administering parks that might result. As a result, Meany suggested to Nichols that the senator introduce a bill to create a state park board which could investigate Moran's proposal and determine what land should be acquired to ensure the integrity of the park. Nichols said he liked the idea, but that the representative of the district that included the San Juans should introduce the bill. Meany was discouraged by "these real or fancied obstacles"; Moran, he feared, would in exasperation "throw the whole scheme overboard."[42]

Moran was in an uncomfortable position. As he told Meany, "I do not care to more than submit the scheme to the State, I do not want to be put in a position where it might appear to some people of narrow minds that I ultimately expected a personal gain from this grant."[43] Yet he recognized that without additional public support the legislature was not apt to act. He confided to Meany his suspicions that "Nichols does not enter into the scheme with a good heart" and expressed distress that his proposal had been turned over to the state Senate's committee on public buildings and grounds, "no member of which has likely ever been among the San Juan Islands, not to mention viewing Puget Sound from the top of the Mountain."[44] Seeking a way out, Moran laid his plan before Scott Bone, editor of the *Seattle Post-Intelligencer*. "While I am not in a position to urge a gift on the State," he wrote, "I really think a movement should be made to intelligently investigate the question of the State acquiring this property." He invited Bone to visit Orcas Island and judge the site's merits for himself.[45] Moran then turned to Meany for help in persuading the editor to make the trip. Bone accepted Moran's invitation, and Meany also prevailed upon the Mountaineers to create a committee "to help the publicity along."[46]

V. J. Capron, who represented Moran's district in the state House of Representatives, lent his support. He told Moran, "I find it rather difficult to get members of the Legislature interested in this matter, [but] I will do the best I can." Capron introduced a bill creating a State Park Board. It passed the House two weeks later and in less than a month was signed into law by Governor Ernest Lister.[47]

But this was a limited victory. The new board was empowered to accept gifts of land for parks, but it had no funds and only advisory powers. Moran had no illusions that passage of Capron's bill presaged prompt action. As he put it to Meany, "Public matters are generally the last to receive attention unless there is a personal interest, that is why we have 'Insurgents' or 'Progressives' in our governmental affairs now."[48] Moran was prescient. The board was made up of state officials already busy with other duties. It accepted a gift of twenty acres near Bellingham and two small tracts near Chehalis, but did little else. Governor Lister had little interest in parks, and without his active leadership there was no way the board was going to move to accept potentially expensive gifts such as Moran's.

In October 1913, E. F. Blaine, a Seattle attorney appointed to serve as Park Commissioner by Governor Lister,[49] inquired if Moran's offer still stood. Moran assured him that it did and invited Blaine and the Park Board to examine the tract. No action seems to have been taken, for early in 1915 Moran was complaining to Joshua Green, a Seattle banker, that the governor and other state officials had done nothing on the matter; nor, Moran noted, had the general public become interested in the proposal.[50]

Green sympathized and offered to help push for the park, but he was hardly sanguine about chances of success. "For some reason," Green wrote, "people do not appreciate and understand the San Juan Islands." In his opinion "so few of them have been down there that it is really [a matter of] ignorance."[51] At about the same time, Representative Capron told Moran that Governor Lister favored the idea of a state park on Mount Constitution and that the legislature had received a petition from many people in San Juan County calling for its establishment. If Moran would withdraw his proviso that the state must purchase additional lands, Capron predicted that the legislature would accept the donation. Moran agreed to the suggestion, noting that once the state had his property it would eventually move to acquire the rest.[52]

Still there was no action. Blaine wrote that State Land Commissioner Clark Savidge was for the park, but thought that before the state could accept Moran's gift the legislature would need to appropriate funds for its management and upkeep.[53] Again, action was stalled. Indeed, when Welford Beaton tried to persuade the editors of the *Post-Intelligencer* to run an article on the proposed park, these former supporters refused. "They seemed to have the idea that it was some pet personal proposition of yours," Beaton told Moran, and that it "did not appeal to anyone but you." Still, Moran continued to try to get publicity for the San Juans. He apparently spent his own funds to underwrite Beaton in the preparation and publication of such pieces.[54]

All this did little good, however, and Moran's proposal dropped so far from sight that in February 1917 E. H. Nash, who now represented Moran's district in the state legislature, wrote to the ex-industrialist asking if, some two years before, he had offered to donate land on Orcas Island as a game preserve. Moran seized the opportunity to explain that he had offered to donate land for a park and that a State Park Board had been created as a result, but that nothing had happened subsequently to carry the plan to fruition. Moran added that the offer was still open and had the support of Henry Suzzallo, who had replaced Kane as president of the University of Washington.[55] Nash pushed to get the gift accepted, but was soon forced to report that the necessity of appropriating money in order to accept Moran's offer once again had resulted in its being "shelved in favor of expenditures which at this time seemed to be more necessary."[56] Nash tried again at the next session of the legislature, but with the same result.[57] The decade ended as it had begun. Moran's offer still stood, but the legislature had taken no action.

In spite of repeated rebuffs, the tide finally began to turn in Moran's favor. Developments outside the state as well as within were responsible. Scenic preservationists had grown increasingly strong and vocal. Led by such men as J. Horace McFarland of the American Civic Association and John Muir of the Sierra Club, they had successfully lobbied for the establishment in 1916 of a separate National Park Service. The new agency's head, Stephen Mather, proved himself a dynamic, charismatic leader who brought parks into the limelight as never before. He pushed both state and national parks, encouraging the appreciation and protection of scenery wherever he went.[58]

In the late summer of 1919, Mather joined Madison Grant on a trip to the West Coast. Grant, although destined to be remembered primarily for his anti-immigration efforts, was also dedicated to saving the nation's beauty. As a respected amateur naturalist, president of the Bronx Parkway Commission, chairman of the executive committee of the New York Zoological Society, and prominent New York citizen, Grant came west with Mather not as a subordinate, but as a co-worker.[59]

Ostensibly Mather and Grant had come west to inspect national parks and to further Mather's dream of a park-to-park highway, a federally aided road that would tie the West's national parks together in a giant loop. In fact, they were also directing a major portion of their effort to encouraging scenic preservation efforts at the state and local levels. On their trip they stopped in California, where they helped set up the Save-the-Redwoods League, and then in Oregon, where they laid the groundwork for subsequent efforts at preservation. When they reached the state of Washington, they continued their campaign.[60]

Soon after their arrival in Washington, Mather and Grant back-packed into the northern part of Mount Rainier National Park. Accompanying them on their inspection trip were Roger W. Toll, the park's superintendent; Everett Griggs and David Whitcomb, two members of the Rainier National Park Advisory Board, a citizen's group that served as liaison between the Park Service and interested Washingtonians; and S. Herbert Evison, a young Seattlite who was an employee of Whitcomb's and served as camp cook. During their trip, Mather expounded on the work he and Grant had done in helping to establish the Save-the-Redwoods League and then, noting the rapidity with which the timber beside Washington's highways was being logged and scenery in the state destroyed, he asked, "Why not get something going up here to save your own trees?"

Mather's listeners were receptive—even Griggs, who was one of the state's leading lumbermen. Two days later, aboard Whitcomb's yacht *Missawit*, the group began putting together the Natural Parks Association of Washington, a group that had the dual purposes of saving roadside timber and bringing about the establishment of a state park system. To give the organization increased prestige, a long list of influential Washingtonians were persuaded to accept vice-presidencies. Among them was Robert Moran. Suddenly the ex-industralist, who had fought for so long with but scattered and ineffectual help, found himself with powerful, organized allies.[61]

Mather and Grant came onto the scene at a propitious time. The Alaska-Yukon-Pacific Exposition, held in Seattle in 1909, had dramatized the potential of tourism in the area. Subsequent developments had reinforced the impression. Paradise Inn in Mount Rainier National Park opened in July 1917 and was immediately popular. Improved automotive transportation and roads were making scenic areas accessible to increasing numbers of tourists and in 1919 the legislature gave the state land commissioner authority to set aside five-acre tracts for parks beside public highways. Moreover, the city of Seattle, which had acquired its first park as a gift in 1884 and gradually done more and more, was now working to make Seattle truly a "city beautiful" and to attract and hold visitors.[62] All that was needed was a catalyst to bring these latent sources of support for state parks together into an active combination. It was this that Mather and Grant supplied.

The Natural Parks Association began almost immediately to draw up proposals for presentation to the next legislature. At the same time, its members cast about for additional support. They found it in the Auto Club of Western Washington, which in turn lined up many of the more influential commercial and civic organizations of the state, and the Washington State Federation of Women's Clubs, which announced its enthusiastic support of the NPA's program. An important element in the NPA's legislative package was a proposal for a two-dollar annual fee on private automobiles, auto stages, and rental cars that would be earmarked for the preservation of roadside scenery. The users of such vehicles, the Auto Club argued, would be the primary beneficiaries of these expenditures and thus could with justice be asked to pay such a tax. State Land Commissioner Clark Savidge, who had reserved a number of tracts of roadside timber under the act of 1919, joined the chorus calling for parks.[63]

Moran was enthusiastic about these developments, although they were not directly aimed at bringing his own park plan to fruition. He recognized that his proposal was being inexorably swept along by the larger movement for state parks in Washington. But he supported the NPA not only because of the indirect help it could be to him; he sympathized with its basic goals. As he told Everett Griggs, there should be at least one state park in every county in the state; indeed, "we can do nothing that will be more highly appreciated by the people as time goes on."[64]

As a result of the Natural Parks Association's campaign, the legislature created a new State Park Commission and gave it greater powers than its predecessor.[65] Meanwhile, Howard Allen, who introduced the NPA's bills into the legislature, kept after Governor Louis F. Hart about Moran's proposed gift. On 15 April 1921, the new commission—made up of Governor Hart, Land Commissioner Savidge, the secretary of state, and the state treasurer—met for the first time. Allen had complained earlier that having a board or commission composed of ex officio members was not sound practice, but added that "the personnel of this particular committee is fortunate . . . [they] all take genuine interest in park matters." When the commission finally met, Allen's predictions were borne out. Among other things, the members voted unanimously to accept Moran's donation and terms. Although it took some months to complete the transfer, it was at last clear that a park on Orcas Island was to become a reality.[66]

Robert Moran's interest in the park continued after its establishment. He later donated additional acres, fought for appropriations for a road to the top of Mount Constitution, and used his own funds for the park when public monies were not forthcoming. Repeatedly, he nagged state officials to insure that the land was properly managed.[67] It was altogether proper then, that the state would christen the tract Moran State Park. Like Heyburn State Park in Idaho, it would surely never have come into being without the efforts of the man whose name it bears.

Unlike the park at Lake Chatcolet, that on Mount Constitution was soon followed by others. Idaho's parks remained in limbo until the 1950s, while Washington gradually built a system of size and quality.

Moran's efforts resulted in Washington's first major state park;[68] still, it would be no more accurate to credit him with being the father of Washington's state park system than it would be to give Weldon Heyburn such credit in Idaho. Moran recognized the potential of the site on Orcas Island and the public good that would come from parks, but he was unable to persuade enough others to move the legislature to action. Only as interest in scenery preservation grew across the United States and spawned a widespread drive for state parks did a scenic preserve in the San Juans begin to verge on reality.

Moran's campaign profited from the rising interest in state parks; it did not create it. Improved transportation and increased tourism; an increasingly felt need for recreation as modern, urban life evolved around Puget Sound; and a reaction against the growing commercial despoliation in the area were the mainsprings of the movement. They would have brought on a drive to preserve Washington's scenery whether Moran had entered the fray or not. They were the forces that Mather and Grant drew upon during their visit to Washington in 1919. Idaho—less urban, its transportation less developed, and its tourism more limited—long remained insulated against such forces. Not until much later were the consequences of development to drive Idahoans into a major effort to preserve, yet make accessible, the state's scenic resources.

Chapter 3

Ben Olcott's Crusade to Save Oregon's Scenery

The trip to the West Coast by Stephen Mather and Madison Grant marked a turning point for the conservation movement in Oregon as well as in Washington and California. Prior to 1919 conservationists in Oregon, as elsewhere, had been interested primarily in the efficient use of resources in order that the economy might be developed to its full potential.[1] Joseph N. Teal, chairman of the Oregon Conservation Commission, reflected this utilitarian view when he proudly declared that his commission might as readily be called an Oregon development board.[2] Only sporadically had those more concerned with preserving natural resources than in making their exploitation more efficient bestirred themselves to action. The Mather-Grant visit marked the beginning of a new era; preservationists now began to crusade militantly for projects and policies aimed at husbanding the scenery of the state.

Early in August 1919, fresh from helping lay the groundwork in California for the Save-the-Redwoods League, Mather and Grant arrived at Crater Lake. The governor of Oregon, Ben W. Olcott, was there to address a meeting of the Oregon Editorial Association. The two visitors seized this opportunity to push their cause with both the assembled editors and the governor, but without notable success.[3]

On 13 August, Mather and Grant journeyed northward from Crater Lake along the east side of the Cascades to the mushrooming mill town of Bend.[4] Arriving in the evening, they dropped in unheralded at the office of the *Bulletin*, the community's daily newspaper. They apparently did not know Robert W. Sawyer, the young editor, but as missionaries for the preservationist cause they had a message to preach and at night, in a strange community, what better place to start than the lighted offices of the local newspaper?

In approaching Bend from the south, Mather and Grant had passed through a wasteland of stumps and slash where miles of ponderosa pine forest had but recently stood. Grant told Sawyer: "I was shocked to see in coming through that your pine trees have been cut away on both sides of the road. . . . By following the method now being used, you are leaving nothing but barren, unattractive slashings for the tourist to see. A growth of pines on either side could be one of the great assets of a great auto highway."[5]

Sawyer listened intently as his visitors expounded on the need to protect America's scenic heritage. He himself had often praised the beauty of central Oregon in his newspaper; he constantly urged residents of the area to take steps to encourage the tourist trade.[6] When his visitors showed no interest in visiting the city's massive sawmills but turned their attention instead to searching for practical means to save central Oregon's scenery, Sawyer approved. Their concern, he said, gave "weight to what so many Bend people feel, that is, that while our big and immediate cash asset is the sawmills, there are still other things here that should be preserved."[7]

Sawyer also liked Mather's plan for a park-to-park highway.[8] Such a project would be next to valueless, however, if the scenery along it were destroyed. Mather and Grant urged Sawyer to work for preservation of the remaining timber along The Dalles-California Highway (later U.S. 97). The young editor "caught the spark and set to work."[9]

The travelers continued their campaign as they proceeded northward. In Hood River they met Samuel Christopher Lancaster, who had engineered the new Columbia Gorge Highway with scenic preservation in mind, and inspected his work approvingly.[10] Once again, however, the visitors were shocked to find roadside trees being logged. In both Hood River and Portland they reiterated the theme they had emphasized in Bend. Mather warned: "You Oregonians are so accustomed to it that you do not realize the charm of your beautiful trees to visitors from less-favored regions. The trees along your highways are a scenic asset of almost incalculable value. If you permit these trees to be cut away and your highways to traverse bare and desolate regions, you will destroy what is, in fact, your greatest tourist asset."[11]

The two urged George M. Cornwall—editor of the *Timberman*, the leading lumber trade journal on the West Coast—to organize an Oregon equivalent of the Save-the-Redwoods League.[12] They met with a group of civic and business leaders—perhaps some of the same men who shortly before, working through the Portland Commercial Club, had persuaded the Forest Service to set aside the Columbia Gorge as a scenic and recreational preserve. They urged action to preserve roadside beauty as well as efforts to secure the extension of Crater Lake park and the improvement of facilities there. The group formed an ad hoc committee of Portland businessmen to seek means to those ends.[13]

From Portland Mather and Grant went north to Seattle. Then Mather went east to Glacier and Yellowstone while Grant returned to California. En route south, Grant stopped at the governor's office in Salem and again urged Olcott to join the preservationists's crusade.[14] Once more he failed to arouse the governor's interest.

Although Mather and Grant apparently left Oregon believing they had laid a solid foundation for a movement of scenery preservation, they were quickly disabused. Cornwall's interest in an Oregon League flagged without the infectious enthusiasm of his two visitors. After his initial report of the Mather-Grant visit, Cornwall gave the League no further mention in the *Timberman* and, after repeated urgings for action from Mather, finally confessed to the Park Service director that he lacked sufficient interest in the project to carry it through.[15] A new organizer would have to be found. The committee of Portland businessmen passed a resolution calling for action but then, like Cornwall, lapsed into inactivity.[16] Grant confessed that he was "getting discouraged at the way things had collapsed" in Oregon after he left.[17]

It was Sawyer who kept the embryonic movement alive. Immediately after the Mather-Grant visit, he issued an editorial plea for the Bend Commercial Club to reverse its earlier stand against the extension of Crater Lake park.[18] Then he set out on the preservationist campaigns that his unexpected callers had urged upon him.

Sawyer was well equipped for the struggle. A native of Bangor, Maine, educated at Phillips-Exeter Academy and Harvard, and admitted to the Massachusetts bar in 1905, Sawyer had practiced law in Boston until 1910. Then, fleeing an unhappy domestic life, he had abandoned his practice and moved to Oregon. Although he started out in Bend working as a millhand, it was not long until his abilities came to the attention of George Palmer Putnam, who gave him a job with the *Bulletin*. Sawyer rapidly gained Putnam's confidence and, when the latter left Bend to become Governor James Withycombe's secretary, Sawyer was put in charge of the newspaper. The *Bulletin* had prospered under Putnam; it continued to do so under its new manager. It became a daily in 1916. A year later Sawyer bought the paper.[19]

But even a growing daily newspaper was not enough to absorb Sawyer's full energies. Deeply interested in public affairs (a verse Sawyer had written celebrating Will R. King had first called Putnam's attention to the young ex-lawyer), keenly appreciative of natural beauty, ambitious and contentious by nature, Sawyer welcomed the opportunity to campaign in the preservationist cause.[20]

Others before had worked to save Oregon's scenery. But earlier efforts had been limited in scope, each an individual project in which some person or group had a special interest. These projects demonstrated that Oregonians could be roused to seek the preservation of endangered scenery, but their infrequency underscored how little was actually being done. Sawyer's goals were at first equally limited; unlike his predecessors, he gradually developed a broader vision.

Sawyer turned first to private industry. Working quietly behind the scenes, he was able to persuade officials of Shevlin-Hixon Company, a large Bend sawmill firm, to donate an extensive tract threatened with immediate logging to the city of Bend for a park. The late Thomas Shevlin, former president of the company, had been an avid outdoorsman. Sawyer argued that a park in rugged, pine-studded Tumalo Canyon, located just a few miles west of town, would make the finest of memorials to such a man. Company officials liked the idea. They accepted it and, their aesthetic sympathies aroused, also agreed not to cut company timber that stood within 600 feet of The Dalles-California Highway and the timber around Dillon Falls on the Deschutes River.[21] Sawyer described the Tumalo tract to Grant as a "magnificent wooded site"; from the restrained Sawyer, this amounted to an enthusiastic endorsement. Grant was exultant: "It is . . . great satisfaction to find that something really has been done on the Coast." Grant suggested that Sawyer hasten the news to Portland to encourage those working for the becalmed Oregon League.[22]

Successful with Shevlin officials, Sawyer next turned his attention to their cross-river competitors at the Brooks-Scanlon mill. Shevlin officials had given the Tumalo tract without expectation of compensation—indeed, they had bought tracts from other timber owners to round out the park site—and they made no demands for in lieu land selections for the roadside tracts they set aside. Harry K. Brooks, general manager of Brooks-Scanlon, was less altruistic; he was reluctant to take any steps that might cost his company money. Sawyer's arguments apparently made little impression; it once again began to appear that the crusade initiated by the Mather-Grant visit was doomed to die aborning.[23]

Then a trip to the coast did for Ben Olcott what Mather and Grant had been unable to do, and new life surged into the movement. Olcott, who was deeply interested in the state's developing highway system, had journeyed across the Coast Range to inspect the Cannon Beach–Seaside road (later U.S. 101). Crown-Willamette Paper Company was logging the dense virgin forest that flanked the route, and the scarred, barren hills left at roadside shocked the state's chief executive. On his return to Salem, Olcott wrote to William Pierce Johnson, president of Crown-Willamette, and urged that his firm hold off cutting timber alongside the Cannon Beach-Seaside road until equitable arrangements could be made for its preservation. Johnson's reply expressed general agreement with Olcott's desire to maintain roadside beauty. The correspondence, released to the press by the governor's office, received wide circulation; Sawyer found that he had suddenly acquired a powerful ally.[24]

Encouraged, Sawyer asked Olcott for help in breaking the impasse with Brooks-Scanlon. The governor responded with a letter to Brooks that proclaimed it "the patriotic and civic duty" of each Oregon resident to endeavor "to preserve our wonderful natural surroundings." As in his letter to Johnson, Olcott held out the implied promise that the company would be fully compensated for any timber reserved from cutting. The Bend Commercial Club added its voice to the chorus urging Brooks to save the endangered strips. Letters were also directed to the company's head office in Minneapolis. In spite of this pressure, Brooks did not capitulate until Oregon's congressional delegation entered the fray. Senator Charles L. McNary introduced a land exchange bill to allow Forest Service stands away from the road to be traded for the endangered strips. With the interests of the company thus protected by gubernatorial promise and pending legislation, Brooks conceded. He informed Sawyer that tracts of timber 300 feet wide would be left uncut on either side of the highway. Sawyer rushed the news to Olcott, and the governor released it to the press.[25]

Olcott's entry into the struggle for scenic preservation must not have come entirely as a surprise to those who knew him well. Olcott had led an active outdoor life. While living in Alaska, he had driven his own dog sled from Nome to Fairbanks and, perhaps even more revealing, he had once taken a job on a ranch in southern Oregon in order to be near Mt. Shasta, which he longed to climb.[26] As governor, he still found occasion to go hiking. Once, for example, Olcott and two companions hiked along the then-roadless coast from Neskowin to Newport; at the end of the journey Olcott sang the praises of the beauty of the area traversed.[27]

Although a Republican, Olcott was a protege of Oswald West, the Democratic governor who had moved to protect Oregon beaches. The two had married sisters, and West had appointed the virtually unknown Olcott as his secretary of state when the incumbent died in office.[28] Thus, Olcott was influenced by his own appreciation of the outdoors, by West's example, and by the urging of Mather and Grant. The sight of the logging operations along the Cannon Beach-Seaside highway was all that was needed to push him into the ranks of those working for conservation based on aesthetic principles.

Olcott quickly assumed the leadership of the movement in Oregon. The Crown-Willamette and Brooks-Scanlon letters had only been a beginning. He reopened the question of facilities at Crater Lake by replacing the committee of Portland businessmen with one of his own.[29] He also appointed a committee to study the Cannon Beach–Seaside roadside timber problem and to recommend appropriate steps there and wherever similar problems arose.[30] Suspecting that legislation would be needed if his goals were to be achieved, Olcott began a search for guidelines in the statutes of other states. A letter from the governor's office in California revealed that a law passed in that state in 1915 empowered the highway department to enlarge right of ways in order to protect roadside scenery. Again, Olcott released the correspondence to the press.[31]

Olcott's efforts met with an enthusiastic response. His actions, the *Oregonian* observed, were "but the voice of the times"; it is not necessary, the paper added, that "every vestige of verdure be shaved from the landscape." On 5 September 1920, L. H. Gregory (later to gain regional prominence as a sports writer) wrote approvingly that the "save-the-trees movement" was gaining momentum.[32]

Members of the State Highway Commission were among those who responded favorably. R. A. Booth, chairman of the commission, assured Olcott that he shared the governor's concern. Booth wrote to Johnson and Herbert Fleishhacker, chairman of the board of Crown-Willamette, urging the cessation of logging in the Cannon Beach–Seaside strips.[33] Simon Benson, another member, suggested that the state legislature give the Highway Commission the power to acquire roadside tracts through condemnation; "something should be done immediately," he wrote.[34]

Concerned citizens urged Olcott on. One called for posting endangered strips with no trespassing signs bearing the governor's signature. The "'red tape' proceedings" already in progress were too slow to be satisfactory.[35] E. E. Gray, an attorney from Astoria, suggested that a recent decision of the supreme court of Maine suggested a way to preserve roadside timber in Oregon. Gray believed Oregon's courts would also hold that the state could regulate the cutting of timber on private land and that the state might "even take timber without compensation" since it was not the product of the landowner's labor—though, perhaps, Gray added, some compensation should be given.[36]

Perhaps drastic measures were needed. Highway engineer Herbert Nunn, sent on an investigating tour, discovered that roadside devastation was worse than previously reported. South of Bend not a tree was left for ten miles; loggers had even cut trees standing within the highway right of way. Nor were logging operations solely to blame. A "particularly beautiful" strip of trees between Eugene and Goshen, which Nunn had sought to save, had been felled by crews installing telephone lines.[37]

The public response so encouraged Olcott that on 16 October he declared that at the next session of the legislature he would have bills introduced to provide for vigorous state action. Although he was not certain what form his proposals would take—he had not yet received a report from his investigating committee—Olcott declared that the time was ripe for action.[38]

Nor was this the only positive step. The Pelican Bay Lumber Company of Klamath Falls was preparing to log land directly east of

Crater Lake. The tract was on the Klamath Indian Reservation and was crossed by The Dalles-California Highway. Walter W. West, superintendent of the Klamath agency, responded favorably to requests that strips on either side of the highway be reserved from cutting. West noted that the final decision would rest with the tribal council, but promised to exercise his influence to gain approval.[39] Mather, hearing of the efforts in Oregon, got in touch with officials in the Bureau of Indian Affairs and "made an arrangement . . . whereby all timber within the Indian Reservations in Oregon, hereafter, within a three hundred foot strip along highways, is to be preserved." The example thus set for private owners is "the least the government can do," the park director told Olcott.[40]

Mather was not the only easterner to notice this sudden burst of activity in Oregon. A representative of *Old Colony* magazine, published in New York, sought an article by Olcott on his program of timber conservation. The governor grasped this opportunity to reach a larger audience.[41] Grant wrote to encourage Olcott. "The present century will probably see the extermination of all the large animals of the world," the New York naturalist wrote. Since "we have only our forest to fall back on . . . those of the present generation who take part in the effort to preserve our great heritage will be entitled to and undoubtedly will receive the thanks of posterity." If "Washington and Oregon continue along the lines [now] laid down," he added, "they will far outstrip the East in aiding conservation." At the same time, Grant warned Olcott to move carefully; he must not arouse the timber owners' fear of "socialistic" action. Cooperation with the owners of stumpage, not confiscation, offered the surest road to success.[42]

Not all reactions were favorable. Fear of what Olcott's proposals might bring led many utilitarians into active, if not violent, opposition. They did not object to the preservation of roadside scenery, but argued that extensive strips of timber along highways were impractical: trees accustomed to the protection of a surrounding forest would blow down when left in exposed belts. Private land owners could not afford to donate the many acres that stood beside the highways of Oregon, while the state government could hardly afford to buy large tracts of timber that windthrow would quickly destroy. Besides, such strips were unnecessary since within a comparatively short time alder and hemlock would cover land logged of its fir "so that it is no longer unpleasant to look at."[43] Some utilitarians preferred setting aside a few carefully selected sites, for such action would not conflict with their basic goal—the planned, scientific utilization of natural resources. On these terms, even Cornwall joined the critics.[44]

The contest between the utilitarians and preservationists was not particularly illuminating. Both used faulty arguments. The former were clearly wrong, as time and experience would demonstrate, when they argued that roadside strips would surely fall victim of windthrow. On the other hand, the *Oregonian*, champion of the preservationist cause, was equally wrong when it contended—ignoring the processes of ecological succession by which forests heal their wounds— that once fir tracts were logged, the rays of the sun would kill the vegetation on the long-protected forest floor, leaving a permanent wasteland of dust and desolation.[45]

The real point at issue, the desirability of leaving a screen of primeval forest standing at roadside, was seldom debated. With the passage of time, however, it became increasingly clear that most utilitarians and lumbermen, though they might favor the maintenance of some form of roadside beauty, saw no reason to leave extensive strips of old growth timber along the highways. Cornwall suggested that it might be well if some of the roadside fir and cedar were removed since "the traveller might welcome changes of scenery occasioned by intervals of timber and open country."[46] Another utilitarian, C. S. Chapman, thought it sufficient to save a "few acres of old growth timber . . . to show the traveller what kind of forest grew in the locality even were most of the rest of it removed." More ambitious programs, he warned, might endanger the lumber industry of the state.[47]

A third consideration also inspired opposition. While the utilitarians found a general withdrawal impractical and feared its economic impact, others thought they detected a threat to individual property rights. One writer observed that "some companies appear to resent efforts to interfere in any manner with unrestricted logging operations" in order to save roadside timber.[48] Gray's argument that trees might be confiscated in the public interest was certainly not designed to quiet those fears of socialistic action about which Grant had warned Olcott. Increasing the Highway Commission's powers of condemnation (Benson's suggestion), seemed only slightly less ominous. Moreover, criticism of those who logged roadside stands was growing. Chapman protested to Olcott against the public sentiment which condemns "to the point of interference the legitimate removal of stumpage along highways." Such criticism does a "moral injustice to a property owner acting within his rights." Hoping Olcott would rein in the preservationists, Chapman argued that "the public should not be led to feel that owners who cut timber along highways are some peculiar kind of an animal to whom harsh names should be applied."[49] Timbermen in Oregon had been the recipients of uncomplimentary epithets during the exposure of timber frauds in the preceding decades; they had no desire for another such experience.[50]

The long-awaited report of Olcott's committee on the preservation of roadside scenery did nothing to reconcile the adversaries. The committee, primarily made up of laymen, turned for advice to Chapman, State Forester F. A. Elliott, and George H. Cecil of the Forest Service. Although Cecil's earlier role in saving the roadside timber in the Columbia Gorge had made it clear that he was not hostile to limited preservation, he may have shared the reservations of others over the more general program that Olcott was advocating— or, like Chapman, he may have changed his position. If he had not, then the committee simply listened to others, for when it reported to the governor it expressed utilitarian views. If Olcott wanted a program that would be faithful to the Grant-Mather ideal, he would have to find it on his own.[51]

Left to his own devices, the governor decided upon a two-pronged attack. On the one hand, he would ask the state legislature for a package of laws designed to protect roadside beauty; on the other, he would create a counter-weight to his utilitarian opponents and their organizations by establishing a Scenic Preservation Association, a body through which the previously unorganized preservationists could make their influence felt.

Olcott turned first to the legislative program. On 24 January 1921, in a special message to the legislature, he announced his proposals and called for "prompt action to assist in the preservation of what should never be lost." His plan, admittedly copied after that of California, consisted of three major parts: first, give the State Highway Commission power to enlarge highway right of ways "for the maintenance and preservation of scenic beauties"; second, outlaw wanton destruction of trees along the roadways; and, third, authorize the Highway Commission to acquire land for parks or parking places "for the use, convenience and accommodation of the travelling public," to take steps to beautify roadside areas, and to protect scenery from desecration. An ambiguously worded fourth proposal, the purpose of which is not now clear, may have been designed, in part at least, to control the erection of billboards, advertising panels, and roadside stands.[52]

Public opinion quickly rallied to the governor's support. The *Oregonian* applauded his efforts to "keep our state the most livable in the Union."[53] A press release from the governor's office noted that virtually "every commercial body in the state has expressed its endorsement. Practically every newspaper in the state, large or small, has commented favorably on it editorially." Letters of approval came from public officials as far away as Massachusetts and New Jersey.[54] State Senator Charles M. Thomas, a political opponent of Olcott's, noted sourly that since the state legislators "were all in favor of the measure" there was no occasion "for the great activity of the governor to secure passage of the bill."[55]

In spite of Senator Thomas's claims, the proposed legislation suffered a mixed fate. HB 311, the bill outlawing wanton destruction of roadside vegetation, passed the House without a single dissenting vote. The Senate amended it to make the bill less sweeping—making it permissible to cut along roads other than highways, to cut so as to clear obstacles from the paths of telephone and electric power lines, and to trim roadside trees—and then passed it by a 21 to 4 vote.[56]

The right-of-ways bill, SB 365, aroused greater opposition. Although it was reported favorably by the Senate Committee on Roads and Highways, a minority sought to have a do-not-pass recommendation substituted. The bill passed on a 20 to 8 vote, but opposition continued when it was transmitted to the House. A number of representatives, largely lawyers from rural constituencies, voted against it, but again without success. On 21 February, two days before the session drew to a close, the right-of-ways bill—the most important single part of Olcott's legislative program—passed the House by a vote of 39 to 15. With Olcott's signature three days later, the bill became law.[57]

The governor's other two bills failed to pass. The parks bill was premature. Little public interest had yet been shown in state parks and Olcott had done nothing directly aimed at creating an awareness of their need. Referred to the Senate highway committee, the bill died there.[58] The House passed Olcott's confusingly-worded fourth proposal, but the Senate postponed action on it indefinitely.[59]

Only half his legislative program had become law, but Olcott was pleased: "I was more than gratified at the spontaneous response received to the call for assistance in this movement. From nearly every town and village, from practically every civic organization, from the schools and churches, and from the heart of the common people all over came encouraging words, and it is out of this feeling that the big accomplishments are to come." Not all of his program had been enacted, but the "opening wedge was secured . . . which I hope will eventually bring about large results."[60]

With the legislative session out of the way, Olcott turned his attention to the second part of his program, the Scenic Preservation Association. On 24 August 1921, what Olcott described as a "score of prominent Portland citizens" met in the executive offices in Salem to lay plans for a statewide organization. Apparently no list of those present has survived, but they seem to have included many of the same men whom Mather and Grant had lobbied for an Oregon League two years before.[61] Not all of the proposed organization's support came from that quarter, however. At least as early as January a group had organized in Jackson County to work for the preservation of scenery; by August, if not before, it was holding monthly meetings. Olcott and his allies used the constitution and bylaws of the southern Oregon group as a model as they set up their statewide association.[62]

After the organizational meeting, Olcott contacted civic and commercial clubs throughout the state and urged the establishment of an organization in each county to work for the preservation of scenic beauty. These county bodies were in turn to choose representatives to serve as directors of the state association. Having issued his call, Olcott repeatedly urged influential groups to cooperate in building local associations; Olcott himself named directors for those counties where no local associations emerged.[63]

In spite of the governor's efforts, progress was slow. The first meeting of the would-be directors was not held until 25 April 1922—some seven months after the Salem meeting. The Scenic Preservation Association of Oregon was not officially established until 16 September.[64] Indeed, the delay was so great that Olcott began to come under attack from some of the more militant preservationists. State Senator Thomas was among the most outspoken:

> We have the law and we have the money. . . . What we do
> not have is a state highway commission strong enough to
> withstand the pressure brought to bear to induce them to
> use all the highway money for commercial purposes. . . .
> Not only does the highway commission fail to do its plain
> duty in regard to scenic preservation along our state roads,
> but the governor lacks the courage to remove them from
> office and replace them with men who will serve the best
> interests of the state.[65]

The Jackson County association adopted a "strong" resolution con-
demning scenic destruction along the Pacific Highway (later Interstate 5) and urging the State Highway Commission to take action.[66]

Such criticism disappeared with the formal organization of the
state association in September. At the inaugural meeting, Olcott, by
now involved in a bitterly contested campaign for reelection, was
named honorary president of the organization. Officers were chosen
and, on Sawyer's motion, the group went on record favoring strong
legislation to restrict roadside signs and billboards.[67]

To the aesthetically motivated conservationists gathered in Portland for the initiation of the Scenic Preservation Association, the
future of their movement must never have looked brighter. But there
were ominous signs. The gubernatorial election campaign and the
emotion-laden economic and social issues associated with it threatened to push the movement for scenery preservation out of the
limelight, or even to destroy it.

Walter M. Pierce, the Democratic candidate for governor, had no
particular interest in the preservation of scenery, although he gave it
occasional lip service. He was primarily concerned with lowering taxes
and with rural problems. Neither issue augured well for the preservationists. The implementation of Olcott's right-of-ways bill would be
expensive, and much of the opposition to his legislative program for
scenery preservation had come from representatives of rural districts.
In addition, the fact that the campaign of the preservationists had been
so much the work of Republicans, and especially of the Olcott administration, did nothing to enhance its standing with the Democratic
candidate.

Nor was this all. Pierce, while in the state Senate, had been a
leading advocate of market roads, which farmers needed desperately.

His criticisms of the large expenditures of the state Highway Commission stemmed in large part from his belief that roads such as the Columbia Gorge highway, the cost of which was hard to justify on economic grounds, reflected priorities that favored well-to-do urbanites over farmers. Pierce's earlier attacks on the Warren Construction Company—Oregon's "paving trust"—had furthered growing public concern that the few were benefiting at the expense of many. He had opposed bond issues for highway construction, favoring a pay-as-you-go approach financed by gasoline and other taxes. The bonds had been approved, but when many of the inadequately ballasted paved roads built with the funds quickly began to crumble, Pierce's attacks on the paving company gained new credibility.

A seven-man Tax Investigation Committee, established by the legislature in 1921, criss-crossed the state in the months that followed. As a member, Pierce pushed his argument that Oregon's tax burden and road expenditures both were inequitably distributed. He proposed a graduated income tax. By the gubernatorial campaign of 1922, even the Republicans had come to admit the need for tax revision, but that party's platform carefully avoided specific suggestions on how to bring it about.[68]

Olcott—hampered by his own weak position in the Republican party and anathema to many for his strong stand against the Ku Klux Klan—squeaked through the Republican primary but was unable to find an effective counterweight to the timely issues espoused by Pierce. He was swamped in the general election.[69]

Olcott's defeat was not the only blow to the Scenic Preservation Association. Following the election, Olcott left the state to enter banking in California. No one else in the movement had worked on preservationist activities on a statewide scale. Even Sawyer, whose later activities were to range broadly, had not yet done much beyond central Oregon. Moreover, although he was the most likely inheritor of Olcott's position of leadership, Sawyer was poorly equipped to assume it. He lived in an isolated, sparsely populated part of the state. His forte was logical exposition and behind-the-scenes persuasion; as a leader he was uninspiring. Without effective leadership, the Scenic Preservation Association crumbled quickly. In 1930, when conditions once again appeared ripe for a statewide organization, a new one had to be built.

Olcott's defeat and departure from the state did not kill public interest in preserving the scenic heritage of Oregon, but except on local levels, these sentiments made little impact.[70] Without Olcott's presence—without a governor who championed the cause of the preservationists and kept the issue before the public, without a leader who could bring together diverse local groups to create a body of sufficient size to influence the decisions of state and federal agencies—the crusade for nature foundered. The sanguine hopes of Mather, Grant, Sawyer, and Olcott were to go unfulfilled, not because their ideas had been rejected—they clearly had not been—but because the great public crusade that they had sought to set in motion was shorn of its leadership when Olcott was unseated.[71]

But preservationist leaders did not give up their efforts. Their initial plans undone, they turned to other means to obtain their ends. They abandoned the unwieldy vehicles of mass public opinion and statewide organization to work unobtrusively within established agencies. Quiet, behind-the-scenes activity by preservationists on the highway commission and within the highway department obtained the appointment of an advisory committee on roadside beauty, and bit by bit resulted in progress toward preservationist goals.[72] In the long run these methods, a far cry from the public campaigns of the Olcott years, were strikingly successful.

On the surface the crusade in Oregon in 1919–22 may appear to have failed, but closer examination reveals that it contributed much to the preservationist cause. It gave the movement's leaders a chance to sharpen their dedication, to gain experience and converts, and to make contacts that proved invaluable in their later, more localized campaigns and in their use of behind-the-scenes pressure tactics. Although the number of sites actually preserved during those three years was small, foundations were laid for major achievements at a later date. While Sawyer tended to give himself too much credit for the impressive park system that had been developed in Oregon by 1948, he was not altogether wrong when he recalled the Grant-Mather visit of 1919 and mused, "All this the result of that summer evening call so many years ago."[73] Sawyer had touched the heart of the matter: although the organized crusade for nature died in 1922, the work of the preservationists went on.

Chapter 4

Conservation by Subterfuge
Robert W. Sawyer and the Birth of the Oregon State Parks

The 1920s were years of accomplishment for conservationists. As one historian put it, contrary "to widely held opinion, the national conservation program did not deteriorate in the 1920s. It expanded and matured."[1] Significant progress came at the state and local levels too. During the decade, state parks enjoyed unprecedented growth and became accepted throughout the North and West.

Although Mather and other national figures were important in encouraging this development, the growth of state parks was primarily the result of leaders whose concern and influence sprang from local sources. Indeed, conservation leaders at local levels sometimes found themselves arrayed in opposition to the very federal personnel who kept the movement alive within the national government. An intricate interplay between federal and local forces took place, but throughout the decade the primary force responsible for the rise of state parks came from within the individual states. Nowhere is this better illustrated than in Oregon.[2]

In the fall of 1927 officials of the National Conference on State Parks dispatched Charles G. Sauers, a longtime leader in the development of Indiana's parks, to the West Coast to proselytize for the growing state parks movement. Sauers urged leaders in Oregon to create a department of conservation, the primary function of which would be the development of a system of parks within the state, but which would also concern itself with other aspects of the management and protection of natural resources.[3] In proposing such an agency, Sauers not only drew upon his own experience in the Department of Conservation of Indiana, but also reflected the policy of the National Conference on State Parks. Ever since its creation in 1921, the NCSP had favored establishing a department of conservation as a vital step in creating a state's park system.[4]

Sauers's proposal seemed logical. It would result in centralization and rationalization of the management of Oregon's natural resources, control of which had hitherto been fragmented. Moreover, it seemed reasonable to expect that a department specifically charged with building a system of parks would do so with greater vigor and dispatch than the state's Highway Commission, which was then directing the effort seemingly only because the first of Oregon's existing handful of tiny parks had been donations that fronted on highways.

Sauers could point to the experience of other states in support of his idea. Those with the most impressive parks holdings all had such departments. In addition, as the number of state parks across the country increased, more and more states were adopting agencies of the sort he proposed. Earlier that same year California had created a Department of Natural Resources and, within it, a Division of Parks under the direction of a State Park Commission. New York, like California a pioneer in the acquisition of state parks, also moved in 1927 in the direction Sauers advocated.[5]

Interest in protecting Oregon's scenery was widespread, as earlier efforts in its defense demonstrated,[6] and when Sauers approached civic leaders in Portland he quickly won support. Some who had allied with Governor Ben Olcott in his abortive parks movement six years before now rallied behind Sauers.[7] But he met implacable opposition from the state Highway Commission. Henry B. Van Duzer, vice president and general manager of Portland's largest lumber company and chairman of the commission, summed up the attitude of its three members when he wrote of Sauers's "fool idea of organizing a Park Comm[ission]."[8]

The Highway Commission's opposition did not spring from any hostility to conservation or parks. Over the preceding months the commission had taken a number of steps to acquire new park sites and preserve roadside beauty. The motives of the commissioners had been mixed. On the one hand, they desired to preserve natural beauty because they wished to keep the state, as the *Oregonian* had put it earlier, "the most livable in the Union." On the other hand, they recognized that scenic beauty would attract tourists to the state. These dual concerns had led the commission to acquire both scenic sites for use as parks and strips of timber along major highways so that travelers would find them pleasant to drive along.[9]

Robert Sawyer, who had continued his preservationist crusade of the early 1920s, was appointed to the Highway Commission in July 1927. Van Duzer caught his enthusiasm and joined Sawyer as a champion of saving the state's scenic beauty. Between Sawyer's appointment and the end of the year, the commission acquired over twice as many sites for parks and scenery protection as in its entire previous history. In 1928, Sawyer's first full year on the commission, the number was even greater.[10]

Sawyer brought more than his activist background and infectious love of nature with him to the Highway Commission. Educated in the best Eastern schools, trained in the law, and editor of what was rapidly becoming one of Oregon's outstanding smaller newspapers, Sawyer was an informed and articulate appointee who for the next quarter century was to be one of the state's most influential figures. Moreover, he was a perceptive judge of the political scene, and he sensed that the nascent parks movement of the state would encounter serious problems if placed in a separately funded Department of Conservation.

An uncertain economy and high taxes—as well as the Ku Klux Klan and a controversial school bill—had been factors in Walter Pierce's victory over Ben Olcott in the gubernatorial election of 1922. In spite of Pierce's tax reforms, much discontent remained. Watchdogs of the public purse made passage of new or increased state appropriations unlikely, especially when such expenditures did not appear essential.[11]

Only limited legislative support, and no funds, had been forthcoming for parks during Olcott's term despite widespread public backing. This experience forewarned Sawyer of the uncertainty of aid from the legislature. In addition, he feared that legislative struggles over parks appropriations would alert owners of potential sites, who would then raise the prices they asked for their land.[12]

The Highway Commission, however, was not dependent on appropriations from the legislature. A few years before, Oregon had pioneered in adopting gasoline taxes and automobile license fees, which were earmarked for the commission. Authors of these taxes had intended to ensure good roads, not parks, but as long as parks remained under the Highway Commission's jurisdiction, funds for them seemed assured.[13]

Olcott's program was not the only one that had encountered legislative and financial problems. Parks in Washington, Texas, and other states faced similar difficulties. Much of the discussion at the annual meetings of the National Conference on State Parks centered on these concerns.[14] But, though Sawyer himself was a delegate to the conference in 1928, there is no evidence that, when he opposed Sauers's proposal in 1927, he had knowledge of actions in behalf of parks beyond those taken on the West Coast.[15] His understanding of conditions in Oregon, rather than the experience of others, was responsible for his belief that the creation of a conservation agency that would have to turn to the legislature every biennium for funds might well halt development of parks in the state.

Sawyer was not content merely to oppose the establishment of a Department of Conservation. He had plans of his own. Before Sauers's arrival in Oregon, Sawyer had suggested that the Highway Commission hire a superintendent of parks. Sawyer argued that neither the commission nor the division engineers of the Highway Department were in a position to provide the continuing, systematic direction essential for a sound park system.[16] The commission underwent frequent changes of membership, which hampered its ability to give continuity to leadership; moreover, appointees were seldom if ever selected because of their views on the protection of scenery. Division engineers had been under instructions to search out potential roadside park sites ever since 1921, but few acquisitions had resulted. Among the division engineers, only Charles W. Wanzer appears to have actively sought out park sites.[17] As Sawyer observed, the engineers were busy with problems of construction, engineering, and maintenance.[18] To Sawyer, only the existence of an official specifically charged with developing and administering parks seemed apt to bring substantial progress over the long run.

Sawyer's proposal was not entirely new. In 1921, at the height of Governor Olcott's efforts to save scenic beauty, Charles H. Cheney had suggested that a parks bureau be established under the aegis of the Highway Commission and that he be hired to head it.[19]

At the time, Portland was a center of interest in parks. The city had recently acquired a number of sites for city parks, including outstanding ones at Crown Point and Multnomah Falls, miles east of the city in the Columbia gorge.[20] As a consultant to Portland's Planning Commission, Cheney had been at the center of this activity. John C. Ainsworth, a banker and leading citizen of Portland, noted that in two months Cheney had obtained gifts of property worth $60,000.[21] Cheney suggested that the state hire him to do the same sort of thing for it. A park bureau, he estimated, could operate for a year and a half on $16,800 and, under proper leadership, bring in gifts worth far more than that.[22] The Highway Commission shelved Cheney's proposal, but it may not have been without effect. Shortly after, N. J. Drew, a Highway Department employee, was signing himself as "temporarily in charge of parks."[23]

At first Van Duzer was unenthusiastic about Sawyer's proposal for a parks superintendent. He seems to have believed that the existing advisory committee on roadside planting and parks could accomplish much the same good at little if any cost.[24] The advisory committee had been in existence since 1924, but after an initial burst of activity had grown moribund.[25] At Van Duzer's suggestion, three new members were now added. Encouraged by this interest from the chairman of the commission it was to advise and invigorated by the new members, the advisory committee was soon actively at work once more.[26]

The creation of the advisory committee had first been suggested to the Highway Commission by Professor A. L. Peck of Oregon Agricultural College. Once created, the committee operated quite independently of the commission. Essentially it was an extra-legal body whose members served indefinite terms and were free to determine the scope of their own activity.

Sawyer was not convinced that the advisory committee was an effective way to solve parks problems, although he did work through it in seeking, together with John C. Merriam of the Carnegie Institution of Washington, D.C., the establishment of a large scientific and scenic park in the John Day Fossil Beds. Sawyer sought to obtain for the Highway Commission "some control over the advisory parks committee" by formally establishing the number of members and length of their terms. "At present, with unlimited terms," Sawyer told Van Duzer, "the situation seems to me to be unsatisfactory."[27]

The disagreement between Sawyer and Van Duzer over the

efficacy of the advisory board was minor. On the other hand, the two were united in opposition to the proposal for a separate department of conservation. Efforts in that direction, they agreed, should be headed off. Indeed, Van Duzer may well have considered strengthening the advisory board as a means of undermining support for Sauers's proposal.[28]

Sawyer and Van Duzer sought to squelch the drive for a separate agency, whether a department of conservation or a parks bureau, without a public confrontation with champions of the idea. Such a confrontation might well have resulted in undue publicity for the Highway Commission's use of gasoline tax receipts and other funds for parks.

When Van Duzer learned that the Portland Chamber of Commerce had formed a committee to push for a parks department, he quietly contacted Herbert Cuthbert, secretary of the committee. Cuthbert agreed to try to head off precipitate action. He relayed to the Chamber of Commerce committee Van Duzer's wish that nothing be done before conferring with the Highway Commission or its chairman and then arranged to have a subcommittee appointed to meet with Van Duzer. It was "composed of five of the most level headed business men we have on our committee," Cuthbert assured him. "They are all solid men with sound judgement and you need not be afraid in discussing the matters we discussed over the phone, with them."[29]

Sawyer applauded the action and added, in reference to Sauers's efforts, "any movement toward that end I should like to see changed about to make it an adjunct of the work we are doing." A volunteer citizens' group, similar to the Washington Natural Parks Association, might be useful in raising funds and in generating other types of support, Sawyer observed. Unlike a separate agency for parks, it would not threaten the control of the Highway Commission or its ability to work out of the limelight in acquiring parks with funds earmarked for the commission's use.[30]

When C. G. Thomsen, superintendent of Crater Lake National Park, sought to enlist in the movement for a separate agency for state parks, Cuthbert dissuaded him. He wrote Thomsen, "I was amazed to find how much this [highway] commission had accomplished in a quiet way along these lines." Sauers's proposal would result in duplication of effort. It would be better to lend support to the Highway Commission, Cuthbert told the superintendent; "they have quite a lot of authority and sufficient resources . . . to accomplish anything that is not on too large a scale."[31] Indeed, even Sauers rallied behind the Highway Commission. When Van Duzer and Roy A. Klein made the commission's approach and record clear to him, the representative of the National Conference of State Parks withdrew his suggestion for a department of conservation and agreed to do all he could to aid the commission in its work.[32]

Sauers's conversion was an important victory, but security had not yet been guaranteed for the Highway Commission's parks program. Sawyer turned to Governor Isaac L. Patterson, himself a supporter of parks, in hopes of insuring continued acquisition and development of park sites. Sawyer and his fellow commissioners were under continuing pressure to extend and improve the state's network of highways. Future commissions, Sawyer knew, were apt to be less conscious of scenic and recreational values. It seemed likely that they would respond to pressure by putting nearly all the available funds into highway construction and sharply curtailing expenditures on parks. Sawyer urged Patterson to seek legislation directing the Highway Commission to spend "annually for as long as necessary at least $100,000 for the acquisition of parks, timbered strips along the highways and other recreational and scenic areas."[33] Legally such a directive was not needed since the Highway Commission already had authority to make such expenditures, but it would strengthen the hand of the present commission and help ensure that future commissioners continued its parks program.

In putting forward such a proposal, Sawyer was abandoning the position that one should avoid making expenditures on parks a public issue. The reasons for this change are not clear. Perhaps he felt emboldened by the presence in Salem of a governor who supported the commission's program, or perhaps he had been inspired to take more vigorous action while in attendance some three months before at the annual meeting of the National Conference on State Parks. Whatever the reason, the change was momentary and without effect. Patterson recognized what Sawyer had earlier: substantial progress was being made, progress that might be threatened by submitting the program for scrutiny by cost-conscious legislators and, through them, by the public. Patterson took no action on Sawyer's proposal; indeed, when he addressed the legislature, he emphasized the necessity of cutting back on nonessential programs.[34]

Patterson soon came forward with a parks proposal of his own, however. On 22 May 1929, he met with the Highway Commission. There was, he observed, "considerable interest among the people of the state on the subject of parks." He noted that William Gladstone Steel, who had led the earlier movement to have Crater Lake set aside as a national park, had publicly proposed that a state park commission be established. The idea had evoked much favorable comment, especially among members of a civic group in Astoria with whom Patterson had just met. He assured the commission of his own interest in preserving roadside beauty and announced his intention of appointing the highway commissioners, together with former commission chairmen William C. Duby and R. A. Booth, to serve as a parks commission.[35]

The commission Patterson appointed was a proven group. Sawyer, Van Duzer, and Charles E. Gates were daily demonstrating their interest in parks, while Booth had been a key figure in Ben Olcott's crusade and Duby the commissioner most interested in roadside beauty during the years just prior to Sawyer's appointment. Indeed, when Sawyer was named to replace Duby on the commission, he had praised Duby's contributions to the highway system and scenery preservation and expressed the hope that he would be able to do as well.[36]

It is not clear how Sawyer and Van Duzer felt about Patterson's parks commission. Sawyer, at least, may have welcomed it. The commission was not to be an independently funded agency of the sort Sauers had proposed, but a body that was to advise the Highway Commission on parks matters. As such, it supplanted the old advisory committee with which Sawyer had never been wholly satisfied.

Patterson himself may not have expected much from the new group. Due to the overlap of membership between the Highway and Parks commissions, it was in effect a body established to give itself advice. The Oregon State Parks Commission met on 24 July 1929, and formally adopted policies and guidelines already being informally pursued by the Highway Commission. It never met again. Except for providing a Parks Commission letterhead, this unpaid and powerless commission accomplished little if anything that the Highway Commission could not have done alone. But perhaps Patterson was not unhappy with the results. By appointing the commission, he had demonstrated that he stood on the side of the angels on a popular issue and helped squelch proposals for an independent agency.[37]

While Patterson was creating his Parks Commission, Sawyer renewed his efforts to win Van Duzer and Gates over to the idea of appointing a parks superintendent. Some time during the summer of 1929 he gained their grudging approval. The first application for the position was dated 23 July, just one day before the meeting of the Parks Commission. Other applications quickly followed.[38] Van Duzer and Gates seem to have conceived of the position as temporary and limited in scope. Rather than hire Mark H. Astrup, a well-qualified candidate heartily recommended by A. L. Peck (the driving force behind the old advisory committee), or one of the other applicants, the commission decided to find someone already employed by the Highway Department. As Roy Klein explained to Astrup,

> the Commission has . . . decided to limit the work for the present to securing timber lands alongside the highway, as that is the most pressing need, particularly in places where logging operations are in progress. Therefore, to meet the present situation, we have decided to appoint one of our engineering employes [sic] to handle this work who has a knowledge of timber and land values and whose job it will be for the next few months to handle this work.

Next spring, Klein added, "the Commission may consider the actual development of the parks areas, in which case we will probably then desire to employ a man who has training and experience in landscape work and park development." Neither he nor the commissioners seem to have suspected that the temporary appointment of "one of our engineering employes" marked the beginning of what was to be a twenty-one year tenure in office for Samuel H. Boardman, Oregon's first State Parks Superintendent.[39]

At first, Boardman's position carried the title of Parks Engineer, a term perhaps chosen because it sounded utilitarian enough to stave off critics of unnecessary expenditures and indicated the rather limited range of activities that he was expected to pursue. As planned, Boardman first turned his attention to roadside timber, but he soon began to give equal attention to scenic park sites.

The position Sawyer had pushed to have created and the man who filled it combined to provide the continuity and security Sawyer had been seeking. It is well that they did. Governor Patterson died in December 1929, and Sawyer was soon removed from the commission following a dispute with the new governor, A. W. Norblad, over road-building priorities. Suddenly, Sawyer was in no position to ensure the continued acquisition and development of state parks.[40]

In the years that followed his ouster from the Highway Commission, Sawyer continued to be active in conservation causes. He was an outspoken champion of sustained-yield timber management, a president of the National Reclamation Association, and a leader in efforts to regulate roadside billboards. His many public services led ex-governor Charles Sprague, shortly before Sawyer's retirement in 1953, to describe the editor from Bend as Oregon's outstanding citizen of the last quarter century.[41]

Sprague may not have been aware of Sawyer's contribution to the state's parks. By that time, Boardman was being publicly described as "father of the Oregon state parks," though Boardman himself admitted that Sawyer was the "yeast that raised the Park Department [sic] into being."[42] Sawyer was indeed responsible. His success in implementing a parks system that had both the security of earmarked funds and the continuity of a permanent superintendent may well have been the greatest accomplishment of his long career of public service.

Chapter 5

Asahel Curtis, Herbert Evison, and the Parks and Roadside Timber of Washington State

From its beginnings, the state parks movement in the Pacific Northwest was intimately tied to efforts to save roadside beauty. Stephen Mather and Madison Grant had emphasized preserving timber along the highways when they campaigned on the West Coast in 1919. Ben Olcott and Robert Sawyer were deeply interested in the problem, and when Samuel Boardman took over as Oregon's first state parks superintendent his initial efforts were aimed at saving roadside timber.

The connection was not accidental. Concerns both for establishing parks and for preserving roadside trees were, in the Northwest at least, products of the automobile revolution. With the widespread adoption of the automobile around 1920 the level of such activity abruptly increased.

Along with crusades for state parks and roadside timber, campaigns were launched to regulate roadside billboards (and the ubiquitous smaller signs that sprang up along roads in an age when autos went slowly enough that travelers could read them); to protect wild flowers and shrubs from hordes of newly mobile bouquet gatherers, who picked and transplanted in such quantities that rhododendron and other spectacular roadside plants had begun to show serious signs of depletion; and to prevent electricity, telephone, and telegraph companies from destroying or mutilating trees along roads in the process of erecting their lines.[1]

Of all these many efforts, none was more ambitious—nor enlisted a wider range of supporters—than that which sought to save stands of roadside timber. Without the trees that gave the area much of its scenic appeal, none of the lesser campaigns would be of much use. Roadside timber was being rapidly felled; caves, canyons, and other sites of the sort that would eventually go into state parks seemed—and often actually were—in less immediate danger.

The most ambitious of the many efforts at saving roadside timber in the Pacific Northwest focused on saving the forests bordering major highways in Washington's Cascade Range. In the end, Oregon was to preserve more miles of roadside timber, but its bordering strips were scattered in different parts of the state. Moreover, the effort was less difficult to bring to fruition there because Oregon's lumber industry had developed more slowly. Throughout the nation only the Save-the-Redwoods League mounted a crusade as concentrated in focus and as fraught with difficulties as that undertaken in Washington. Because of the uniqueness of the redwoods, however, the League enjoyed a level of support from outside the state that preservationists in Washington never had.[2] From first to last, local residents dominated the crusade for roadside timber in the Evergreen State.

No one epitomized this effort better, or was more important to it, than Asahel Curtis. Born in southern Minnesota in 1874, Curtis moved to Washington with his family while still a child. Curtis's father died when the boy was just thirteen, but Asahel managed to get an education in the Kitsap County schools nonetheless and in 1894, following in the footsteps of his older brother Edward, embarked on a career as a professional photographer. Asahel remained in that profession all his adult life, while keeping active in a variety of civic and outdoor organizations. Curtis spent 1897–98 in Alaska, drawn there by gold fever, and for a time in 1903 worked in San Francisco. In 1904 he returned to the Pacific Northwest to take a job as a photographer for the *Tacoma Ledger*. He then moved to Seattle, which served as his base of operations for the rest of his career. From 1904 to 1906 he was a staff photographer with the *Post-Intelligencer*, and then in 1906 opened his own studio in the heart of the downtown business district. There Curtis both plied his trade and developed the contacts so important later in his campaigns to protect Washington's scenic beauty.[3]

As a photographer, Curtis had varied interests. Like his brother, he frequently photographed Indians, but unlike Edward's studies, which tended to be carefully posed and romanticized, Asahel's less sentimental pictures received only modest acclaim. He also took many commercial views, which not only helped to make his studio prosperous but also reflected the streak of local boosterism that was a part of his makeup. But the younger Curtis was most noted as a nature photographer: his scenic views enjoyed wide popularity. Most showed Washington scenes, Mount Rainier being his favorite subject.[4]

Curtis had apparently loved the outdoors since his boyhood. He had begun leading climbing parties up Mount Rainier and other peaks by 1908. He was a founder of the Mountaineers, a Seattle-based alpinists' organization in which he participated throughout his active life.[5] Such interests, coupled with his growing influence in Seattle, led to his being selected in 1912 for the Seattle-Tacoma Rainier National Park Joint Committee, a body formed that year to push for "a practical and well defined policy" for development of the park. Curtis may well have been the driving force behind the creation of the committee. In any case, he was elected its chairman and served on an eight-man executive committee that hammered out a plan for the park for presentation to Secretary of the Interior Walter L. Fisher.[6]

The idea of a joint committee had originally been broached to the New Seattle Chamber of Commerce, the Tacoma Commercial Club and Chamber of Commerce, the Seattle Commercial Club, and the Rotary clubs of Seattle and Tacoma. Each organization approved the idea and appointed a representative to serve in the group. Since Seattle and Tacoma had been squabbling for years over whether the peak should be called Mount Rainier or Mount Tacoma, the decision to form a joint committee was a refreshing departure.[7] By simply calling their body the Rainier National Park Joint Committee, the members sidestepped the issue of the proper name for the mountain itself and proceeded instead to try to spell out their common ideas about development of the park.

The end product of the committee's work was a nine-point proposal calling for creation of a Bureau of National Parks, improved access, facilities and protection for Rainier Park, and the preservation of roadside timber along routes leading to it. The last, especially, was a harbinger of things to come. As the committee put it, the "park approach would lose a great deal of its beauty and interest through the cutting away of these wonderful trees. As matters stand, the forest border of the highway is gradually disappearing. The cutting of the trees cannot be permanently stopped unless the acreage along the roadway is taken over by the Government." The group proposed land exchanges to bring the timber under governmental control. For twenty years and more, Curtis and his allies were to push for preservation of these stands.[8]

Following its report, the joint committee hired Samuel Christopher Lancaster to lobby in Washington, D.C. As a highway engineer who had laid out parkways and tree-lined boulevards in Seattle and as an enthusiastic and articulate lover of nature, Lancaster was well qualified for the task. His efforts may have been responsible for the funds that were soon forthcoming for road-building in the park. When construction began, Lancaster played a key role in the work.[9]

Gradually, the joint committee—and Curtis—retreated from the limelight, but neither stayed away long. When Stephen Mather and Madison Grant visited Washington in 1919, they sought out the committee. Mather, Grant, and a group of Washington residents made the arduous hike into what one member of the party described as "that wonderland of parks and meadows" to the north of the mountain. It was there that the idea of forming a Natural Parks Association of Washington was first broached.

For some reason, Curtis was not a member of this party, but Herbert Evison was. Young, enthusiastic, and articulate, Evison quickly became a leading figure in the NPA. He served as its secretary and primary spokesman. Too junior to have much personal influence, Evison worked assiduously to enlist Curtis and others in the cause. As a result, the NPA quickly became an influential body, outstripping the old Seattle-Tacoma joint committee because of its greater vigor and broader purpose.[10]

Curtis was a member of NPA from the first; his name appears on its letterhead as one of twenty-seven vice presidents. Curtis may have thought he was only lending his name to the cause, for he does not appear to have been intimately involved in the NPA during its first months. Gradually, however, Curtis's interest rose as he watched Evison and the organization in action.[11]

In January 1920 Evison announced the first of the Natural Parks

Association's efforts. For most people, the existence of the organization was itself news, for it had been established only a few months before. Evison revealed that Mather, as Director of the National Park Service, was requesting $100,000 from Congress to build a road to Mount Rainier National Park from the northwest. The road, first proposed by the Seattle-Tacoma joint committee in 1912, was to run along the Carbon River, bringing Seattle sixty miles closer to the park and opening the high parklands and meadows to the north of the mountain to motorists. Perhaps not coincidentally, the area Mather proposed opening was the one he, Grant, Evison, and others had camped in the year before.

Evison had qualms. "It seems almost a shame to think of offering anything so great to the not-very-energetic tourist," he wrote, but he welcomed Mather's proposal nonetheless. For its part, the NPA had a land exchange bill under preparation that would bring the whole route, much of which lay outside the park (and even beyond neighboring national forest boundaries), under control of the Park Service. Such an exchange was needed, Evison explained, "so that the menace to that timber [along the proposed highway] may be removed." The Manley-Moore Lumber Company had already scheduled logging along a key portion of the route, but had "consented to leave it all untouched" until an exchange for land north of the park could be authorized.[12]

Victory came quickly. A road was built to the park boundary, and exchange legislation was soon passed and signed into law by President Warren G. Harding. But this was a minor route in a remote area. Faced with no real opposition, the NPA had only to overcome inertia to gain victory. Unfortunately, subsequent efforts to connect the route with other roads within the park failed; it was destined to remain a dead-end route of little significance. Still, this initial triumph spurred on members of the NPA in their efforts to save Washington's scenery.[13]

Subsequent challenges proved more difficult. State officials had no funds with which to buy parks, so the NPA tried to move into the breach when emergency situations arose. In 1921, "a fine virgin timber park" on the Stevens Pass highway seemed in danger, so the association raised funds to take over and operate the eighteen-acre site until the state could do so. "Should the experiment prove successful," one NPA official told Moran, "it is planned to extend it to other areas."[14] A similar effort to save a stand of cedars on the

Parks of Washington

LEGEND:

Highways	(solid line)
Rivers	(wavy line)
Cities	○
National Parks	■
State Parks	●

CANADA

IDAHO

OREGON

PACIFIC OCEAN

Columbia River
Spokane River
Snake River
Yakima River
Naches River
White River
Carbon River
Nisqually R.
Hood Canal
Willapa Bay
Grays Harbor
Lake Chelan
Puget Sound

BLUE MOUNTAINS
CASCADE RANGE

PULLMAN
CLARKSTON
WALLA WALLA
Whitman Mission National Historical Site
Steptoe Butte
SPOKANE
PASCO
WENATCHEE
ELLENSBURG
YAKIMA
North Cascades National Park
Deception Pass
BELLINGHAM
Larrabee
San Juan Island National Historical Park
Olympic National Park
EVERETT
SEATTLE
BREMERTON
TACOMA
ENUMCLAW
Federation Forest
Mather Memorial Parkway
Mt. Rainier National Park
Mt. St. Helens National Volcanic Monument
OLYMPIA
Millersylvania
ABERDEEN
Twin Harbors
LONGVIEW
VANCOUVER

Snoqualmie Pass highway followed, but the costs of such efforts were a strain on the NPA (and on Evison).[15] The group turned to the legislature to get laws to make the state more active in acquiring parks and in roadside protection, thereby relieving the NPA of the burden of purchasing land itself.

Mather and Grant stepped forward to aid the NPA. Mather donated $500 to help acquire the Stevens Pass timber, and Grant returned to Seattle to lend personal support. At a meeting of the association in August 1921, Grant addressed the group:

> [L]et me plead with you to do this thing on a big scale . . . If you spend . . . now you will receive a great deal for it; if you postpone it you will save very little for it. If you do now you will have almost the only spot on earth that is unspoiled; and we can keep one portion of this land of ours in a condition fit to live in, fit to fight for, and which will show to those that come after us some part of the beauty that nature has lavished upon us.[16]

Encouraged by Grant's eloquence, Evison was sanguine about prospects for state action. Signs of support were forthcoming from a variety of civic groups, the state Republican organization adopted a platform for the forthcoming elections supporting scenery preservation, and State Land Commissioner Clark V. Savidge announced that in 1919 he planned to ask the legislature to amend the state park law, which allowed him to set aside five-acre parks along highways, so as to permit larger withdrawals and setting aside land for the protection of roadside timber as well as parks.[17] After speaking to the state Good Roads convention, Evison wrote Robert Moran that "public interest in the matter appears to be very general and strongly in favor of as quick action as possible to build up a good state park system."[18]

Evison may well have been right. The NPA's package of parks-related legislation was introduced at the legislature's 1921 session by Howard W. Allen, and after some suspense key portions were enacted, although the five-acre limitation remained.[19]

Evison reported the legislative victories to Moran, Curtis, and others.[20] Cheered by these successes, Curtis stepped up his involvement. When John Culp wrote Curtis shortly after Evison's report, seeking support for a national park near Wenatchee to honor Americans who had died in World War I, Curtis replied that Culp would find it easier and quicker to get a state park: "The sentiment in favor of State Parks is, I believe, very strong and when the legislature meets again, it is quite probable that we will secure some [more] constructive legislation."[21]

Still, finance was a nagging concern. In his letter to Culp, Curtis acknowledged that there was in the legislature "a mood to curtail all expenditures whether it is real constructive work or not." Unwilling to appropriate tax monies for parks and roadside timber, the legislature had created a State Parks and Parkways Fund and earmarked up to $50,000 for the biennium, to be derived from 25 percent of all fines for highway violations outside of cities. The legislature also created a force of highway police, which meant among other things that a significant number of fines would actually be levied. This financial sleight-of-hand failed to work, generating only some $15,000 for the Park and Parkways Fund over the next two years, far too little to achieve the goals of the NPA and its allies. Obviously, new legislation would be needed.[22]

Evison remained optimistic. Having seen the bulk of the NPA's legislative package passed in 1921, he anticipated a similar victory when the legislature met again in 1923. He was confident enough to look beyond the question of finances to long-range needs. He wanted the state to undertake a scenic resources survey. As he told Curtis, "If our state park development is to be logical and ordered, calculated to meet the recreational needs of all parts of the state, it cannot be handled in a hap-hazard manner." He proposed creating a body of experts which—with the help of the NPA, local chambers of commerce, the auto clubs, and others—would survey the state's recreational potential and formulate a long-term plan of action.[23] Evison brushed aside the question of financing such a study, but to Curtis that issue was central. "Go ahead and try," he said, "and see where we get off. So far we haven't succeeded in getting a thing done"—at least not anything that required funding through taxes. Curtis clearly anticipated little change when the legislature met again in 1923.[24]

Moran shared Curtis's pessimism. The watchword of the present, Moran wrote as the legislature reassembled, is economy and lower taxes, which "can go to such extremes as to be poor business for the future of the state." He explained that

[w]e of the northwest are just beginning to realize the value of our natural resources in climate and scenic beauty, and if we are to reap . . . full value from the tourist trade there has got to be money used in preserving scenic spots of timber along the highways [and] also more money to improve the state parks. . . . It would be shortsighted policy to do otherwise.[25]

Moran's interpretation of the public mood was based on more than general observation. Only a short time before, the editor of the *Friday Harbor Journal*, the key paper in Moran's beloved San Juan Islands, had told Moran in no uncertain terms that if the legislators made "a blanket appropriation" for scenic highways and parks, "they should receive universal condemnation." The crying need was for tax reduction, the editor argued; "'economy' should be the watchword of this legislative session."[26] The feeling, it appeared, was widespread.

Whatever the public mood, new sources of support would have to be found if parks were to be adequately funded and scenic roadside timber saved. A variety of proposals were forthcoming. J. J. Donovan, one of the state's leading lumbermen as well as vice president of the NPA, suggested increasing auto license fees and earmarking 10 percent of each year's highway funds for parks until the necessary acquisitions had been made. Since this funding would come largely from licenses and gasoline taxes, both user's fees, no new taxes on the general public would be needed. Donovan was anticipating the sort of funding that Oregon was to begin using soon after for its parks program, but his proposal went nowhere. At a time when highway construction needs far exceeded available funds, the idea of reducing construction money by 10 percent had little appeal.[27]

Others in the Natural Parks Association had more practical ideas. Curtis helped frame a package of four new proposals for the 1923 legislature. These included: (1) eliminating the five-acre limit on purchases by the State Land Commissioner for roadside parks and the requirement that the legislature approve donations of land for parks (the requirement that had held up acquisition of Moran State Park for so long); (2) amending the Motor Vehicle Act so that all receipts from non-urban fines, not just 25 percent of them, would go into the Parks and Parkway Fund; (3) calling upon Congress to transfer to the state unused military reservations that had scenic or recreational value; and (4) levying an excise tax on outdoor advertising and placing the proceeds in the Parks and Parkways Fund (a proposal inspired by legislation passed shortly before by Connecticut and Vermont).[28]

For all Evison's optimism, only a portion of the second NPA legislative package became law. The main setbacks came on the vital question of funding. The proposed tax on billboards lost, despite arguments that since outdoor advertising detracted from scenic beauty it was equitable that advertisers be charged with some of the costs of protecting it. In addition, only 50 percent of the fines for motor vehicle violations in rural areas was earmarked for parks.[29] Worse still, in the months that followed, receipts from this source proved much smaller than anticipated; some of the larger counties, whose local authorities collected the fines, simply failed to forward the state's portion. Evison maintained that four or five times as much would have to be appropriated by the 1925 and 1927 legislatures "if we are to accomplish what we should."[30]

Although disappointed, the NPA was not prepared to give up the struggle. The Washington Natural Parks Association joined others in arranging a statewide conference on scenic resource preservation. Representatives of some forty organizations—including the Auto Club of Washington, the State Federation of Women's Clubs, the State Chamber of Commerce, and the State Press Association— gathered in Seattle in March 1924. They issued a joint call for a state park policy commission, apparently hoping that such collective action would force the legislature to respond. Nothing concrete resulted. After the conference, the groups went their separate ways, and leadership was left to the same handful of stalwarts who had supplied it before.[31]

At this time Evison and Curtis revived the old campaign of 1912 to save timber along the White River west of the Cascade divide, for it was in imminent danger of being felled. The Chinook Pass highway through the area was nearing completion; once opened, this road was sure to be a main route to Mount Rainier National Park. No place in the state rivaled Rainier in the minds of champions of the state's scenery; if there was a route whose beauty must be protected above all others, this surely was it. But doing so would be no small undertaking. Miles of prime Douglas fir timber were involved.[32]

The NPA was not alone in its campaign to save the White River stands. The moribund Seattle-Tacoma joint committee reorganized in 1924 as the Rainier National Park Advisory Board. Curtis once again served as chairman. He quickly molded the new body into a respected and effective voice that concerned itself not just with timber along White River but with much else as well. A major portion of the group's strength came from Curtis himself. As one superintendent of Mount Rainier National Park explained, Curtis's "keen powers of observation and excellent judgement of country make his opinions of no small value."[33] His understanding of people and the political scene and his friendship with a host of civic and business leaders were no less valuable.

To Curtis and Evison it was clear that major new sources of support were necessary to meet the threat to the White River stands—to say nothing of timber elsewhere along the Chinook Pass highway. Accordingly they tried a new tack. Since neither highway funds (including fines) nor direct appropriations seemed apt to be forthcoming in sufficient quantities to meet pressing needs, the association proposed a $1,500,000 bond issue for parks and parkways. Robert Moran was among those who endorsed the idea. Clifford Babcock provided the basic argument: the advocates of parks and parkways were building for the future, and through bonds future residents of Washington were being asked to help pay for the benefits they would enjoy. In the end, this idea also went nowhere. Evison grumbled that it was time to "quit fooling around, trying to get money from this fund or that, and concentrate on securing an outright appropriation out of the general fund."[34]

At this juncture the preservationists suddenly received help from an unexpected quarter. The National Conference on Outdoor Recreation met in the nation's capital in May 1924. There, William B. Greeley, chief of the Forest Service, announced his support for the preservation of roadside timber for scenic purposes and for the exchange of private roadside stands for national forest timber located away from the highways. Greeley further indicated that he would support a congressional bill, which the NPA was then preparing, to achieve these goals.[35]

Greeley's support was important. The Forest Service held many of the most scenic stretches of roadside timber in the West, but lacking clear guidelines from Congress (and from their own leaders), its personnel had waffled on the question of scenic strips. Some, believing that the Forest Service should manage its holdings for maximum economic return, thought that exchanges for scenery protection were unwise. Others, although sympathetic to efforts to protect scenery and sometimes willing to place selected stands in scenic reserves (as had been done earlier in the Columbia River Gorge), believed they lacked legal authority to make exchanges with private landholders. Because of this division, the Forest Service had frequently given mixed messages to the advocates of scenery preservation. Greeley changed all that. He—and thus his minions—would henceforth support legislation authorizing exchanges. No longer could Forest Service officials take a purely utilitarian stance on the subject and expect support from headquarters.[36]

But however encouraging Greeley's statements were, political developments inside the Evergreen State soon cancelled them out. If things had seemed bad in the face of the disinterest of governors Ernest Lister (1913–19) and Louis F. Hart (1919–25), they grew far worse when Roland H. Hartley assumed the governorship in 1925. Evison, Curtis, and their supporters now had to deal with outright hostility from the governor on the one hand and with political chaos on the other. Further progress suddenly appeared unlikely, and much of that already won seemed in danger of being lost.

Hartley was an unlikely governor. The product of an impoverished boyhood, he had grown up ambitious, eager for acceptance, but insecure. A fortunate marriage aided his rise to a position of local importance in the lumber business, but Hartley remained a man of limited abilities. Irascible and unpolished, he was given to fits of temper in which he would harangue and abuse anyone who crossed him. Compromise and concession seemed beyond him. He did not trust others to act out of anything other than gross self-interest. Moreover, Hartley had little political experience, having served but a single term as mayor of Everett and another as a state representative. In the legislature, Hartley followed the Republican line, but he was not a member of the party's inner circle. He was a late-arriving outsider there, just as he was in the state's lumber industry.[37]

When Hartley first sought the governorship in 1916, his platform had a single plank: The state should protect the open shop and "industrial freedom." In 1924 his platform was only slightly broader, emphasizing the need for ending waste in government. As he bluntly put it, "The people are entitled to a dollar's worth of service for every

dollar of public money expended." Despite charges of corrupt political practices and opposition from the Republican establishment,
Hartley rode these simplistic nostrums to the gubernatorial nomination in 1924. Republican stalwarts and public-spirited citizens such as
Curtis watched with some trepidation as Hartley won in the general
election that followed.[38]

Hartley's inaugural address repeated his calls for economy in
government. He told the assembled legislators, "we are too much
governed. The agencies of government have been multiplied, their
ramifications extended, their powers enlarged, and their sphere
widened until the whole system is top heavy."[39] He was particularly
critical of the state's highway program. One lawmaker summed up
Hartley's address as "the gloomy, sordid recital of the extreme
materialist."[40] It was indeed.

The first months of Hartley's administration did nothing to
lessen concern. The state careened from crisis to crisis as the governor
lashed out at first one enemy, then another. Parks were among the
targets of his budget-cutting axe, if not his overt wrath. He vetoed a
$50,000 appropriation for state parks and a bill giving the State Parks
Board the power of condemnation. In the end, parks received only
$12,900 for the biennium. Moran called Hartley's approach "a
narrow-minded policy." Evison agreed and feared that worse was yet
to come. Nobody knows what the governor will do, he told Moran,
adding that Hartley "does not seem to be able to get anything he
wants, [but] he seems abundantly able to keep others from getting
what they want or need."[41]

Advocates of parks and roadside protection despaired of
progress as long as Hartley remained in office. When one citizen
proposed making a site he favored into a state park, Clark Savidge
replied lamely that the State Parks Board "is not sure of the advis-
ability of establishing another park at this time."[42] Internal squabbling exacerbated problems. As pessimism spread, the Natural Parks
Association crumbled. It had been in financial straits since 1922, and
a membership drive the following year proved insufficient. Only the
legislative successes of 1921 and 1923 had kept the organization viable
by encouraging donors; now, with defeats, not victories, to anticipate, donations dried up.[43]

With the demise of the NPA, primary leadership in the movement for scenery protection passed to Asahel Curtis. Unlike Evison,

Curtis was financially secure; he was also sufficiently influential in his own right not to be left impotent when the NPA collapsed.

In an attempt to insure Evison of continued influence, Curtis had the young Seattlite named assistant secretary of the Rainier National Park Advisory Board. The move helped but little. Evison wanted the RNPAB to move aggressively to bring the Kiwanis, Rotary, Lions, and similar groups into the parks movement. Curtis demurred, preferring a more low-key approach. To bring in so many groups, he argued, "would give us a pretty large number to educate without bringing in any additional influence that would aid us in development work." Evison had to acquiesce. For the moment he was left without a role to play.[44]

Curtis, on the other hand, was increasingly active, attacking on a variety of fronts. He worked closely with Robert Moran seeking appropriations for and additions to Moran State Park, he used the Rainier National Park Advisory Board to generate pressure for scenery protection, and he sought to persuade the Washington State Chamber of Commerce to assume the NPA's role of primary voice for scenery protection.

Curtis's work with the Chamber of Commerce seemed the most promising of these efforts. As a statewide group with a large, influential membership and solid financial support, the chamber could accomplish more than the NPA ever had. Perhaps the basic weakness of the NPA was best indicated by the fact that thirteen of its twenty-seven vice presidents were from Seattle.

In the summer of 1927, the state chamber agreed to Curtis's proposal that it create a State Park Advisory Board to work with state authorities "to coordinate the plans of the various communities in the matter of selection of State Parks and their proper development from the standpoint of protection of the objects that make them worthy of being State Parks."[45] Chamber leaders asked Curtis to head the group. He agreed, hoping that he would also be able to persuade Moran, Whitcomb (who was by this time president of the Seattle Chamber of Commerce), and others of recognized stature to join him. Among other things, he wanted to use the chamber's advisory board to bring about the sort of state recreational survey that Evison had pushed for earlier.[46]

But when Curtis approached the state, through Clark Savidge, he received a lukewarm reception. Savidge indicated that "because of the situation existing in our State" the parks board wanted to discuss the matter with Curtis privately.[47] Later, Curtis revealed what supposedly lay behind his hesitancy: "The State Park Commission [sic] approved the idea but felt it was not an opportune time for fear they would be laying themselves liable to the charge that they were calling in outside help because they could not properly administer the parks."[48] Other factors may well have been involved. H. W. Rutherford, who was then employed in the relatively powerless position of State Parks Superintendent, told Evison "it is extremely difficult to get anywhere with the board comprised as it is now." Evison agreed. Reorganization was needed; authority should be centered in one man who would attend to the system rather than assigned to a three-man board that had two members always "ready to throw a monkey wrench in the machinery" but never ready to give constructive attention to parks.[49] The only change, however, was that Harry A. Young replaced Rutherford as parks superintendent. Moran implied in a letter to Curtis that Young's appointment was part of Hartley's attempt to build a political machine. What is clear is that Curtis thought little of Young's subsequent performance and blamed him for some of the troubles that beset the state's park system in the months that followed.[50]

If Curtis and his allies hoped things would get better after the gubernatorial election of 1928, they were badly mistaken. Hartley survived censure by the state House of Representatives (on a 60 to 33 vote), a recall movement (sparked partly by his war on the University of Washington and its president Henry A. Suzzallo), a referendum to put highway funds (and the patronage and power that went with them) beyond his grasp, and an effort by old-line Republicans to wrest control of party machinery from him. In 1928, against all odds and the opposition of most of the state's newspapers, Hartley won reelection.[51]

Things promptly got worse for champions of scenery protection. When the legislature met in 1929, Hartley vetoed an appropriation of $200,000 for the highway along Carbon River to Mount Rainier National Park and all appropriations for state parks, which he described as "nick-naks."[52] Savidge wrote despairingly to Curtis, "Only those of us who have put our heart work into getting a system of parks for our state before the choice spots were gone can understand our feelings as we stand in the presence of the disaster that has come to them. I think it is the greatest length to which the Governor has yet gone. . . . We will not have a penny to spend for we can not even use our receipts." Having no remaining options, the State Park Board began closing parks.[53]

Curtis was distraught, but he did not lay all the blame at Hartley's door. Superintendent Young, the State Park Board, and the legislature had contributed too. Curtis told Moran, "At the present time we appear to be wholly lacking in any leadership . . . in State Parks, with such a fear of power of the Chief Executive of our state that no one dares lift a voice." There was little Curtis could do that he had not tried already, and he confessed "I have grown just a bit weary . . . [from being] blocked at every turn."[54] To make matters worse, at this juncture Herbert Evison left the state to become secretary of the National Conference on State Parks.[55] Curtis and Evison had had their disagreements, primarily on methods, but they had been an effective team. Henceforth Curtis would have to fight his battles—and overcome his moments of depression—without Evison as an on-the-scene ally and confidant.

Curtis may have been growing weary, but he did not give up. He simply shifted his focus away from state parks. Curtis became involved in the contest between the Forest Service and Park Service over control of the greater portion of the Olympic Mountains, across Puget Sound from Seattle; in efforts to bring development to Mount Rainier National Park without doing damage to its beauty; and in the campaign to save timber along the Chinook Pass (Naches) highway, which had taken a back seat to more urgent concerns during the first years of the Hartley administration.

The issues to which Curtis now turned his attention were fraught with controversy, but at least they seemed to offer room for accomplishments; the same could not be said for state parks as long as Hartley occupied the governor's chair. Even the cooperation of the National Conference on State Parks and its field representative, Charles G. Sauers, failed to bring a shift in the balance of power.[56]

Curtis had additional reasons for changing emphasis. Activity was continuing on other issues about which he had strong feelings. In 1926 the State Federation of Women's Clubs mounted a drive to raise $62,000 to save a stretch of virgin timber along the Sunset Highway; the Weyerhaeuser Timber Company alone donated $5,000.[57] At about the same time, the Tourist Committee of the Seattle Chamber of Commerce recommended building an aerial tramway to the summit of Mount Rainier. As chairman of the Rainier National Park Advisory Board, Curtis was bombarded with arguments pro and con.[58] Also, debate over the proposed Olympic National Park was heating up. Curtis was soon pulled into that controversy too.[59]

For the moment, saving timber along Chinook Pass highway was his greatest concern. Since 1912 Curtis had lobbied without much success for steps to save the trees along this route, especially those along the White River portion. Only the fact that most of the highway had not yet been opened protected most of the stands.

By the late 1920s developments were pushing the issue to the forefront. Highway construction would soon connect Yakima to the park by way of the Naches River and Chinook Pass; there the route would turn north along the White River toward Enumclaw, Tacoma, and Seattle and connect with a highway from the south that the National Park Service was building along the Ohanapecosh River. Completion of these highways had been urged in 1912 by the Seattle-Tacoma joint committee, and by others both then and later, but construction had been repeatedly delayed. Officials of the Park Service wanted the highway to run through the park, but the best route lay to the east of it. To solve this problem, they proposed extending Mount Rainier National Park eastward to the crest of the Cascades and Crystal Mountain, which extended as a spur from main summit. Even without a new highway, the NPS would have welcomed this change, for it would provide a better boundary than the existing one which followed section lines.

After some initial reluctance, authorities in the Forest Service were persuaded to accept the transfer of the proposed addition from their jurisdiction to the Park Service, a concession they found acceptable largely because the area contained little merchantable timber. The state of Washington also had reservations about the transfer, for it hesitated to build a highway that would be partly under the control of the Park Service, fearing the NPS would seek to charge entrance fees or tolls to through traffic as well as park visitors. This concern was alleviated when the Park Service agreed to wording in the congressional act of transfer that assured state control of the highway and made clear that tolls could be charged only to travelers turning off the highway into the park itself. As chairman of the Rainier National Park Advisory Board, Curtis was in the midst of the involved discussions triggered by the proposed changes.[60]

With these compromises agreed to, construction was soon proceeding apace. As it did, the threat of logging along the access roads leading to the park became more pressing than ever. As early as 1912, Curtis had urged the saving not only of timber within the park and along the highways to it where they passed through national forests, but also privately owned roadside timber beyond the national forest boundaries toward Enumclaw. In the late 1920s he and others renewed their agitation to save these stands.

At this point Stephen Mather reentered the picture. In 1928, while on an official inspection of Mount Rainier National Park, Mather became an enthusiastic supporter of Curtis's dream. He threw his own considerable influence and enthusiasm into the effort to save all seventy-five timbered miles of what he labeled the "Cascade Parkway." Mather won support for the idea from Charles Donnelly, president of the Northern Pacific Railroad Company, and from Henry S. Rhodes, president of the Rainier National Park Company. Meanwhile, Park Service and Forest Service personnel joined Curtis in organizing supporters and promoting the proposed parkway, some fifty-five miles of which ran through federally owned land.[61] Curtis also discussed timber exchanges with officials of the White River Lumber Company and solicited support from civic and commercial groups.[62]

In January 1929, Mather left Washington, D.C., en route to Seattle, where he intended to aid local efforts in behalf of the parkway. He suffered a stroke, however, during a stopover in Chicago. Rushed to St. Luke's hospital in critical condition and barely able to speak, Mather managed to say "Cascade" to Horace M. Albright, his closest aide. Eventually Albright was able to determine that Mather meant the Cascade Parkway—he either wanted a progress report or to encourage his lieutenant not to give up working for it. In the days that followed, Mather mentioned the Cascade Parkway again and again to visitors.[63]

As news of Mather's condition spread, tributes poured in, and friends organized the Stephen T. Mather Appreciation Association to commemorate his unparalleled contributions to the nation's parks. Curtis was a member from the first. Following Mather's death from a second stroke on 20 January 1930, Curtis proposed to the association that the parkway Mather had championed be named the Stephen T. Mather Memorial Parkway. The Rainier National Park

Advisory Board had gone on record twelve days before in favor of naming it in Mather's honor. Forest Service officials joined those of the National Park Service in endorsing this idea. Conservationists across the nation lent support to the Mather Appreciation Association and the proposed parkway. Evison lobbied in Washington, where the National Conference on State Parks was headquartered.[64]

Responding to these pressures, Secretary of Agriculture Arthur M. Hyde prepared an Executive Order dated 24 March 1931 setting aside a strip of land extending one-half mile on either side of the road for the entire fifty miles that it lay inside national forest boundaries; he designated it the Mather Memorial Highway. Secretary of the Interior Ray Lyman Wilbur followed suit on 23 April 1931, doing the same thing for the twelve-mile stretch of the highway that passed through land added to Mount Rainier National Park only three months earlier.[65]

The Mather Memorial Parkway was now a reality, although it still did not include the ten miles of timber that lay west of the Snoqualmie National Forest boundary. To add this land required action by the state of Washington. The state Automobile Club was already working toward this end and had plans to sponsor an enabling act when the legislature next met. The Rainier National Park Advisory Board quickly offered its support. As chairman, Curtis named a committee to coordinate its efforts with various other commercial and civic organizations, commenting that "real action would be expected" from the committee.[66] Ironically, the trees that were the subject of these efforts were those which the Seattle-Tacoma joint committee had sought to have preserved some two decades before when the campaign to protect roadside timber was just beginning.

Curtis and his allies hoped to have the parkway formally dedicated during the late summer of 1931. However, highway construction lagged behind schedule, and it was decided to postpone ceremonies until the following summer when the roadwork would be complete and greater attendance could therefore be expected. Nonetheless, in August 1931, a congressional delegation came west to join an inspection tour of the route. Governor Hartley was among those in the party.

The governor was notorious for his manipulation of highway

funds to curry support or punish opponents. With another gubernatorial election approaching, he may well have been thinking about
how he could turn the parkway to his advantage. Or he may simply
have been eager to win the applause of the assembled dignitaries,
representing as they did the sort of social leaders he had long viewed
with a mixture of envy and dislike. For whatever reason, Hartley
seized the opportunity to announce one of those startling reversals
that had come to mark his political career. He not only lauded the
parkway, but also declared that he would seek to have the state
extend it beyond the national forest boundaries.[67]

Curtis leaped to take advantage of this unexpected windfall. By
the time of the parkway's dedication the following summer, he and
others had already drafted a bill to extend the parkway for introduction in the 1933 legislative session and had begun organizing support
for it.[68]

Dedication ceremonies took place on 2 July 1932 at a site near
Tipsoo Lake and Chinook Pass. Some six feet of snow prevented
permanent placement of the bronze plaque dedicating the parkway to
Mather. Instead, it rested on an easel that Curtis provided. As part of
the proceedings, Governor Hartley addressed the assemblage. Again
he lauded the parkway and promised to seek its extension.[69]

In 1929 Curtis had complained that the members of the
"legislature will not [vote to] pass anything over the Governor's veto
and a few of them have no inclination to do anything without first
securing his approval."[70] Now, three years later, Hartley was on
Curtis's side, and the latter worked hard to turn the governor's
support to his own ends. As the legislature gathered in Olympia,
Curtis's corps of lobbyists pulled out all stops, countering concerns
about windthrow in roadside strips and the threat to state school
endowment lands that some thought exchanges represented. Once
the legislators' fears were assuaged, Curtis saw his bill quickly enacted. A similar act for timber along the Snoqualmie Pass highway
soon followed. Perhaps Curtis took perverse delight in knowledge
that, although Hartley had long opposed state parks, under this
legislation the state would administer the extension of the Mather
Memorial Parkway as a park.[71]

The battle won, Curtis penned a letter of thanks to Hartley,
saying "your pledge of support was of great value . . . and aided
materially in influencing others to join in this work."[72] There was

probably a great deal more that Curtis would have liked to have said, most of it not so flattering.

Curtis also wrote Evison. "When we started no one believed it could be done," he told his longtime ally, "and outside of you and one or two others, I had little support, but fortunately it wasn't needed. Your valuable work on the eastern end helped to overcome obstacles there and once the Federal reservation was set aside the rest was not so hard." Curtis also wrote to C. J. Buck of the Forest Service, thanking him for his encouragement and invaluable support.[73] Hartley, the late-arriving opportunist of the campaign, received no credit in these reviews of events—and deserved none.

But victory was not complete. Questions soon arose about the constitutionality of state participation in the planned exchanges, and the legislature stalled appropriations for timber surveys that were necessary if the exchanges were to be carried out. As a result, they were never consummated. The Mather Memorial Parkway was destined to terminate at the western boundary of the Snoqualmie National Forest; some fine roadside stands of big timber remained outside its protection.[74]

Despite the missing ten miles, Curtis had reason to celebrate. Moreover, other developments about this time helped compensate for the blocking of the White River exchanges. With a new governor in Olympia, the 1933 legislature appropriated more funds for state parks than ever before. W. G. Weigle, a respected Forest Service retiree, was hired as the new state parks superintendent and charged with resuscitating the system. Parks activists were delighted.[75] Their campaigns may not have prevented Hartley from gutting Washington's state parks, but at least they were able to insure that a residue of holdings and interest would survive him, a residue that provided Weigle with a starting point.

As a new day dawned for Washington's parks in 1934, Curtis described them in an article for the *Argus*, an influential Seattle journal. Washington had possessed state parks for years, he said, "but with no funds for development they were largely useless." The state had accomplished what it had "principally through the generosity of its citizens." Curtis did not mention his own role—just how generous he had been of his own time and talent—but those on the inside knew how vital it had been.[76] When he died in 1941, the *Seattle Post-Intelligencer* observed:

If he had been no more than a photographer . . . [his] influence would have been profound. But he was more. The intimate acquaintance of the region which he gained in his work was translated, at one point after another, into steps for its development. It is useless to attempt to list all his activities, but the highway system in Rainier National Park, the parkway of trees which line the Naches Pass Highway just within the national forest boundary and the Lake Washington bridge represent some of the efforts which engaged him in recent years.

Washington and the Pacific Northwest need more men with the breadth of interest that was displayed by Asahel Curtis during his life.[77]

Curtis's work with parks, although less well known and on the surface less successful than his work for Mount Rainier National Park and the Mather Memorial Parkway, is an important part of his legacy to the cause of scenic preservation. Herbert Evison's, even less well known, was important too.

Chapter 6

Samuel H. Boardman
The Preservationist as Administrator

For Oregon state parks 1929 was a memorable year. With Samuel H. Boardman assigned to give full-time attention to parks and roadside timber, there at last seemed a good chance that the beginnings made under Ben Olcott and Robert Sawyer would not prove abortive.

Boardman's appointment as Parks Engineer was a direct result of Sawyer's efforts, but it was also a product of the scenery preservation movement under way across the nation. Sawyer and Charles Sauers, Herbert Evison and Asahel Curtis, Stephen Mather and Horace Albright were, like Boardman, all representatives of the rising concern for the protection of scenic beauty. But Boardman was not a typical product of this movement. Indeed, he stood apart, largely oblivious to it through much of his long career.

Sam Boardman felt a great responsibility to protect scenery for future generations. He embarked on his crusade out of a sense of personal, almost religious conviction. When he received public support and a chance as a public official to advance his cause, he welcomed the turn of events, but that the chance came was almost accidental.

In August 1929 Boardman was working with a highway department oiling crew in southwestern Oregon. He liked his assignment—the area was rustic and unspoiled, the climate conducive to outdoor work—and he was perturbed when told to report to Highway Engineer Roy Klein in Salem. To Boardman such instructions could mean only one thing—reassignment to a desk job in the state capital—and he was "mad about it." On 13 August Klein informed Boardman that he had been selected for the new post of Parks Engineer. Instead of the transfer he had feared, Boardman was handed an assignment to savor. Moreover, it was one for which he was better equipped than anyone could have foreseen at the time, including Klein, who apparently first suggested Boardman for the job.[1]

Boardman was born in Massachusetts on 13 December 1874. He attended public schools and Wayland Academy in Beaver Dam, Wisconsin. Subsequently he worked as an engineer for the Denver Union Water Works, Denver and Rio Grande Railroad, Colorado Fuel and Iron Company, and Great Southern Railroad. In 1903 he moved to Oregon, where he worked as an engineer for the Spokane, Portland and Seattle Railroad and the Oregon Railway and Navigation Company.[2]

In 1904 Boardman left engineering to homestead a dry, forbidding tract along the Columbia River east of Arlington, for he had learned that a federal irrigation project was to bring water to the site. Others did the same, but as "the years went by with no water the settlers kept dropping out until there were only five of us left. . . . Thru thirteen sand-snuffing years Mrs. B and I fought that shifting desert." As a part of his struggle, Boardman began planting trees— poplars and locusts—in "sheer defense against the burning sands of the desert"; he wanted, he later explained, to provide "the green coverage of the creator's awning." When water finally arrived, new settlers followed, and a town bearing Boardman's name sprang up. His original grove served as a source of cuttings for others. He also persuaded local authorities to establish a tree nursery on the public school grounds, to institute an Arbor Day program in which the students set out trees around the school and along the rights of way of local roads, and to provide free trees for schoolchildren in nearby communities. The area fast became a tree-studded oasis.[3]

Although the area prospered, the Boardmans did not. Their savings were used up before the advent of irrigation, and Boardman's wife left the homestead to take a teaching job. Boardman himself took employment as an engineer when he could find such work. Then in 1919 he went to work for the State Highway Department. But his interest in trees continued. In his new position he pushed for plantings along the highway rights of way throughout the arid reaches of eastern

Oregon and "sold" the idea to Roy Klein, William C. Duby, and Governor Walter Pierce. Probably none of them was difficult to persuade. Klein would soon prove himself a staunch supporter of parks. Duby, while chairman of the State Highway Commission, secured the condemnation of a privately owned and poorly maintained camp site at historic Emigrant Springs and pushed through the commission expenditures for the acquisition of roadside timber along what was then known as the Old Oregon Trail Highway (later Interstate 84). The purchases were the largest made by the state to that time for the protection of scenery. And Pierce, although personally little interested in scenery, had apparently decided that there was political mileage to be gained in its defense: he had begun giving speeches that sounded for all the world like those of Ben Olcott.[4]

Boardman himself described what followed:

> Having no money to buy trees, it was up to me to produce trees. . . . With a highway hoopie provided, two barrels as water containers, a bucket, [and] an assortment of trees, I started out from The Dalles on this wayside tree planting, three years later terminating the planting at Ontario. Five thousand trees were planted, all taken from native resources. . . . The first two years was a fight. Grass fires set mostly by passing engines and cigarette butts destroyed the young trees. Cattle were also destructive. . . .
>
> Most of the trees were planted in sand blown up from the river, containing little fertility. I gathered droppings from animal life to fertilize the trees. When the gradient permitted, I dug small ditches from the hillside leading to the tree[s]. Remember, the area I was planting has only eight inches of rain a year. . . .
>
> The towns of Wasco, Moro, and Grass Valley set a day aside, closed down all business; the oil companies furnished tankers for watering the trees; [and] the trees were furnished by the Boardman School. Thousands of trees were planted along the Sherman Highway. The approaches to Hermiston, Stanfield, Echo, and Pendleton were planted. Trees were given to property owners to plant along the highway, particularly at Biggs Junction, Arlington, Irrigon, and Umatilla. . . . At Emigrant Hill and near Union

trees were planted behind the snow fences eventually to take their place.[5]

There was widespread public support, but there was also opposition to Boardman's activity. The Grange in northeastern Oregon sought to end spending on tree planting, small though it was. In contrast to other parts of the country, where it had long since disappeared as a political force, the Grange still had enormous influence over public affairs in Oregon. Over Boardman's protests, the Highway Commission meekly ordered a halt to the planting. Acting in his role as commission secretary, Klein explained to Boardman that results did not seem to justify the expense. Bitterly disappointed, Boardman lashed back, but to no avail. The program on which he had lavished so much time and effort came to an end; lacking care, many of the young plants soon died. Boardman continued on with the Highway Department, working at maintenance and other mundane tasks.[6]

Boardman's love of trees continued. While working in southwestern Oregon, he learned of the Save-the-Redwoods League. He and his wife contributed time and money to its campaigns, and in recognition of their efforts the League named a stand the Mrs. Samuel H. Boardman Memorial Grove. Neither this nor Boardman's earlier efforts went unnoticed. When the time came to select a Parks Engineer from among the department's employees, his name was quickly forthcoming.

Boardman wasted no time in getting to work. He learned of his assignment on 13 August 1929, and spent the rest of the day conferring with Klein regarding his duties. The next morning he went over the past year's correspondence dealing with parks and then went to Sodaville in the afternoon to see L. A. Simons about additional acreage for the small park there. On Thursday Boardman borrowed Klein's Buick and drove to Bend to confer with Sawyer. The two left for Klamath Falls immediately following dinner. They hoped to save a strip of pines on Quartz Mountain, along the highway between Klamath Falls and Lakeview, that was in imminent danger of being logged. The Boardman era had begun.[7]

Klein, Sawyer, and Van Duzer anticipated that Boardman would give most of his attention to the preservation of roadside timber. The rapid growth of the state's lumber industry, the expansion of its highway system, and the development of practical logging trucks had combined to increase greatly the threat to roadside trees. At the same time, the burgeoning auto tourist traffic was making protection of roadside timber a utilitarian as well as an aesthetic concern, for trees were an important part of the scenery that lured tourists to Oregon. The three were not disappointed. Boardman worked hard to persuade the Forest Service to reserve timber fronting on highways, to get landowners to trade roadside tracts for stands away from the highway, and when all else failed to get the Highway Commission to purchase selected strips of timber. Indeed, up to 1938 timber acquisition accounted for a third of the commission's total expenditures for scenic purposes.[8]

But Boardman's enthusiasm for natural beauty was too great for him to restrict his work so narrowly for long. He soon gave as much attention to park sites as to timber along highways, and by 1931 parks had assumed a primacy that they maintained thereafter. Boardman tackled his new job so eagerly that Sawyer, fearing he would monopolize Highway Commission meetings, felt compelled to suggest that Boardman submit the bulk of his information to the commission in writing.[9]

Boardman's dedication and ability, if not his loquaciousness, won the admiration of commission chairman Van Duzer. Within three months of Boardman's appointment, Van Duzer was writing to Sawyer, "I don't know how it appeals to you but it seems to me that he was a particularly fortunate suggestion."[10] Years later Sawyer recalled to Boardman, it was "only after you were appointed to the position . . . with your personality and superb performance that Van became enthusiastic" about having a full-time employee in charge of scenery protection.[11] Perhaps because of the change in Van Duzer's outlook, the term Parks Engineer quickly dropped from use and Boardman came to be referred to as what he had in fact been from the first: State Parks Superintendent.

Sawyer stayed on the Highway Commission for just over a year following Boardman's appointment. This was a period of orientation for Boardman, and Sawyer did all he could to facilitate his transition from oiling crew to administration. Sawyer examined potential park sites at Boardman's request, investigated others on his own, and above all helped to persuade his fellow commissioners of the wisdom of many purchases. This was a boon to Boardman; he later confessed to Sawyer, "after you left I don't remember of a commission asking me for a park. They all had to be brought to the commission and then a fight to get the commission to accept them."[12] But it was clear that the Boardman-Sawyer partnership could not last. Sooner or later Sawyer would leave the commission and Boardman would be on his own. That time came in September 1930, when Governor A. W. Norblad replaced Sawyer with M. A. Lynch, a grocer from Redmond who had little interest in parks.

During the 1930s the gulf between those who wanted to "improve" parks to increase recreational use and those who would protect them insofar as possible in their natural state grew wider; clashes became more frequent. To the former parks were instruments through which the nation's need for recreation could be at least partially met. Conrad Wirth of the National Park Service described development as making more areas available for "true recreation for the multitudes." President Franklin D. Roosevelt agreed; to him parks were a "part of our great program of husbandry, the joint husbandry of our human resources and national resources." To preservationists such talk was disquieting. A writer in *Nature Magazine* described Civilian Conservation Corps work as a "wild orgy . . . [that] bids fair to solve the wilderness problem in much the same way as the Turks set about solving the Armenian problem—by annihilation." Another preservationist proclaimed that man cannot alter nature without disfiguring it, adding "Oregon does not need to be 'prettified.' She needs to be conserved." In short, one scholar noted, the Depression was "a time of triumph and despair for nature lovers." They welcomed the increase in funds for use on lands they championed but were concerned because these funds were often used for purposes incompatible with their own.[13]

There was no question as to where Sam Boardman stood in the conflict between recreationists and nature lovers. "There is little left today that may be called primitive," he wrote. "Strange as it may seem, the more the world civilizes the primitive, the more barbaric we become." Through the state's parks, Boardman sought to maintain "a haven of primitiveness . . . preserved in all its naturalness." He put it bluntly to State Highway Engineer R. H. Baldock: "Development should be kept to a very minimum." Use of parks should be allowed only insofar as it did not harm the inherent nature of the areas involved. Uses that required development so extensive that a site's original character would be lost—overnight camping, for example—should be banned.[14]

Boardman brought no ready-made set of principles to his superintendency, nor was anything of the sort provided by the Highway Commission or the short-lived State Parks Commission created by Governor I. L. Patterson. The latter simply directed Boardman to "create and develop for the people of the State of Oregon a state parks system, to acquire and protect timbered strips on the borders of the state highways, . . . and to preserve the natural beauty of the state."[15] No record of the Highway Commission's basic directive remains—Klein gave it to Boardman orally during their meeting on 13 August—but it was, in all probability, equally vague. Boardman's insistence on keeping Oregon's parks natural was a product of personal conviction rather than direction from his superiors.

Boardman's experience at Joseph Park was especially important in shaping his outlook. Latourell Falls were the heart of the park. The upper falls plunged in a thin ribbon down the side of the Columbia River Gorge and into a picturesque pool. The stream then spilled over a lava lip to form the lower falls, which dropped in a final cascade toward the river below. Boardman later recalled his actions there:

> I conceived the idea that it would be a wonderful thing if a trail were constructed along the face of the cliff where the hiker could stand between the two falls. The trail was blasted into the side of the cliff. But what happened? The very foundation upon which depended the beauty of the entire picture had a great gash across it. The aesthetic sense of the individual curdled before reaching the beauty spot.
>
> It was fortunate that this lesson came early in my park career, for it taught me that man's hand in the alteration of the Design of the Great Architect is egotistic, tragic, ignorant. I received caustic criticism for my disfigurement, but it was unnecessary. From then on, I became the protector of the blade of grass, the flower on the sward, the fern, the shrub, the tree, the forest. . . . We live through trial and error. My error at the falls taught me humbleness when I stood before my maker.[16]

As his ideas evolved, Boardman, the former planter of trees along the highways of eastern Oregon, came to oppose the introduction of nonindigenous species into parks and roadside strips. Entreated by the Bend Chamber of Commerce to "do up" Peter Skene Ogden State Park on the arid rim of Crooked River Gorge, Boardman's only concession was to drain a sump of irrigation water behind the highway embankment. "To bring in the artificial would, to me, be a desecration to the natural setting," he told Sawyer.[17]

Throughout the Depression Boardman sought to take advantage of federal funds without opening the way to excess development. Doing so was not easy. Most available money came through the CCC. Boardman was suspicious of its planners and those in the National Park Service, which advised the CCC on parks projects. He complained that they liked "to hang the garland on the crag, festoon the stars and moon," and were "never down to earth where practicable things . . . are built." Their landscape architects were a special anathema. A blind man scattering seeds at night could do a better job of beautifying, Boardman maintained.[18] He told one Park Service official, "I am no landscaper, but I love the untarnished wilderness. I cringe when the landscaper sets his hand to improve the natural as the Creator designed it. . . . I am an unpolished park gent, uncouth in my language, and have my tobacco expectoration to deposit, but in those very deficiencies Oregon has its insurance in me. Because of it, the natural stays natural."[19]

Boardman voiced his frustration to Sawyer:

> I put in an application for a CCC camp for the cleanup and improvement of our new holdings on the Salmon River cut-off. They wanted to know if I couldn't have the State Forestry people handle the work—no gingerbread in sight on such a project. I am having a scrap with them to plant the Nehalem Sandspit . . . to Holland Grass [to stabilize it]—no gingerbread. Both the Salmon River and Nehalem Sandspit projects represent the natural type of work the CCC should be doing. . . . You think you have troubles. Just wait until you get in the CCC business.[20]

Somehow Boardman managed to get CCC crews to undertake work he judged vital. He characterized it as "fire insurance mainly" and even resorted to subterfuge to get it done. On one occasion, despairing of getting workers for cleanup in roadside timber south of Bend, he put in an application for a park development project. When the crews arrived, he put them to cleanup work, ignoring the tasks they had been sent to do.[21]

But cleanup—"pre-suppression of fires," Conrad Wirth called it—did not make up the whole of the CCC work in Oregon's parks. Seventeen parks received complete picnic facilities. At Saddle Mountain, CCC crews built seven miles of road to open the site to vehicular traffic and make practical the installation of day-use facilities. In time Saddle Mountain became one of the finest, most popular parks on the Oregon coast. Boardman hastened to reassure Sawyer and other nature lovers that, in spite of all this activity, "I am not doing any damage."[22]

The CCC's accomplishments in parks and roadside timber, Boardman once wrote, "would not be done in the next twenty-five years by the state"; in a more generous moment, he amended the figure to fifty years.[23] Whatever the time span, there was no question but that the CCC had inaugurated a new era for Oregon's parks. Earlier, the state had spent nearly all of its limited parks funds on land acquisition. What little development there was came as the result of the efforts of civic organizations—such as the Bend Civic Club, which improved Lava River Caves Park—and of interested individuals. The state's first major expenditure for development was $3,000 spent on trails at Silver Creek Falls in 1935.[24]

Nothing illustrated the new emphasis as well as developments around Silver Creek Falls. On 30 March 1935, the Highway Commission reached agreement with federal authorities for a CCC camp in the state park property by the falls. The camp lasted until 1938; World War I veterans then took over, staying on until 1941. During this time, federal crews worked on eighty-eight separate projects in the park—including boundary surveys, the construction of trails and picnic facilities, the laying of water and sewer lines, and the erection of a visitors center, maintenance buildings, and other structures. The federal government paid 97 percent of the cost—$410,000. In addition, after the federal programs ended, the state fell heir to the camp facilities, which represented a $50,000 investment. It promptly converted them for use by church and civic groups.

Adjoining the state park was Silver Creek Falls Recreational

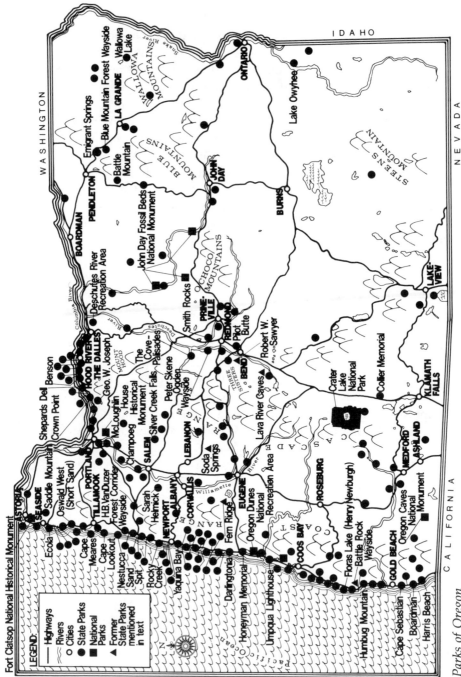

LEGEND:
— Highways
○ Rivers
● Cities
● State Parks
■ National Parks
▲ Former State Parks mentioned in text

Fort Clatsop National Historical Monument

WASHINGTON

IDAHO

NEVADA

CALIFORNIA

Parks of Oregon

Emigrant Springs

Blue Mountain Forest Wayside

Wallowa Lake

WALLOWA MOUNTAINS

Snake River

LA GRANDE

Battle Mountain

BLUE MOUNTAINS

PENDLETON

BOARDMAN

JOHN DAY

BURNS

Lake Owyhee

STEENS MOUNTAIN

John Day Fossil Beds National Monument

ONTARIO

Deschutes River Recreation Area

Columbia River

Deschutes River

OCHOCO MOUNTAINS

Smith Rocks

PRINE-VILLE

REDMOND

Pilot Butte

Robert W. Sawyer

LAKE VIEW

HOOD RIVER
THE DALLES

Shepards Dell
Benson
Crown Point

Saddle Mountain

Oswald West (Short Sand)

Geo. W. Joseph

MOUNT HOOD

The Cove-Palisades

Peter Skene Ogden

Silver Creek Falls

McLoughlin House Historical Monument

Champoeg

SALEM

Collier Memorial

BEND

Lava River Caves

THREE SISTERS

Soda Springs

LEBANON

KLAMATH FALLS

Crater Lake National Park

PORTLAND

TILLAMOOK

H.B.VanDuzer Forest Corridor

Sarah Helmick

ALBANY

CORVALLIS

NEWPORT

Ecola

Cape Meares

Cape Lookout

Nestucca Sand Spit

Rocky Creek

Yaquina Bay

SEASIDE

ASTORIA

Darlingtonia

Honeyman Memorial

Umpqua Lighthouse

Fern Ridge

EUGENE

Oregon Dunes National Recreation Area

Willamette River

COAST RANGE

CASCADE RANGE

ROSEBURG

MEDFORD

ASHLAND

Oregon Caves National Monument

Floras Lake (Henry Newburgh)

Battle Rock Wayside

COOS BAY

GOLD BEACH

Humbug Mountain

Cape Sebastian

Boardman

Harris Beach

Pacific Ocean

N

Demonstration Project, a part of the Roosevelt administration's efforts to show the virtues of properly planned and administered outdoor recreation. The project consisted of two recreational camps constructed by the Works Progress Administration. Upon completion of the project, the Highway Commission took over the property for a consideration of one dollar; federal expenditures on it had totalled $1,150,000.

Boardman cannot have been entirely happy with what was occurring around Silver Creek Falls, a spectacular natural site convenient to the main population centers of the state. Work there frequently smacked of the "gingerbread" projects against which he so often inveighed. But he seems to have recognized that a sort of *quid pro quo* was necessary and fought hard for federal funds to develop it. By giving recreationists a relatively free hand at Silver Creek Falls, he diverted attention from other parks and thus was able to keep at least those natural and untrammeled.[25]

Protecting the naturalness of parks and waysides was not the only guiding principle behind Sam Boardman's efforts. Gradually three others emerged: early acquisition of sites before desecration crept in or prices became prohibitive; utilization of federal and private funds for acquisition and development whenever possible; and maintenance of high scenic standards for sites acquired for parks. These too were products not of directives from Boardman's superiors but of his own experience.

Farsightedness seems to have been the biggest factor behind these policies. Boardman saw himself as responsible not just to the Highway Commission, or to contemporary Oregonians, but to "generations yet unborn." He believed he was preserving natural areas for a time when they would be needed even more than they were in his own day.[26] Nothing illustrates this better than his purchases of cutover lands along highways. Unable to buy roadside timber in the quantities he desired, Boardman bought up many acres of comparatively valueless cutover. It would be decades before this land could yield another crop of timber, but when that time came Boardman wanted to be sure that Oregon would have timbered strips fronting on its highways.[27]

A tract near Newport on the Oregon coast provided an especially good example of Boardman's vision. Examining it for possible purchase, Boardman found it "an exceedingly foul section due to dead standing timber. . . . The storms will level your matured timber if you leave it standing." Even so, Boardman thought the tract should be acquired: "I would wholly depend upon the young growth (which is fine) for my future scenic asset." Indeed, he suggested that perhaps the owners would be amenable to donating the land to the state "if this timber was [first] logged off." In Boardman's eyes, the site had scenic potential; little matter that the potential would not be manifest to most others for years to come.[28]

Boardman also planned ahead by insisting that the limited available state funds be used to acquire additional acres rather than to develop those already owned. He purchased park sites that he had no intention of developing and recommended to his eventual successor, Chester H. Armstrong, that certain tracts be left completely undeveloped for as much as fifty years.[29]

Boardman's desire to preserve natural areas inviolate made prompt acquisition a necessity. But it was hard to accomplish. Pressure to put all the Highway Commission's funds into roads was great. Commissioners who lacked Boardman's vision had difficulty seeing the need to control areas not in immediate danger of destruction, which in any case might not be developed for decades. Commissioner Leslie Scott once commented that he could not understand why there was so much concern over saving roadside timber, for "trees are only a place for birds to roost." Commissioner Henry F. Spalding went even further. Boardman recalled the commission meeting of 11 February 1932 when Spalding gave him "the most complete verbal tongue lashing my august person has ever been decorated with. Times were tough . . . and the Commissioner thought it sacrilegious to be spending money on parks when people were tottering on the verge of starvation." Boardman at times even had to fight to get the commission to accept gifts. To men such as Scott and Spalding the specter of the rising cost of park sites was of little concern; to Boardman it made early acquisition all the more imperative.[30]

Lacking money from the state, Boardman turned to outside sources. He was highly successful. President F. M. Ballard and Secretary Henry Newburgh of the Blacklock Sandstone Company of San Francisco turned down higher offers for property on the Oregon coast when the commission was "in the throes of indecision." Boardman described their actions, which led to acquisition of what became Henry Newburgh State Park:

A great deal of the time we were without option. At one time when everything had gone awry, in desperation I wrote asking a personal option for one year which they gave me. I took the option with the thought that I would find some angel who would buy the property and give it to the state for park purposes. I wound up at the end of the option with no angel, just the tail of the devil in my hands. Still they went on with us holding to the general purpose of the original negotiations. To Oregonians who read this, always remember that two Californians practically gave us one of the finest parks in our state park system.

Although Ballard and Newburgh actually sold the land to Oregon, they did so for well below market value.[31]

Others provided similar help. Highway Commissioner Ben Chandler persuaded the Menasha Woodenware Company to donate 112 acres to round out Umpqua Lighthouse State Park. The Louis W. Hill Foundation, continuing Hill's own interest in protecting Oregon's scenery, donated 175 acres to the Cape Lookout Park. Rodney L. Glisan, Florence Minott, and Louise and Caroline Flanders donated an area, including substantial summer homes, that became the nucleus of Ecola State Park. And, when Boardman was unable to persuade the commission to spend $5,000 for an eighty-acre addition to Silver Creek Falls park, Henry Crawford bought the land and held it for Boardman until the commission finally agreed to its purchase. A bit later the Ladd and Bush Bank did the same thing with another tract nearby.[32]

The Oregon Roadside Council was a continuing help in arranging donations. Established in 1931 through the efforts of Jessie M. Honeyman and the State Federation of Garden Clubs, the organization was affiliated with the National Roadside Council. The Oregon council—and Honeyman in particular—shared Boardman's dedication for saving the natural. It campaigned for the preservation of roadside timber, for the regulation of billboards along the highways, and, less openly, for the acquisition of state parks. One longtime activist in the group later recalled how Boardman, when he wished to generate pressure in support of an acquisition then before the Highway Commission, would telephone Honeyman. She in turn would quickly organize a campaign to deluge the commission with letters, telegrams, and phone calls so as to demonstrate public support for the proposed purchase.[33]

Even with such help, Boardman was not always successful in obtaining donations. He was unable to get any real help in his efforts to acquire the giant springs at the head of the Metolius River for a park. The S. S. Johnson Company of San Francisco owned the surrounding timber. Its president, S. O. Johnson, would not agree to an exchange of land unless he were given three times the amount of timber on his tract and an alternate mill site of his choice. Eventually Johnson built a summer home on the land and fenced off the springs. The timber itself was not cut, apparently more because of Johnson's desire for an attractive summer home site than out of any sense of public-spiritedness. Not until years later, after Boardman had retired and Johnson's son had assumed control of the site, did negotiations providing public access to the springs finally come to fruition. The site never did become a state park.[34]

Boardman had other defeats, including Quartz Mountain, where he began his parks work. Unable to persuade Forest Service officials to protect roadside stands there by exchanging federal timber away from the road for privately held timber fronting it, and able to obtain only enough state money to purchase seventy-five acres, Boardman watched helplessly as hundreds more were cut. But such setbacks served only to sharpen his dedication. As he wrote Sawyer: "Quartz Mountain failures must not be the composite of our biographies. Way out in the beyond await the unborn who must live because we were not false to our heritage to serve and save."[35]

The final basic concept in Boardman's philosophy demanded that new parks be of high scenic quality. "We have the foundation of a real park system," he wrote in the mid-1930s, "I hope that its standard will never be lowered and that quantity will never take the place of quality. It's a constant fight to keep the 'weeds' out of the setting."[36]

Boardman's concern was reflected in his criticisms of Secretary of the Interior Harold L. Ickes for lowering the quality of national parks. Boardman charged that, in trying to get sites away from the control of Secretary of Agriculture Henry A. Wallace, Ickes "took in any old thing for a park"—something that should not be allowed to happen to Oregon's parks system. Boardman also warned against letting political pressure influence acquisition, something he believed had happened in California to the detriment of overall quality.[37]

Boardman was not interested in land that required development for recreational use, in picnic areas lacking in scenic qualities, or in sites intended merely as stopping places to break the monotony of travel. To be sure, he inherited some such sites, but he devoted his efforts thereafter almost exclusively to acquiring and protecting genuinely scenic locations. The tiny park surrounding the mineral spring in the center of Sodaville, for example, was all but forgotten under Boardman. He also gave almost no attention to such places as the boating and picnicking site on Fern Ridge Reservoir, near Eugene, that would undergo extensive development under his successors.

A tour of California in February 1941 strengthened Boardman's commitment to his basic principles, especially his policy of protecting the natural. In reporting to Highway Engineer R. H. Baldock, Boardman criticized what he had seen in California. The state's officials planned to keep Point Lobos, "their star park . . . in its natural state; sort of a curiosity, like the horse in time to come. . . . It is more or less a duplication of our Rocky Creek Park. It can't hold a candle to Cape Lookout, Ecola, Short Sand, Yaquina Bay, etc." In a letter to Newton B. Drury, Chief of California's Division of Beaches and Parks, Boardman was more specific:

> It was a wonderfully instructive trip to me. Instructive in things you have done and should not have done. . . . There seemed a strong tendency to intrude with man-made things among the God-given things that you originally obtained to conserve. This seemed to me to apply both to national and state parks. It seemed to me that in sheer desperation you were keeping one park, Point Lobos, as a reserve so that there would be one example depicting what all the parks were like at one time.
>
> In park after park I observed the lines of the technician's blueprint intertwining and overpowering the living designs of the great Architect. Maybe the times call for this but it seems sacrilegious to me. To me a park is a pulpit. The more you keep it as He made it, the closer you are to Him.[38]

Perhaps Boardman's observations in California lay behind his attempt in 1943 to put the principles guiding his stewardship of Oregon's parks down on paper for the first time. The result was a list mixing basic tenets and less important procedural practices. In fact, as adopted by the Highway Commission, Boardman's policy statement merely articulated and endorsed what had long been his standard procedures.[39]

Nowhere did Boardman's approach to park building come more clearly into focus than on the Oregon coast. Soon after assuming leadership of the state's parks, Boardman came to recognize that the 430 miles of beaches, rugged headlands, and spectacular vistas represented a very special opportunity. The new Roosevelt or Coast Highway (later U.S. 101)—which closely paralleled the shoreline through much of its distance—provided easy access to potential park sites, little development had occurred, and property values were still low. Boardman sought to insure that the opportunities thus presented did not slip away. Repeatedly he pointed to California, where most of the coast was privately owned and the few coastal parks had been obtained only at great expense. The same thing, he insisted, must not be allowed to happen in Oregon.[40]

Bit by bit Boardman arranged donations, transfers of federal land, and state purchases. Much of the cutover land the commission bought was along the Coast Highway. The cumulative effect was great, but Boardman was dissatisfied. There was too much land, and his piecemeal acquisitions were too slow.

An alternative approach occurred to him. In the 1920s both California and New York had passed bond issues for use in building state park systems. In 1936 Boardman proposed the same approach to save Oregon's coastline. The depression had driven land values down. He estimated that the many miles of narrow strips between the Coast Highway and the state-owned beaches, ranging from 50 to 1,000 feet wide, could be purchased for $500,000. It seemed a remarkable bargain; California's Point Lobos park alone had cost over twice that. Boardman proposed issuing state bonds at 3 1/2 percent interest to raise the needed funds and to retire them over ten years out of current revenues. The idea went nowhere. Governor Charles H. Martin was opposed in spite of his interest in parks. New bond issues seemed too fraught with political and economic danger. Boardman's supporters in the parks movement were equally unenthusiastic, dismissing the idea as an impractical pipe dream. The superintendent had to struggle on as best he could.[41]

Even without a bond issue, Boardman's efforts had already

yielded impressive results. Late in 1936 he and Richard Leiber, head of the National Conference on State Parks, toured Oregon's parks. Leiber and his companions came to the state unaware of what Boardman had wrought. Used to the larger, more developed parks of places like his own Indiana, Leiber confessed that his group at first had difficulty seeing "the many parcels of land" set aside by the Highway Commission as parks at all.

> Yet, as we advanced over the magnificent Oregon coast highway, passing Harris [Beach] State Park, Crystal River, San Sebastian and finally landing for lunch in Humbug Mountain State Park with its stupendous myrtle trees, a great light came over us. Here then is a state which takes some 400 miles, leads its highway along the ocean, winds about through groves of marvelous trees and protects the surroundings from artificialities and desecration. When I had adjusted my vision, it became plain to me and filled me with boundless enthusiasm, that here is an American commonwealth that proposes to say that native scenery is sacred, that the people of the state should own this scenery and control it, that it should be preserved for all time to come in its native stateliness. . . . Instead of waiting for a changed order Oregon has taken the lead and aims to preserve that which is still pristine. . . . We older park men can learn a great lesson [in Oregon].[42]

Of course, what Leiber was describing was the product of Sam Boardman more than of the state as a whole. But Boardman's ability to inspire others to share his vision lay behind his remarkable success in arranging donations of land and in repeatedly wringing funds from reluctant highway commissioners.

As the years passed Boardman's scenic taste, as well as his parks philosophy, matured. At first his appreciation was restricted to what Joseph Wood Krutch once termed green and damp scenery, but it gradually broadened. When Boardman had first arrived at the summit of the Cascades to cross from "the Eastern Oregon sagebrush land," he was entranced by what he saw: "a panorama of velveted fields, white-water streams, forests tall and straight reaching for the blue, an enchanted land so picturesque that the visitor stood bewildered by its beauty." As head of the state's parks, Boardman wrote, "I distinctly remember the first park I blocked off. Its boundaries on the east, the Cascade Range; on the north, the Columbia River; on the south, the California line, plus certain areas they have gerrymandered from us from time to time; the west, our incomparable coastline. I knew it was impractical, but justifiable."[43] Boardman's work in eastern Oregon had been directed not to saving scenery but to changing it through the planting of trees. Only that part of the state east of the Cascades was, he felt, unworthy of park status.

By the time Boardman began to appreciate possibilities in the semi-arid and desert lands east of the mountains, he had developed a system that some were criticizing as unbalanced. Boardman's argument that preserving the sea coast "means as much to Ontario, Bend, [or the town of] Boardman as it does to any coastal area" failed to quiet the discontent. It seemed to many in central and eastern Oregon that, in parks as in so many other things, the western third of the state was getting far more than its fair share.[44]

Gradually others awakened in Boardman an awareness of the virtues of the land he had sought at first to transform and then to ignore. John C. Merriam, director of the Carnegie Institution and a leading paleontologist who had worked in the John Day country, presented him with a "grandiose plan" to make the John Day Fossil Beds into one of the outstanding scientific parks in the country. Merriam envisioned a huge preserve, stretching from Kimberly to Picture Gorge. For years the park as he conceived it failed to materialize, for neither the Highway Commission nor the Carnegie Institution had the funds to carry out so large an undertaking. But the smaller Thomas Condon–John Day Fossil Beds State Park was established as a direct outgrowth of Merriam's proposal, and later became the heart of John Day Fossil Beds National Monument.[45]

Merriam also proposed a park in the Burnt Ranch vicinity, near Mitchell. Unfamiliar with the area, Boardman asked Sawyer about it. Sawyer arranged for Boardman to visit the site with Phil F. Brogan, the leading popularizer of Oregon's geology. The result was Painted Hills State Park, with its fossilized redwoods and pastel-tinted slopes.[46] Sawyer and Brogan also pushed Boardman to establish a park at The Cove, in the gorge near the confluence of the Deschutes, Metolius, and Crooked rivers. Boardman saw the huge canyon with its perpendicular walls of columnar basalt and intervening ramparts of weathered multi-hued sandstone as "one of the most marvelous, spectacular settings in the State." Eventually he acquired over 4,000 acres there to create The Cove–Palisades State Park; thereafter, he repeatedly lauded it as one of Oregon's premier parks.[47]

In time Boardman began pushing for dryland park sites on his own. In 1953, following his retirement, he urged Governor Douglas McKay and others to give park status to the area around Owyhee Reservoir in southeastern Oregon. There is, Boardman declared, only "one volcanic scenic attraction superior to it in the state . . . Crater Lake." During his long tenure as head of Oregon's state parks he had shown no interest in the area.[48]

Boardman's interests were also broadening in other ways. Originally he had seen parks as preserved scenery. He eventually came to see them as a means of preserving scientific sites too. Geology as much as scenery lay behind the creation of John Day Fossil Beds, Painted Hills, and The Cove–Palisades parks. With this shift, promotional literature began to give renewed prominence to some of the earliest parks, such as Peter Skene Ogden and Lava River Caves, which were of scientific interest.

Cape Lookout became one of Boardman's favorites. An expert from the U.S. Bureau of Biological Survey considered this park to be more outstanding scientifically than California's Point Lobos. Stanley G. Jewett, head of the U.S. Fish and Wildlife Service, observed 154 species of birds on the cape, and Boardman had marshy areas of little scenic value added to the park because of their nesting value for birds. National Park Service personnel surveyed the area and compared its rain forest flora favorably with that in the Olympic National Park in Washington.[49]

Boardman's growing scientific interest also led him to acquire Darlingtonia Wayside, a marshy tract by the Coast Highway that featured the insect-catching pitcher plant. Late in his superintendency he even set aside stands of western juniper in the Bend-Redmond area and authorized surveys to determine the feasibility of a park near Mitchell to preserve outstanding stands of sagebrush, the plant that symbolized better than anything else all that he had once struggled to change in eastern Oregon.[50]

Boardman also came to see parks as a means of preserving historic sites. Existing legislation gave the Highway Commission no authority to establish historic parks, but Boardman did what he could, justifying acquisitions on other grounds. He added Cape Sebastian, Ecola, and Battle Mountain parks, each of which had historic connections. He incorporated a logging museum in Collier State Park, located in the ponderosa pine belt just east of the Cascades. In 1939 Boardman announced that he intended to survey the state's historic sites so that "they may be included in the general park system." Little came of the plan at the time. In 1943 he gladly accepted into his fold Champoeg State Park, formerly under an independent board. It was the only purely historic park in the system, but in light of the variety that Boardman was developing in the parks system, the state legislature considered Champoeg's transfer to Boardman and the Highway Commission a logical step.[51]

As time passed, Sam Boardman felt increasingly inhibited by the limitations of the parks enabling act and the Highway Commission's control of the purse strings. The constant struggle to wring money from reluctant commissioners was growing old. Turnover exacerbated the problem. He complained to Sawyer that commissioners "hardly stay long enough to learn their names."[52] As his interests diversified, his difficulties increased. Commissioners who might have been persuaded to spend funds on roadside parks and timber were more hesitant about preserving historic monuments and scenic attractions away from the highways. He was able to persuade the commission to finance a few parks off of paved highways—Saddle Mountain, The Cove, and Painted Hills—but he remained dissatisfied.

Boardman began to campaign for basic changes in parks legislation. The keynote was struck when he declared, "Sooner or later there must be a separate Parks Department." Arguments that financing would be even more difficult if the legislature had to allocate funds from the state's general fund failed to move him. So too did claims that large amounts were saved through ties to the Highway Department, whose heavy equipment could be utilized in parks as needed rather than maintained on a permanent basis with parks funds.[53]

However subconsciously, what Boardman seems to have really wanted was a freer hand for carrying on his basically one-man operation. To be sure, there were people working under Boardman, and he in turn was responsible to the Chief Highway Engineer and, beyond him, the Highway Commission. But Oregon's state parks were in fact little more than the shadow of Sam Boardman—and had been at least since Sawyer had left the commission in 1930.

That things would have been much better under a separate Parks Department is doubtful. The day when dedicated amateurs could shape and run government programs had largely passed. Planners, technicians with specialized training, and the give-and-take of inter-agency cooperation had come to the fore during the Progressive Era and gained an even stronger place in public affairs during the New Deal years.

The Oregon State Planning Board was indicative of the new order. Created on 1 February 1935—although it had been preceded by a voluntary Oregon Planning Council in 1934—the Planning Board was a direct outgrowth of the New Deal's emphasis on coordinated analysis of and plans for solving societal problems. Within two months, it was making recommendations and issuing reports that were to have a great effect on parks and tourism in Oregon. One, made public on 25 March, called for an Oregon State Travel Development Division. The legislature quickly responded, creating the Travel Information Division to encourage tourism.

Other reports followed. Between 1935 and 1938 the Planning Board made more than fifty studies of Oregon's resources, their use and conservation. The one most directly affecting state parks was *A Study of Parks, Parkways and Recreation Areas in Oregon*, completed in 1938. This report analyzed the status of parks and recreation areas, suggested improvements, and established a set of standards by which parks might be judged. One result was Governor Julius Meier's appointment of an advisory State Park Commission. Also directly relevant to Boardman's efforts was the board's survey entitled *Preservation of Oregon Roadside Timber*. Another study, carried out by the Pacific Northwest Regional Planning Committee—composed of planning leaders from the northwestern states—surveyed scenery preservation problems in the Columbia River Gorge. Boardman accepted all of this, and cooperated with it, but he was unenthusiastic. He never felt comfortable with the "Endless Governmental red tape" of planning meetings, group reports, and New Deal "alphabetical units."[54]

The Planning Board did not see a separate Parks Commission as the key to solving the problems that the superintendent faced.

"Oregon's combined assets of roadside beauty, scenic charm, and outdoor recreation" were as threatened by "the apathy of many Oregon citizens toward protecting scenic resources" as they were by the lack of strong state policies of preservation and agencies specifically charged with carrying them out. Many who had known Boardman personally had been won over by his zeal and vision, but most Oregonians remained unconverted. Under the circumstances, more than an independent agency was needed if Boardman's frustrations were to end. Not surprisingly, his campaign for a separate Parks Department, like his earlier call for a bond issue, went nowhere.[55]

The Planning Board was correct. Changes were under way that were far more threatening to Boardman than the absence of an independent Parks Department. Outdoor recreation prospered in spite of the Great Depression. In 1936 Oregon's new Travel Information Division spent $50,000 on advertising to lure tourists to the state. The results were startling: visitation in 1936 showed a 40 percent increase over the year before. One observer complained that the volume of tourist travel in Oregon had become "virtually unmanageable." Between 1936 and 1941 tourism in the state continued to climb, out-of-state visitors increasing from 500,000 to 800,000 per year. Recreational demands, spurred on by the increasing acceptance of the recreation-oriented New Deal philosophy of parks use, were becoming so great that even Boardman had to bend a little.[56]

Boardman remained adamantly opposed to overnight camping, however. He warned Baldock that with camping "grass will turn to the dust of earth, bush and foliage will wither and [only] stunted stumps will remain." Boardman's solution was simple: let tourists stay in private facilities. "Near-by will be the ever present tourist camp. It is not a far walk to the shrine of His handiwork." Boardman turned to Newton Drury, among others, for support. "Some of your notable citizens," he told the director of California's parks, "are complaining to our Governor because we have not provided overnight camping in our State parks"; knowing Drury's personal feelings on the subject, Boardman asked for data on overnight camping in California to aid in the fight against such "mutilation."[57]

World War II interrupted the growth of tourism. Suddenly the Park Superintendent, who had been struggling against the rising calls for development within the parks, had to struggle no more. Touring the country had become a sign of lax patriotism, or so the everpresent signs demanding "Is This Trip Really Necessary?" would make the public believe. Oregon's Travel Information Division eliminated "for the duration" advertising aimed at enticing visitors to the state; and gasoline rationing completed the job of virtually eliminating the highway-based tourist industry. Facilities that had been inadequate in 1940 were now more than sufficient. Relieved of pressure to develop parks, Sam Boardman turned to additional acquisition, free to expand the parks system using the criteria he had established for it.

Acquisition was not the sole concern during the war, any more than it had been earlier, but it *was* Boardman's primary concern. And during the war he found less opposition to his emphasis than at any time since the advent of the New Deal. Expenditures for development had taken up 17 percent of the parks budget during the thirties; during the war the figure dropped to 7 percent. However, an overall reduction in expenditures on parks (perhaps resulting from a feeling that spending not aimed toward the war effort was somehow un-American) and the everpresent commission apathy hampered Boardman's efforts. So too did the military, which intruded in a variety of ways—building defense facilities, barring public access to sensitive areas, and sending casualties to Shore Acres park for recuperation. In exasperation he wrote to an acting regional director of the Park Service:

> What is the army doing to National and State Parks in California? They are raising more or less heck with my parks, especially along the coast line. I am putting up as stiff a battle as possible, it's sort of a preliminary training before the lads meet the Japs. . . . Can't a sergeant be God-awful ornery? I have been thrown out of a couple of my parks. Did I write you about getting a fourteen hundred acre seashore park in northern Curry County the middle of February and having the Navy take it away from me a week later for an airport? Damn Hitler and his satellites.

But Boardman persevered. Indeed, compared with the hostility of Commissioner Spalding, or the flood of tourists on the eve of war, the problems he faced during the conflict were minor, difficult though they seemed to him at the time.[58]

World War II brought higher employment and incomes, but less to spend it on. Savings mounted. With peace, tourists returned with a rush. Money in their pockets made travel possible; the long, drab years of strife made it desirable. Oregon had never had over 800,000 visitors in any one year before the war; in 1946 over 1.2 million entered the state. Tourist spending rose more than 50 percent above the old seasonal record of $51 million.[59]

Boardman's philosophy of parks administration suddenly seemed outmoded. Tourists came demanding facilities; the state, wishing to bolster its third largest industry, had no real option but to meet their demands. The old argument that preserving scenery would attract visitors was no longer sufficient. Tourists wanted to look at scenery, but also to get out into it. Unless parks were to be desecrated through unregulated use, facilities were necessary. Planners, landscape architects, and professional administrators, not dedicated nature lovers, would have to be called upon. Overnight camping, against which Boardman had struggled doggedly for years, continued to be banned, but it was clearly coming—and so was much else that Boardman had long opposed.[60]

Boardman fought a rear guard action against the forces unleashed by these new conditions, but his dominance was over. As indomitable as he had been through the years, Boardman was not strong enough to stem the tide rising against him. He had failed to change with the times—indeed, had fought against doing so with all the considerable vigor that he could muster.

Boardman continued on as Parks Superintendent until 30 June 1950, when he reached mandatory retirement age. But the capstone of his career came three years earlier when the American Planning and Civic Association awarded him its prestigious Amory Pugsley medal, the first given since 1938, for his outstanding contributions to conservation. His approach, deemed so odd when Leiber first came into contact with it in 1936, was receiving national recognition. When he finally did step down, Boardman had an impressive record of accomplishment to look back upon. In 1930, at the start of his career, Oregon had possessed a total of 6,444 acres of parks and roadside timber preserves; when he retired nineteen years later there were 57,195 select acres in the system.

Scenery preservation and the maintenance of the primitive nature of Oregon's parks were never entirely abandoned in the years that followed, but they never again dominated as they had earlier. Nothing illustrated the change better than the Highway Commission's choice to succeed Boardman: Chester H. Armstrong. Like Boardman, Armstrong was an engineer already working for the Highway Department, but he lacked Boardman's infectious enthusiasm and love of the untrammeled. With commission encouragement, Armstrong cut back on acquisitions and pushed development. He introduced overnight camping, opened parks that Boardman had kept undeveloped, and added others that were almost wholly recreational. When he did acquire new land it was almost always to provide room for more facilities rather than to protect scenery.[61]

Both Armstrong and Boardman recognized that a major watershed had been crossed. After his own retirement in 1960, Armstrong wrote that the commission had directed him "to place more emphasis on construction and development and less on acquisition." Armstrong clearly felt comfortable with the charge. His own ten-year tenure, Armstrong noted with a touch of pride, "is known as the 'Construction Period.'"

After retiring from the superintendency, Boardman stayed on part-time with parks, working as a consultant and writing short histories of parks and events with which he had been involved, but he was clearly uncomfortable with the new emphasis—which he had seen coming. His son Kenneth later recalled that Boardman had been unhappy with the choice of Armstrong as his successor.[62]

It was not ego that lay behind Boardman's unhappiness as much as it was his continuing conviction that the preservation of scenery was an almost sacred duty—and that too much remained to be done to turn from it to the lesser tasks of recreational development. His idealistic, crusading spirit was admirable, but out of step with the times. The fifties called for a different kind of leadership. Chester Armstrong was clearly not what preservationists wanted at the time, but Sam Boardman was no longer the sort of leader they needed either. Time had passed him by.

Chapter 7

Robert E. Smylie and Idaho's State Parks
A Study in Belated Action

While parks burgeoned in Oregon and developed slowly in Washington, they remained almost unheard of in Idaho. Heyburn State Park, the reserve that had come into being in 1911 because Congress refused to create a national park around Lake Chatcolet, remained under state auspices. But there was nothing resembling a movement for state parks in the Gem State, no Moran or Curtis, no Sawyer or Boardman at work there. In this, as in other ways, Idaho shared more with its Rocky Mountain neighbors than with Oregon and Washington.

The 1950s brought an end to this inaction. Led by Governor Robert E. Smylie, Idaho set out to build a state park system that could rival those elsewhere. Both a concern for saving the scenic beauty of the state and for capturing the tourist trade lay behind this development. In spite of maneuvering by Smylie's political opponents and the protests of fiscal conservatives, in the end this combination swept all before it.

But Smylie did not have to begin from scratch. In addition to Heyburn State Park, a handful of other reserves languished under state jurisdiction when he assumed the governorship in 1955. By the time Idaho obtained Heyburn Park, it had already set aside a beautiful timbered tract on Payette Lake. However, although Ponderosa State Park was later created from a part of the reserve, the legislature seems to have been more concerned with preventing sale of the land than in creating a park when it set the area aside in 1909.[1]

It appropriated no money for use on the "park"; indeed, like state forests, the tract was placed under the State Land Board whose purpose was to manage Idaho-owned property profitably. Toward this end, the board leased summer home tracts and gave out a hotel concession on the Payette Lake Reserve. It apparently sought to keep some beaches and access thereto in state hands, but only to increase the value of potential leaseholds that did not front on the water. Only gradually did Idaho's officials come to believe that the state ought to do something at the lake for those who could not afford leaseholds or summer homes. Even then, the realization was restricted in its application. As with Heyburn's proposal for Lake Chatcolet, the development of camping facilities at Payette Lake, which began in the 1920s, failed to lead to any larger parks movement.[2]

The sale of leaseholds on Priest Lake, in Idaho's northern panhandle, followed soon after the sales at Payette Lake, and represented essentially the same thing—a quest for profits rather than parks. A decade later, the state also established Spalding Park, located on the Clearwater River at the site of the first mission to Idaho's Indians.[3] In the years that followed, little development occurred there. As precedents that he could draw upon in his own battle for parks, Smylie found little of value in Idaho's handful of holdings.

Nor was Lava Hot Springs particularly useful to the governor. These mineral springs in southeastern Idaho had been transferred to the state by Congress in 1902 and declared a state park by the legislature in 1913. Yet regardless of its title, Lava Hot Springs was never a state park in the normal sense of the term. It was a hot springs resort, appreciated not for its scenic or recreational potential, but for the supposed curative powers of its waters. Like Platt and Hot Springs national parks, Lava Hot Springs gained park status because of the popularity of spas during the period. Their story is peripheral to the mainstream of park history.[4]

In looking back, Robert Smylie was distressed because Idaho had done so little to create parks during the 1920s while much of the rest of the country was pushing rapidly ahead. Idaho's only progress came from some improvements at Heyburn Park (whose value was diminished as excursion boats became less popular and ceased to ply the St. Joe) and from the incidental gains from the sale of leaseholds at Priest and Payette lakes. But the rest of the Rocky Mountain states did even less. In 1928 the only other state "parks" in the entire Rocky Mountain region were two hot springs reserves in Wyoming. Like Lava Hot Springs, these were not the fruits of the park movement then sweeping the country, but of the quest for medical cures.[5]

There were reasons for the relative inactivity of the Rocky Mountain states. First, many in the region shared Heyburn's beliefs in state's rights, which resulted not just in opposition to what he called "Pinchotism," but in distrust of all kinds of conservation and conservationists. Conservation was associated with the locking up of resources. As one regional spokesman put it, "we have reached the limit of proper park reservations and the States should vigorously oppose any further enlargements, or the creation of more parks in the public-land states." Although the writer had national parks in mind, state parks would have the same effect on economic development.[6] To work successfully for state parks in a region where such views were common, in a region where leaders had long been arguing that development was the main need, was a difficult if not impossible task. Nevada serves as a case in point. When Governor James G. Scrugham pushed during the 1920s for a system of state parks, including one centered around Indian ruins near Overton, his opposition campaigned against him on the slogan "Live cities instead of dead ones." Scrugham failed of reelection.[7]

A second reason for the absence of a viable state parks movement in the Rocky Mountain region was that the federal government owned most of the scenic and recreational sites (some 65 percent of Idaho was federally owned). As a result, park supporters tended to look to federal authorities.[8] The situation was similar in Arizona. In 1928 when the National Conference on State Parks invited Arizona's governor, W. P. Hunt, to send delegates to its annual meeting, Hunt replied that to do so would be futile; "all areas in this State suitable or desirable for state parks are already included in federal reservations of one kind or another." Hunt saw little he could do to further the state parks movement, although he insisted he was sympathetic to it. Many in Idaho and other parts of the Mountain West seem to have held similar views.[9]

The third basic reason for the initial failure of the state parks movement in the mountain states was the absence of leaders with the dedication, capacity, and authority to push it ahead. Such leadership played a major role wherever the movement prospered. Governor Ben

Olcott, Robert Sawyer, and Samuel Boardman provided it in Oregon. William E. Colby, Newton Drury, and their many allies, especially those in the Sierra Club and Save-the-Redwoods League, provided it in California. In South Dakota it was supplied by Peter Norbeck, in Indiana by Richard Leiber and Charles Sauers, and in Connecticut by Albert M. Turner. In Idaho Weldon Heyburn was the sole major figure associated with state parks during the period from statehood, in 1889, to 1950. But Heyburn died in 1912, shortly after the park bearing his name was created, and a state park had never been his real goal. With the exception of Nevada and of Utah, where Governor George Dern led an abortive parks movement in the 1920s, the other mountain states produced even less leadership in the parks movement. Circumstances simply turned the attention of local leaders in other directions. In Montana, for example, the struggle against the Anaconda Copper Company's political machine absorbed the energies of public-spirited citizens and activity on behalf of parks languished.[10]

The 1930s saw few advances. Some states in the region used the Civilian Conservation Corps to lay the foundations for park systems, but Idaho did not.[11] One writer in the *Idaho Sunday Statesman* noted in 1938 that over half of the states were using CCC workers in their state parks and argued that Idaho, by then one of only five states without a park system, could surely do the same if a program were started.[12] The suggestion went unheeded. Idaho's forests were suffering from a devastating infestation of white pine blister rust. The bulk of CCC labor available to the state was directed to that threat and to forest fire control, although crews did build visitors' facilities and other improvements at Heyburn Park. For its part, Heyburn remained under a special commission whose authority was limited to that single tract; commissioners were in no position to lead a push for a statewide parks system. Major expansion of Idaho's parks would simply have to wait.[13]

With the end of World War II, tourism boomed. Idaho was unprepared. As State Land Commissioner Edward Woozley put it, "Unfortunately we have not foreseen the tremendous demand for recreational sites that we now have. Many of our more desirable beaches have been sold and leased." Woozley went on to argue that "recreational areas should be properly developed, maintained, and operated for the use of the general public."[14] At last an awareness of the value of parks was developing in Idaho, but there was a long way to go if the state were to catch up with its neighbors to the west. While

Oregon had some 140 state park areas and Washington about 70, Idaho had only 4.

In 1949 the state legislature appropriated $25,000 for a Reclamation and Land Improvement Fund. Part was used to build roads in Sawtelle Park and for improvement at the Pilgrim Cove area of Payette Lake. The same legislature transferred Heyburn Park to the State Land Department, but failed to appropriate any funds for it or for what it called "picnic areas" (such as Spalding Park) that were also under the Land Department. Fortunately, concessions and fees at Heyburn Park produced nearly enough money to make it self-sustaining.

Even more revealing, the state turned down the offer of Virgil T. McCroskey, a retired pharmacist and nature lover with a desire to repay society some of what he believed he owed it. Earlier McCroskey had given Washington a park site on Steptoe Butte, north of his home near Colfax. Now he offered to donate over 2,000 acres along a forested ridge that rose above the Palouse wheat fields in Idaho's Benewah County northeast of Steptoe Butte, plus the twenty-five-mile-long private road that traversed it. Even McCroskey's offer to use his own funds to "improve and maintain the drive as long as I am able" failed to persuade Idaho's legislators to accept the gift.[15]

In 1953, the State Land Board created a Parks Division within the Land Department and prevailed upon the legislature to appropriate, for the first time in the state's history, funds for general parks use. The move was urged by Woozley and Smylie, then attorney general and a member of the Land Board.[16] The $25,000 appropriation was a modest beginning, but when Smylie was elected governor a year later the corner was turned. Under pressure from Smylie, appropriations for parks increased steadily during the years that followed and, more important, additional legislation created a professional Parks Department. By the time Smylie left office in 1967, Idaho had a firmly established park system and was irrevocably committed to protecting the state's scenic and recreational resources.

Smylie's interest in parks was of long standing. As a youngster in Iowa during the 1920s, he had been impressed by that state's park system. He later recalled that during the twenties, nearly "every slough had a state park sign on it." Idaho had far greater scenic and recreational potential than his boyhood home; like Iowa, he believed, it should seek to preserve and develop it.[17]

Encouraged by relatives in Caldwell and across the Snake River in Nyssa, Oregon, Smylie came to Idaho in the early 1930s to attend college. He was graduated from the College of Idaho in 1938, and then earned a law degree from George Washington University in 1942. He practiced law in the District of Columbia while in the Coast Guard during World War II and returned to Idaho when peace came in 1945. It was propitious timing for Smylie, a Republican. Long out of power, his party swept the state in 1946. The new attorney general, Robert Ailshie, promptly appointed Smylie one of two assistant attorney generals. When Ailshie died in office a few months later, Governor C. A. Robbins named the thirty-three-year-old Smylie to replace him. In 1950 Smylie won election to a four-year term of his own.

Smylie was an active supporter of Dwight D. Eisenhower's presidential campaign in 1952 and served as one of the general's advisers on western affairs. The West, Smylie argued, viewed centralization as "a real threat." But, unlike Weldon Heyburn, Smylie did not seek refuge in state's-rights arguments, and, unlike some of his Republican contemporaries, he did not fall back on antisocialist rhetoric. To Smylie, the problem was not too much government activity, but a federal bureaucracy grown insensitive to local interests and needs. To open up the government to the people, he proposed to bridge the gap between the Interior Department and the public it served through an advisory committee of people "whose business interests and experience qualified them to give unbiased and technically sound advice on Departmental problems, especially in the West."

State parks were another matter. In a period when a group of resort owners on Puget Sound were fighting a bond issue for a county park as "socialistic," Smylie called for the establishment of a system of state parks in Idaho. Such a program would not exacerbate the problem of government indifference to local concerns; indeed, state jurisdiction over parks might help alleviate the problems by reducing the distance between the populace and the agency in charge.[18]

Personable and progressive, Smylie epitomized the "new" Republican image encouraged by Eisenhower's strategists. Along with exposure gained as an adviser to the president and his own obvious talent, this image carried the forty-year-old Smylie into the governorship in 1954. During his campaign Smylie emphasized the importance of reorganizing the management of the state's natural resources and of attracting tourists. State parks, he pointed out, could play a key role in this.

In 1955 when Smylie took over as governor, Idaho spent a mere $40,523 a year on parks. Montana spent about the same; only Colorado, New Mexico, Utah, and Nevada spent less. Outside the mountain states the figures were much higher. The gap between the Rocky Mountain–Intermountain Basin area and the rest of the country that had developed in the 1920s was still great.[19]

Smylie quickly took steps to end Idaho's laggardly status. He prevailed upon Leon G. Green—head of the Department of Health, Physical Education, and Recreation at the University of Idaho—to direct a survey of the state's recreational resources and recommend "a comprehensive overall plan" for their "preservation and development."[20]

Smylie's approach was in character. Informal and direct, he liked to take matters into his own hands. He wrote his own speeches, typed many of his own letters, and valued action over procedures and political posturing. Lacking either legislative authorization for Green's study or funds with which to compensate him, Smylie simply asked Green to prepare it as a public-spirited citizen interested in scenery preservation. Green rose to the challenge.

Green's report was just what Smylie needed. The governor used it to justify hiring the state's first director of parks and as the basis for his repeated recommendations to the legislature that it create a Department of Parks. Smylie and Green feared that parks would languish if they remained under the Land Board, whose primary responsibility was profitable management of the state's lands. A fisherman, hunter, and lover of the outdoors, Smylie treasured Idaho's scenery and believed that its parks deserved more careful stewardship than the Land Board had given them. Green's report argued the same position.[21]

Smylie was hardly sworn in as governor before Virgil McCroskey reappeared with his offer to donate the land along Skyline Drive for a state park. In 1953 McCroskey had tried a second time to give the site to Idaho, only to be rebuffed again. Now he came not only with an improved offer of 4,400 acres (which he promised to maintain at his own cost for fifteen years), but also with considerable support from the Palouse country. This time the legislature accepted the donation, although only by a three-vote margin in the lower house. Smylie was delighted. "Future generations will thank Mr. McCroskey," he wrote after signing the bill, "and I feel certain they will applaud the State's decision to accept his gracious gift."[22]

Another of Smylie's first acts as governor was to mount a search for "an experienced Parks man to take charge of the program and plan for improving present facilities, developing land under state supervision, and making recommendations for further acquisition. . . . Such a person is hard to acquire, but is vitally necessary to proper advancement of the Parks system." In April 1958 he found one in John W. Emmert, a retired former superintendent of Glacier National Park who was willing to work for the small sum Smylie was able to wring from available funds. On paper Emmert was only a part-time employee, but he devoted long hours to bring planning and direction to Idaho's parks for the first time.[23]

With Emmert in the fold and with Green's survey as ammunition, Smylie turned his attention to the legislature. In his State of the State message on 6 January 1959, Smylie noted that "we have established a Park Service that is headed by a qualified administrator for the first time, and . . . have managed our water resources with skill and benefit to the State." However, he continued, "our endeavors in these fields suffer from a lack of coordination. . . . Separate agencies deal with separate phases of the problem and no single agency is charged with assisting the Governor in . . . long range planning." Smylie called for the creation of a consolidated Department of Natural Resources "headed by a Commissioner of cabinet rank, appointed by the Governor . . . [and] furnished with a planning commission which could draw broadly on the skill and talent of our entire citizenry."[24] The latter was an effort to establish in Idaho the sort of intermediary between the people and the bureaucracy that he had urged on Eisenhower. Although Smylie did not explicitly say so, it was clear that he intended that a new Parks Bureau, its personnel hired and promoted on the basis of professional merit, would be a part of the Department of Natural Resources.

The legislature, dominated by Democrats, took no action. Smylie later recalled, "At that time there were maybe eight or ten State Land Board jobs that were patronage jobs; the Board was controlled by the Democrats, and the Democrats controlled the state legislature. I think this was the basic reason we didn't go any place that year. You couldn't give them enough assurances that they weren't going to do their [party] faithful in the eye."[25]

A second setback soon followed. The Democrats, having regained control of the State Board of Land Commissioners, fired

Emmert as parks director and replaced him with three regional directors. Among them was Allen J. Coleman of Sandpoint, a party stalwart without training or experience for the job. The Coeur d'Alene Wildlife Federation commented angrily that the parks system was "floundering in political confusion," but State Land Commissioner John G. Walters, who also was State Democratic chairman, denied the charge. The parks, he claimed, were being operated "in a more efficient manner than ever before." Whether any of that efficiency was a result of Coleman's appointment is of course doubtful, but that was a question Walters chose not to pursue. Indeed, his only defense of the new appointees seems to have been to appeal to Idahoans' chauvinism. As he put it, "those of us who have lived many years in Idaho are just as cognizant of what we need in the way of parks as is someone who came into the state only 18 months or so ago."[26] Smylie said the change was purely a matter of patronage politics. His charge rings true in spite of denials by Democrats on the board.[27]

Having been twice rebuffed in 1959, Smylie tried again with the next legislature. This time he was more specific regarding parks: "The present Division of Parks and Recreation Resource Administration should be reconstituted so that it is led by a professionally trained and qualified Director, and staffed by personnel selected and employed on the basis of a merit system of nonpolitical personnel administration."[28] Al Coleman offered no rebuttal. Detected in financial irregularities during his brief tenure as regional parks director, he reportedly had fled the state to avoid prosecution.[29]

With a slim Republican majority in each house of the legislature and having separated the question of parks from the larger question of reorganizing the administration of natural resources, Smylie may have been optimistic about the chances of his proposal. Nevertheless, he was again disappointed. His parks bill, introduced by the House State Affairs Committee, passed the House on a 30-28 vote, but died in the Senate's Forests and Public Lands Committee.[30]

Undaunted, Smylie was determined to try once more at the next session of the legislature. Building toward that time, he named a Commission on Natural Resources Organization and Administration under Donald R. Theophilus, president of the University of Idaho, to survey the state's natural resource administration and to recommend needed changes. No doubt Smylie expected the commission's recommendations to approximate closely those he had already made himself. He also sought and obtained support from the Idaho State Wildlife Federation.[31]

Even more important steps were taking place behind the scenes. In the fall of 1959 E. Roland Harriman invited Smylie to his ranch near Island Park. Informal discussions about donating the 14,700-acre ranch to the state for use as a park followed. Railroad Ranch had belonged to the Harrimans and their associates for nearly fifty years. Located on Henry's Fork of the Snake River near the juncture of Idaho, Montana, and Wyoming—and near Yellowstone National Park—the site included well-watered meadows that had never been more than lightly grazed, forested hills, nesting sites of sandhill cranes and the rare trumpeter swan, and superb trout waters. Deer, elk, moose, and bear abounded under near-primeval conditions.[32]

There were tax advantages to the Harrimans from such a donation, but more than that lay behind the proposed gift. Roland and his brother Averell had spent most of their lives in New York, but both had been coming to the ranch since boyhood. They loved the place and over the years had sought to protect its pristine beauty and wildlife. In doing so they were following in the footsteps of their father. Edward H. Harriman, the railroad tycoon, was an avid outdoorsman and supporter of the early conservation movement. He was a friend of John Muir's and an ally in his efforts to prevent the damming of Hetch Hetchy Valley in Yosemite National Park. Bit by bit the elder Harriman had purchased land along the Hudson River in an effort to protect it from despoliation. Following his death in 1909, his widow Mary donated the 20,000 acres her husband had accumulated to the state of New York. The donation, made in his mother's behalf by young Averell in his first public appearance, became a key part of the Palisades Interstate Park and was the largest single donation to it. Now, nearing the end of their lives, the brothers wanted the ranch preserved in perpetuity too. Averell wrote, "we just could not face the prospect of its becoming nothing more than an uncontrolled real estate development with hot dog stands and cheap honky tonks, and . . . we could foresee the necessity of preserving such property for future generations." As he said later, "it just seemed the natural thing to do."[33]

At first the Harrimans were not sure whether to donate to Idaho or to the federal government, but, impressed by work the Idaho

Department of Fish and Game had done in restoring the Henry's Fork and protecting wildlife habitat in the vicinity, they decided upon the former. By the fall of 1961 they were ready to act. Eagerly, Smylie set to work to hammer out an agreement with Roland Harriman. It was a golden opportunity, but fraught with problems. Harriman insisted that negotiations be kept secret and that a final agreement be signed by the end of 1961. Smylie acceded to these demands, and to meet the deadline had to fly to New York in December to sign the agreement. Smylie's frequent absences from the state had already drawn criticism, and this time when he left, unable to announce why he was going, the *Boise Statesman* criticized him sharply. Condemnation quickly turned to praise, however, when Smylie returned with the signed agreement. "It will doubtless be one of the outstanding state parks of the nation when it is finally established and operating," Smylie proclaimed. No one disagreed.[34]

More than a donation was involved. Smylie had prevailed upon the Harrimans to include in the agreement a proviso that Idaho must have a professionally trained park service at the time of transfer. If Idaho's legislature, ever penurious, wanted to accept the Harrimans' multimillion dollar gift, it would also have to accept Smylie's proposal for a professional Parks Department.[35]

When the legislature met in 1963 Smylie laid both his Parks Department proposal and the agreement with the Harrimans before it. Theophilus's commission had made more modest recommendations for restructuring resource administration than Smylie had hoped for, so he backed off from his larger plan of reorganization. Instead, he concentrated on getting a parks bill so as to "make a modest start in the right direction." In his State of the State message, Smylie made a strong plea for his proposal:

Because State Parks and recreation areas constitute one of the State's great remaining natural assets we should have a modern structure for Parks Administration. Here, time is of the essence. . . . We should create a professionally staffed career park service to plan for, and to develop . . . what can well become the most adequate state park system in the United States. We need to identify and hold these areas in public ownership while there is still time. This is now a

Governor Oswald West. (Oregon Historical Society)

Samuel Christopher Lancaster. (Oregon Historical Society)

Senator Weldon B. Heyburn. (Idaho State Historical Society)

Governor Ben Olcott. (Oregon Historical Society)

The St. Joe River winding through its sunken valley to Lake Coeur d'Alene; Lake Chatcolet to left. (Idaho State Historical Society)

An Asahel Curtis view in Moran State Park. (Washington State Historical Society)

Robert Moran (front row, third from left) and party of distinguished visitors atop Mt. Constitution in Moran State Park, 1923. Photo by Asahel Curtis. (Special Collections, University of Washington Libraries)

Mt. Baker from Moran State Park. Asahel Curtis photograph; distance foreshortened for dramatic effect. (Washington State Historical Society)

Robert W. Sawyer standing above a central Oregon rimrock, c. 1925.
(University of Oregon Library)

Timber along the White River route to Mt. Rainier, 1914. Photo by Asahel Curtis. (Special Collections, University of Washington Libraries)

Asahel Curtis (seated) and friend atop Mt. Shuksan, self portrait. (Special Collections, University of Washington Libraries)

Governor Roland Hartley (left) and Edmond S. Meany at the dedication of Mather Memorial Parkway. Photo by Asahel Curtis. (Washington State Historical Society)

Dedication ceremonies for the Mather Memorial Parkway. Asahel Curtis photograph. (Washington State Historical Society)

Robert W. Sawyer (left) and fellow journalists, c. 1925. (Oregon Historical Society)

Herbert Evison during
his tenure with the
National Park Service.
(National Archives)

Karl Onthank.
(University of Oregon
Archives)

Henry B. Van Duzer.
(Oregon Historical
Society)

Edmond S. Meany in his outdoor
garb. (Special Collections,
University of Washington
Libraries)

Samuel H. Boardman at overlook on
the Oregon coast. (Oregon Parks and
Recreation Division)

The Oregon Coast in Samuel H. Boardman State Park. (Oregon Parks and Recreation Division)

The lodge at Silver Creek Falls State Park, constructed by the Civilian Construction Corps. (Oregon Parks and Recreation Division)

A portion of the Civilian Conservation Corps' Recreation Demonstration Area at Silver Creek Falls. (Oregon Parks and Recreation Division)

Civilian Conservation Corps improvements in Silver Creek Falls State Park. (Oregon Parks and Recreation Division)

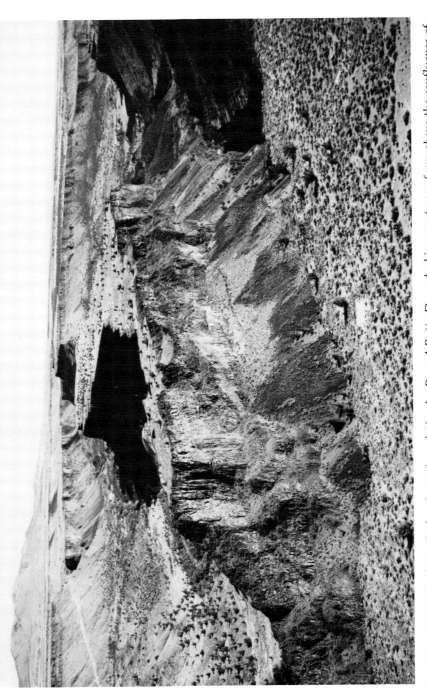

The Cove–Palisades State Park prior to inundation by Round Butte Dam, looking upstream from above the confluence of the Deschutes (right) and Crooked rivers. (Oregon Parks and Recreation Division)

Beneath the Crooked River rimrocks in The Cove–Palisades State Park. View taken prior to inundation of the area from the building of Round Butte Dam. (Oregon Parks and Recreation Division)

The Oregon Coast in the Samuel H. Boardman State Park; Thomas Creek bridge in distance at right. (Oregon Parks and Recreation Division)

Governor Robert Smylie typing a speech in his office. (Idaho State Historical Society)

Governor Albert Rosellini with his daughters in a campaign photo. (Washington State Archives)

Governor Tom McCall fly fishing in the restored Willamette River. (Gerry Lewin)

Robert Straub with aerial photographs of disputed highway location on the Oregon Coast. (Oregon Historical Society)

Glenn Jackson being sworn in as chairman of Oregon Highway Commission (Governor Mark Hatfield, center). (Oregon Historical Society)

thrice made recommendation. I hope that this session can summon the resolution to take action.[36]

Once again, Smylie was rebuffed. Two park bills were introduced. Senate Bill 25 passed the Senate on a 44-0 vote, but the House postponed consideration indefinitely. House Bill 35, a similar measure, fared no better. It passed in the House 62-0, but the Senate killed it by voting 23-20 to excuse the State Affairs Committee from reporting it out. As before, opposition to Smylie's proposal came primarily from Democrats. And, also as before, the governor believed their motivation came not from any fear that a Parks Department would generate excessive demands for funds, but from a desire to maintain control over positions to which spoilsmen could be appointed. Smylie had some consolation, however; the legislature did vote to accept the agreement with the Harrimans. If Idaho could somehow get a professionally trained Parks Department, Railroad Ranch would eventually become a state park.[37] The *Idaho Evening Statesman* contended that accepting the gift will "serve as notice to all the world that here in Idaho we are ready to measure up to the task of preserving . . . areas of majesty and grandeur in our great outdoors."[38] The claim was clearly premature.

In the face of these setbacks, Smylie's attention now turned to the site of the former Farragut Naval Training Station on the shore of Lake Pend Oreille. Shortly after the Second World War, Governor C. A. Robbins had the state acquire the surplus military tract. It was the last major piece of shoreline property apt to become available on the popular lake, but Robbins had no authority to purchase it for a park; he adopted the subterfuge of acquiring it as a "wildlife refuge." The site sat unused, studded with concrete foundations and other remains from the Naval Training Station, until Smylie's administration. As a spur to its renovation, Smylie signed an agreement with the Girl Scouts of America to use the site for the 1965 Senior Girl Scout Roundup. With volunteer labor and donated material, as well as state funds, site preparation was rushed to completion. By the time 12,000 Girl Scouts gathered, Idaho had a new state park.

Idahoans, proud of the attention that the gathering brought, grumbled but little about expenditures at Farragut, although some residents of the southern part of the state did complain that an equal amount was not being spent on parks in their area.[39] The State Land

Board, doubtless trying to defuse the protests of fiscal conservatives and antisocialists, argued:

> In tourism, as in any other business, we are essentially in competition for the dollar. This applies to our entire state, as well as to the individual private campground owner. We must develop outdoor recreation opportunities that are significantly attractive to persuade the potential visitor to visit our state rather than one of our neighbors. . . . If we can accomplish this by virtue of our State Parks system, the private segment will be in an excellent position to accommodate these people on their travels within our state.

The "forthcoming Farragut State Park" was one of those specifically identified as having the capacity to attract and hold such visitors.[40]

When the legislature met again in 1965, Smylie was in a stronger position than ever. He was now in his third term. Moreover, the Republicans at last enjoyed a comfortable margin in the legislature— six in the Senate and five in the House. Democrats still controlled the Land Board, but the Republican majority in the legislature was sufficiently large that chances of overcoming Democratic opposition to a nonpartisan Park Department looked good. Acceptance by the 1963 legislature of the Harrimans' offer, with its proviso that Idaho must have a professionally trained Park Department, added to the pressure for action. In addition, hard on the heels of the agreement to hold the Girl Scout Roundup at Farragut Park, Smylie had arranged to hold the 1967 World Boy Scout Jamboree there.[41] Just what role this played in convincing legislators that parks were not a luxury, but a wise investment, is impossible to determine. This and other developments, however, were clearly pointing in that direction and probably helped to keep Idaho's Republican party, which was drifting to the right, supportive of the governor's proposal.[42]

Events in Washington, D.C., also strengthened Smylie's hand. In August 1964, after a three-year study by the Outdoor Recreation Resources Review Commission and at the urging of President Lyndon Johnson and Secretary of the Interior Stewart Udall, Congress created a federal Land and Water Conservation Fund. Senators Henry Jackson of Washington and Frank Church of Idaho served as floor managers for the bill. The new law meant that considerable federal aid, some $250,000 to start with, would be available to Idaho for state parks and other conservation projects if the state would do the planning required under the law.[43]

When Idaho's legislature reconvened in 1965, it was welcomed with yet another proposal for a Parks Department. The new bill was a carefully worded compromise hammered out with the aid of Darrel Manning, a Democrat, and other leaders of the House. The wording made it clear that a Parks Department would do the planning and provide the liaison with the federal government that was required if Idaho were to tap the Land and Water Conservation Fund. Just how important eagerness for federal funds was in determining the final outcome is unclear. The park bill met no significant opposition in the House, passing after minor amendments 71-0. In the Senate, however, it passed by a margin of 26-17 and then only after intense maneuvering and a series of even closer votes. Even after the final vote, Senate Democrats were not stilled; they insisted the vote was "illegal and invalid." Be that as it may, Governor Smylie happily signed the bill.[44]

Having finally won a professionally trained, non-political Parks Department, Smylie believed that continued progress had been insured. Just how important the new department was became clear in the years that followed. Smylie's conservative Republican successor, Don Samuelson, was little interested in conservation and recreation. Indeed, Samuelson's stand on open pit mining in the scenic White Clouds area so angered Ernest E. Day—Smylie's appointee to head the Parks Board—that he resigned in disgust and marshalled the Sierra Club and similar forces in open war against the proposal. Day protested that "the idea that we have to carve up every nook and cranny of the quality areas of Idaho is specious reasoning and not in the best interest of the citizens of Idaho and the United States."[45]

Things got only slightly better after Samuelson left the statehouse. He was replaced by Cecil Andrus, a Democrat who had consistently voted against Smylie's park bills while in the Senate. Andrus was an avid outdoorsman and mining in the White Clouds was the key issue in his campaign against Samuelson, but he long remained only lukewarm in his support of parks. Smylie later expressed amazement that Andrus had not done more in support of parks as a means of creating a clear distinction between his own administration and that of Samuelson. However, his voting record while a state senator hardly leaves room for surprise. Indeed, Samuelson voted in favor of Smylie's parks proposals more often than Andrus did. State Senator Art Manley's later claims that the Parks Department had been a bipartisan creation is only true for the House; it ignores the opposition of Andrus and other key Democrats in and out of the state Senate.[46]

Gradually Andrus's interest increased, however. In 1976 he reappointed Day to the Parks Board, and when Harriman State Park was finally deeded over to the state in that year, he not only welcomed the acquisition but saw to it that Smylie received his full share of credit for all he had done to bring the donation—and a parks system—into being.[47]

Progress continued after Smylie left office in 1967, but not primarily because of subsequent governors. Instead, it resulted from the work of Wilhelm M. Beckert, selected as Director of the State Parks Department, from his successors, from the staff of trained personnel that they built up, and from the support that they received from the public, the legislature, and the federal government. No longer was there a governor in the vanguard. Repeatedly, Smylie had pushed the legislature to create a parks department. When it finally did, it ensured the continued presence of champions of parks in the state's government regardless of who sat in the governor's chair.[48]

Idaho still may have to pay for its long neglect of its scenic resources. Heyburn Park, like the state tracts at Payette and Priest lakes, was managed so as to be largely self-sustaining. This was accomplished first by logging parts of it, then primarily through leasing summer home sites to private citizens. The leases were issued even though the act of Congress and the deed through which Idaho got the land specified that failure to use it as a public park could result in repossession by the federal government. By the 1970s these private leases had become a source of concern, in part because of sewage and garbage pollution. Beckert's department struggled to bring the situation under control, but the action came too late to prevent major problems. The Coeur d'Alene Tribal Council—unhappy with the condition of the lake that they had surrendered and convinced that the state was unwilling to manage it properly, or perhaps simply seeing a chance to gain valuable property—took steps in 1975 to get the federal government to reclaim the park for the tribe. Tribal attorney Robert D. Dellwo asserted: "The future for the people who use the park would be much brighter under the tribe." At the very time that Idaho had at last begun to care for its parks, it stood to lose its finest holding because of earlier neglect. The suit for return of the site to the federal government went in favor of the state in the federal district and appeals courts, but only after Idaho had ended leaseholds in the park. Wording of the decision made it clear that Idaho might subsequently lose the park if leaseholds were reinstituted.[49]

The dispute over Heyburn Park does not negate Robert Smylie's contributions. His fight for parks was one of many indicators of the rising national concern with conservation and recreation during the 1950s and 1960s. But it was an indicator of something more. Idaho had come a long way from the days of Weldon Heyburn, whose opposition to the conservation policies of Theodore Roosevelt and Gifford Pinchot was a manifestation of a major regional countercurrent. It had also come a long way from the 1920s, when Idaho had stood apart from the state parks movement that was blossoming in much of the rest of the country. With Governor Smylie, Idaho joined the mainstream.

The techniques Smylie used in working for parks were remarkably similar to those utilized earlier by Ben Olcott, Robert Sawyer, and Asahel Curtis. Smylie lobbied and maneuvered, he worked through private organizations, and he sought through persuasion and publicity to build support. With Smylie as with his predecessors, what he wrought in the end was the result of his own efforts and of important allies from outside the state, rather than the support of the local citizenry.

There were echoes of the Depression era in Smylie's efforts too. The professional, bureaucratic agency Smylie proposed was what was emerging across the land during Sam Boardman's tenure as head of Oregon's parks. And the availability of federal funds influenced events in Idaho in Smylie's day as surely as they had elsewhere during the New Deal years.

Still, what Smylie created was new. In scope, in organization, and in purpose he addressed the needs and reflected the ideas of his own day. As earlier, the argument that parks would bring automobile tourists played a key role, but Smylie used this argument in fresh ways. His predecessors had utilized it to persuade reluctant guardians of the public purse to spend money on parks; Smylie did too, but through it he also sought to generate political support for his program and his party. The public, he believed, had become sufficiently interested in recreation and conservation to understand how expenditures on parks could attract tourists.[50] Roadside trees were no longer an issue, nor were roadside parks that were essentially rest stops. Even scenery preservation had ceased to be central; the presence of scenic resources in Idaho was seemingly taken for granted. What Smylie envisioned were large parks with enough recreational potential to attract and hold tourists, while at the same time meeting the recreational needs of Idaho's own. Americans were visiting and appreciating the outdoors as never before. Smylie's program was a direct response. When President Lyndon Johnson spoke in behalf of the "new conservation" in 1965, Robert E. Smylie had already been championing it for over a decade and had already won major victories.[51]

Chapter 8

All the Governor's Men
Parks and Politics in Washington State,
1957–1965

E ven after Roland Hartley left the governor's mansion, Washington continued to lag behind Oregon in the development of its state parks. For all of W. G. Weigle's efforts, progress came slowly during his superintendency (1933–41). CCC crews carried on construction projects in Moran State Park and elsewhere, but new acquisitions during the Depression were limited. Sam Boardman exaggerated only slightly in 1943, when he wrote with characteristic bluntness: "I doubt if there is a state in the nation that can outdo us. . . . California can compare with Oregon in number but not in quality. Washington has nothing."[1]

Bit by bit Washington inched forward, but the state—like Idaho and many others—was unprepared for the hordes that flooded its parks following World War II. Looking at the host of visitors, the limited budgets, and the overtaxed facilities, one writer for the *Seattle Times* expressed concern that the system might be overwhelmed and irreparable damage done. But it was not; indeed, the 1950s saw considerable progress. In January 1961, when Frank F. Warren stepped down as a member of the State Parks and Recreation Commission, he reviewed with pride accomplishments during his twelve years of service. In 1950, he noted, Washington had forty-one developed parks; by 1960 it had sixty-five. In 1950 the state's park system embraced 55,000 acres; by 1960 it encompassed 75,500. In 1950 1.64 million people visited Washington's parks; by 1960 the number had grown to over 7 million. During the same period, budgets for parks rose from $1.1 million to over $2.4 million per year.[2]

Progress did not come without difficulty. Many members of the seven-man Parks and Recreation Commission seem to have viewed themselves as responsible for getting as much as possible for their home districts from what the *Seattle Times* called the "park barrel". Haphazard, uneven development resulted. Furthermore, although intended as a policy-making body, the commission frequently involved itself in administrative matters and, while in theory the commission was nonpartisan, the party in power often used appointments to reward political supporters. This was especially the case after the election of Albert D. Rosellini as governor in 1956. Maneuvering for positions on the commission became so intense in 1957 that the state Supreme Court finally had to settle the resultant controversy.[3]

Budgets were a source of problems too. In 1957 the legislature increased vehicle license fees, earmarking the bulk for state parks. Two years later, faced with a projected deficit and pressing demands for schools, Rosellini moved to shift $1 million of this fund to other agencies for the coming biennium. He supported parks, the governor insisted, but the state faced a fiscal emergency that required drastic action. Legislators rejected the switch; indeed, they increased the parks budget and resorted to other means of solving the state's financial difficulties.[4]

The budget problems, though real, were not severe enough to halt expansion of the parks system. What followed was another matter. In the early 1960s parks became a major political issue, one that—coupled with other developments—threatened to bring down the Rosellini administration. As Washington's state parks staggered from crisis to crisis, much was revealed about their social and political milieu. The picture was hardly flattering, either to Rosellini or to the state.

Patronage lay at the heart of the matter. Rosellini, the son of immigrant parents, had grown up in a poor part of Seattle where he had been drawn into politics during the New Deal years. A self-styled champion of the working-class poor, Rosellini managed to get an education and gradually worked his way up in politics. When he assumed the governorship in January 1957, after eight years of Republican control in Olympia, he saw himself as the outsider who had made it to the top; he was not about to forget either those like himself or those who had helped him to rise.

A scramble for place quickly followed. Hordes of jobseekers descended on the capital. As political analyst C. E. Johns put it, "administration henchmen" in their eagerness to "pass out the gravy . . . did not use moderation, or you might even say good common political prudence." Washington's civil service system was weak; only the departments of highways and public assistance had effective systems for merit hiring and promotion. Not surprisingly, Republican heads rolled at all levels. Rosellini was candid about giving preference to friends of his administration: "You can call it a spoils system or whatever you want. . . . Of necessity you have to have people who are going to carry out your policies and are going to be loyal." Meanwhile, Rosellini appointees were pressured to contribute to political slush funds for the governor's personal and political expenses. Allegations of favoritism in state purchasing and of other irregularities surfaced. There was, the Seattle *Argus* observed, an "ever-growing stench" in Olympia.[5]

At first all of this touched but lightly on state parks. The members of the State Parks and Recreation Commission had all been appointed by Rosellini's Republican predecessor, Arthur B. Langlie. They stayed on in their supposedly nonpartisan positions to fill out their terms, after an abortive effort to force out three of them. John R. Vanderzicht, Langlie's appointee as state park superintendent, was able to survive Rosellini's first term—the sole Republican department head to do so. Parks continued the steady growth shown during the earlier years of Vanderzicht's administration, and during his campaign for reelection Rosellini announced plans for major expansion in the years ahead.[6]

In November 1960, voters reelected Rosellini, seemingly more impressed with his programs for attracting jobs than with charges of impropriety in government. Urged on by the League of Women Voters and organized labor, however, they also passed Initiative 207, designed to reform the state's civil service system. Fearing a freezing in of employees, Rosellini asked department heads to weed out deadwood and those who had opposed his reelection before the new law went into effect on 9 December. He also named Samuel O. Long, former head of central personnel (and thus patronage), to serve as interim director of the new civil service system; he replaced career civil servants in charge of personnel for the formerly independent departments of highways and public assistance with other political supporters. With reelection behind him, Rosellini seemed to one newspaper editor to be seeking to clear out "any remaining vestiges of a Republican toehold in state government." As firings proceeded, Long admitted that at least some employees were terminated for political reasons.[7]

Time was running out for Vanderzicht. He held his position at the discretion of the Parks and Recreation Commission and thus neither Rosellini nor Long could remove him. But the terms of four Langlie appointees expired at the beginning of 1961, and Rosellini promptly appointed his own, giving him a majority on the commission for the first time. Rumors circulated that the superintendency might go to Long, for whom Rosellini was clearly seeking a spot. Concerned citizens protested, urging Rosellini to keep the commission nonpartisan, but the governor was noncommittal.[8]

Early in May Rosellini told the publisher of the *Ferndale Record* that the removal of the parks superintendent was only "a remote possibility. . . . I assume that as long as Mr. Vanderzicht's work is satisfactory to them [the commissioners] he will be retained." Be that as it may, on 18 June Vanderzicht announced that he would resign as of 1 August. He was reluctant to do so, he said, but "I had a little chat" with the commissioners, "and they would like a change and under those conditions the only thing to do is resign." Whether this represented anything more than politics was not clear; the commission refused to make its reasons public, but hints of financial and administrative irregularities did leak out.

Some reports credited Long with bringing Vanderzicht down. Like Rosellini, Long was an avid supporter of the state's experimental Youth Conservation Corps, which was funded through the parks department; indeed, Long was named to head the program when it went into operation in the summer of 1961. Vanderzicht, on the other hand, publicly opposed diverting scarce park funds to such a program and in so doing committed what Rosellini must surely have considered an act of political disloyalty.[9]

At this juncture, the State Personnel Commission refused to approve John R. Chambers, a thirty-eight-year employee of the parks department, as assistant director. Disappointed and frustrated by divisions in the department, Chambers took early retirement shortly thereafter. Rosellini then named Sam Long acting assistant director without even bothering to consult with the Parks and Recreation Commission. Protests over the handling of Vanderzicht's removal and the apparently growing politicization of parks mounted.[10]

Clair V. Greeley, chairman of the park commission, sought to defuse criticisms by announcing a nationwide campaign to recruit as the new superintendent "the best possible man, one with full park experience." The statement was a lightning rod for protest and also a veiled jab at Vanderzicht, who had been named to the park commission by Langlie and had then maneuvered himself into the superintendency at the expense of a parks professional brought in from Indiana. Vanderzicht, Rosellini noted, had been a restaurant operator without parks experience before Langlie named him to the commission in 1949. The governor added that Long, a former schoolteacher, would not be the new superintendent. Rosellini endorsed the idea of nationwide recruitment. Because of his own "deep interest in parks," the governor told Greeley, he would be making suggestions regarding the selection of a superintendent. Indeed, the governor went on to add, "we must obtain the best professionally qualified individual possible."[11]

For acting director during the recruiting process, Rosellini prevailed upon authorities in Yakima to grant Edward V. Putnam a leave of absence from his position as superintendent of its parks district.[12] Putnam and Long soon found themselves engaged in a struggle for control of the department and, despite mutual denials, perhaps for the position of superintendent as well. The parks commission divided four-to-three into pro-Long and pro-Putnam factions, with the result that Putnam found himself with less and less real authority. Representatives from the state Parent-Teachers Association, which was much interested in state parks, attended commission meetings and found that the commission had "almost completely usurped the administrative function of the Director of the Department." Moreover, the split ran through the department from top to bottom, hindering work at all levels.[13]

The problems in Washington's parks system were no secret. They were fully covered in the state's press and, Greeley and Putnam reported, a topic of informal discussion among delegates at the annual meeting of the National Conference on State Parks in the fall of 1961. The *Seattle Times* warned editorially that "even the best systems can deteriorate rapidly if both its policymakers and administrators remain mired in dissension and confusion." Much of the controversy centered around Long, the paper noted, but added that Rosellini "must bear ultimate responsibility." Only prompt selection of a qualified professional superintendent could restore authority and confidence.[14]

The advice was unnecessary. Rosellini and the parks commission were moving swiftly toward a decision. On 21 November Sam Long resigned as assistant parks director effective 1 December. Long explained, "I want to give the new director of the department, whoever he may be, a free hand in choosing an assistant." Long expressed a desire to stay on as administrator of the youth corps "as long as it pleases the commission," but instead Putnam accepted Long's resignation and placed him immediately on terminal leave. Putnam, too, was about to leave the parks department; his four-month term as acting superintendent was scheduled to conclude on 1 December.[15]

A new superintendent had not been selected by the time Putnam's term was up, so John Chambers was recalled from retirement to serve as interim acting director. By 12 December the field had been narrowed to three men: Clayton E. Anderson, head of the recreation division of the Oregon parks department; William N. Parke, a career man with the United States Forest Service; and Loyd Bransford, also of the Forest Service.

Rosellini lobbied for Parke, but the commissioners wanted Anderson. In the end, the governor accepted their choice, but only after four members threatened to resign unless he respected the commission's legal authority to make the selection. At their January meeting, having wrung the recommendation they wanted from Rosellini, the commissioners formally appointed Anderson director of state parks.[16]

Anderson was not unknown in the state. He had a bachelor's degree from the College of Puget Sound (now University of Puget Sound) in Tacoma and had done graduate work in recreation there (as well as at the University of Oregon and Oregon State University). He had also once worked at Mount Rainier National Park, although his main professional experience had been as director of the Willamalane Park District in Oregon and then with the Oregon state parks department.[17]

The choice was not without its critics. Putnam stated bluntly, "they got the wrong man," for between Anderson and Parke "there is no comparison in their abilities, background and qualifications." He called the selection political, adding "they have to be awfully careful or they are going to have Sam Long back there." In its lead editorial on 25 January, the *Seattle Times* lent tacit support to Putnam's position. Anderson, the paper noted, "does not have as extensive a parks-and-recreation background as one or two of the other candidates for the job."[18]

Anderson's selection was probably little influenced by politics, although Rosellini's initial opposition might seem to suggest the opposite. To be sure, Blaine Whipple, executive secretary of the Oregon Democratic party, did write to assure Rosellini that Anderson was a good Democrat who would be "an asset to your administration in terms of political background, knowledge and ability." Rosellini also placed personal telephone calls to Oregon and obtained further assurances. But Anderson was really the commission's choice. He would appear to have gotten the job because a majority wanted a young man with enthusiasm and vigor—characteristics that had been a major part of Sam Long's appeal. Anderson fit the bill; he was thirty-eight, while Parke was fifty-four and Bransford fifty-five.[19]

Having agreed to the commission's choice, Rosellini met with Anderson. The governor told him, Anderson later recalled, that he wanted Washington to have the best state park system in the country. When Anderson replied that was precisely what he hoped to build, Rosellini asked how long it would take. "Five years," Anderson estimated, to which Rosellini replied incredulously, "So *long*?" In retrospect, it seemed to Anderson that the governor was only looking forward as far as the next election.[20]

At the time, his meeting with Rosellini seems to have stirred no qualms in Anderson. Indeed, he welcomed the challenge. The appointment of a new director, he wrote, provides opportunity for "a fresh start in implementing a renewed, vigorous state parks program in Washington." But Anderson hardly got off to a propitious start. Rosellini had a secretary assigned to Anderson who reported back to the governor's office on what Anderson said and did. For his part, Anderson, seeking to establish the professional integrity of the parks department, refused to make the donations to the governor's "slush fund" that were expected of a department head, to sell tickets to

Democratic fund raisers, or to appoint people sent to him by the party's state central committee. The governor met privately with the director and tried to convince him of the wisdom of being more flexible, but to no avail.[21] Whatever frictions resulted from all this went largely undetected outside the administration, but on other fronts Anderson was not so fortunate. Before the end of February he found himself in a storm of public controversy.

Asked about Sam Long during an interview shortly after his appointment had been announced, Anderson replied that neither Rosellini nor the commission had mentioned Long to him. Yet once in office one of Anderson's first major acts was to name Long head of the new Youth Development and Conservation Corps (YDCC), which replaced the earlier experimental program. In so doing, Anderson split the commission wide open. At its meeting on 26 February Clair Greeley tried to block Long's appointment. A majority countered by calling new elections and replacing Greeley as chairman. Further turmoil was added when three top employees of the department presented their resignations. Others could also be expected to quit, Anderson noted, because of the "turbulence in the department the past six months."[22]

The next day the *Seattle Times* again made the department's problems the subject of its lead editorial. The reaction to Anderson's naming of Long had been predictable, it stated, and asked "Why is it imperative that a place be found for Long in the Parks Department?" Perhaps C. E. Johns, writing for the *Argus,* provided the answer. Anderson, he said, was eager to let people know that he was "a good Democrat," but in the process had shown "surprising naivete about how to get along in the goldfish bowl of public administration." Johns observed that Anderson "appears new to the stratum of politics in which he finds himself. His elevation to parks director has been a little heady."[23]

At first Rosellini announced that he would stay out of this latest feud and that Anderson should be given a free hand in personnel matters. But the governor soon changed his mind. Rosellini had a genuine interest in parks and outdoor recreation. More important, he had plans to make them—and the luring of additional tourists to the state—a major concern of his administration. He called a "mandatory" meeting of the commission for 5 March. It was his intention, the governor told the press, to order the commission to stick to policy matters and leave running the department to Anderson. "We'll crack a few heads together," he promised, for "I consider the continued development of a good park system, now and for the future, one of the most important assignments in state government. . . . I'm not going to let one member or seven members stand in the way of doing a good job." Chastened, even Clair Greeley admitted that it was time to "bury the hatchet."[24]

Nor did Rosellini stop there. A man of strong personal loyalties, he appreciated Sam Long's talents and faithful service. Nonetheless, he realized that if there were to be peace in the parks department, Long had to go. Reluctantly, the governor asked his lieutenant to step aside.

On 6 March Long withdrew as a candidate for head of YDCC. He did so, he said, at Rosellini's request and in order to save the youth program. Long could not, however, resist taking a final swipe at his critics. He insisted that the youth corps was something in which he had been interested since "long before I drafted this legislation." He added that he was qualified to run it because of his training in education, his administrative experience, and his work with the earlier experimental program— at the time the only youth corps in the country. Long also said that two of the park commissioners had been trying to hamstring the program. If they did not stop, he would propose to the next legislature that it create a separate youth authority as California had recently done.[25]

The air cleared and controversy for the moment behind them, Rosellini and Anderson prepared for constructive action. The governor named Anderson to head an Inter-Agency Outdoor Recreation Commission (IORC) to study Washington's recreation needs, plan for coordinated action by state agencies dealing with outdoor resources, and recommend legislation to the next session of the legislature. Rosellini anticipated that the bill to establish a Land and Water Conservation Fund, which was then before Congress, would pass; under its terms the work of the IORC would make Washington eligible to tap federal funds. Rosellini asked for a master plan by December 1962. To carry out a statewide survey that would serve as the basis for their recommendations, the IORC hired Walter S. Horchler and gave him a full-time staff of four.[26]

Work proceeded apace. A preliminary report on 19 September noted that the study would only cost about $30,000; in comparison

Oregon's survey cost $130,000 and California's $300,000. By February Rosellini was ready with a special message to the legislature in which he outlined the state's recreational needs, with a program to meet them, and with a report to back up his recommendations. State parks, the study showed, already served roughly as many people in Washington as did national parks and did so with far less land and money. It also made clear that the demand for outdoor recreation was rising sharply, especially for water-oriented activities, and that the cost of recreational land was rising with it. Rosellini was eager to acquire new land for state parks before escalating costs put it out of reach.

At the heart of his program was a package of proposed legislation: SB 380, which would provide for the use of pleasure-boat fuel taxes (an estimated $1.5 million per year) on water-related recreational facilities; SB 381, calling for a $10 million bond issue for park acquisition and development, the bond issue to be repaid out of fees on corporations; SB 382, which would repeal current laws by which taxes on pleasure-boat fuel were refunded (or used on highways if refunds were not applied for); and SB 383, which would create a fifteen-member Outdoor Recreation Development Board to establish priorities, distribute funds, and coordinate the actions of various state agencies. The package, Rosellini told Oregon's Governor Mark Hatfield, would make $23 million available for the acquisition and development of parks over the next ten years.[27]

Sensing rising interest in outdoor recreation, Rosellini pushed the proposals hard, calling them the key program of his administration. In the end, only the bond issue passed—perhaps, as some charged, because Rosellini was not effective in working with the legislature. Nonetheless, his effort in behalf of his outdoor recreation program was a major factor in leading C. E. Johns to write that Rosellini had "taken on a higher stature than his opponents had expected."[28]

In the meantime, Clayton Anderson was busy trying to bring lasting order to the parks department. He sought to eliminate confusion and contests for authority by drawing up an administrative manual that would clearly define responsibilities and the chain of command. To increase efficiency and reduce political influence on the department, he sought to attract qualified professionals, often from out of state. And to provide a better sense of direction and priorities, he hoped to formulate a master plan for parks development. Obviously, the work of the IORC would greatly influence the last of these, so while Horchler and the interagency committee did their work Anderson focused most of his efforts on developing the administrative manual and a professional staff.[29]

For a time, things seemed to go reasonably well, although nagging problems continued to surface. Environmentalists, led by the Western Federation of Outdoor Clubs, protested overly zealous cleanup logging in Deception Pass Park. Others complained when the state proposed to trade away a valuable site at Fort Ward, on Bainbridge Island, on the grounds that it lacked an adequate water supply for a park. Local residents, who had wells of their own, dismissed that argument as preposterous, and others pointed out that the department itself had admitted that it needed more waterfront parks on Puget Sound. A *Seattle Times* editorial said the incident showed "limited vision by the state director of parks and recreation."

Some of Anderson's appointments also caused grumbling; Rosellini questioned increased expenses for the parks commission; embarrassing comparisons between Oregon's and Washington's parks appeared in the press from time to time; and in July 1962 Albert H. Culverwell, head of the state parks historical program for nine years, resigned in disgust citing departmental morale problems and interference with his work by Commissioner Joseph S. Whiting. The resignation led to a brief effort in the legislature to abolish the parks commission, giving parks independent departmental status or placing them under the Natural Resources Board.[30]

But all these were minor irritants, the sort that any administrator trying to bring order into a long-troubled department might expect. Indeed, both Anderson and Rosellini seem to have thought things were going reasonably well. In April 1963 Anderson noted to Marshall Dana of the Portland *Oregon Journal* that the legislature had just passed the department's budget intact. "This is the first time in State Parks history this has ever been done, so I feel we are making some progress."[31]

Yet there were ominous signs. Demands for patronage continued to strain relations between Anderson and the Democratic party's power structure. Kay MacDonald, a Rosellini assistant, put the latter's position baldly in discussing the appointment of summer rangers: "We want these people to associate their jobs with the

Governor. . . . The whole idea here is to please the existing state organization."[32]

The relative tranquility that the public saw came to an abrupt end in the summer of 1963. On 30 July Elmer Anderson, the department's supervisor of recreation, sent a bitter letter to Clayton Anderson. Since his "knowledge, experience and ability . . . [were] not wanted under the present departmental administration, and it has become an impossibility for me to do any part of the job without complete disregard or destructive criticism from the Director," Elmer Anderson told his superior, he was resigning to become director of parks for Clark County, Nevada. Orders had been issued straight from the director to the supervisor of recreation's staff, ignoring the chain of command; the result was "low morale and frustrations . . . [which are] obvious at the present time." The press promptly picked up the story. Clayton Anderson believed that this and other damaging items were leaked to the *Seattle Times* by people in the office of the Democratic state central committee who were incensed by his inflexible stand on patronage.[33]

In any case, a new controversy over parks was anathema to Rosellini. With his outdoor recreation package under consideration and the vital bond issue scheduled to be voted on in the fall, he could hardly afford signs of renewed trouble in the parks department. Clayton Anderson denied that there were problems of morale in the department and tried to explain away Elmer Anderson's charges as the grumblings of a malcontent. But the issue would not disappear, partly because the charges sounded so similar to those made by Culverwell when he had resigned a year earlier and partly because Rosellini knew and respected Elmer Anderson's work. Quietly the governor assigned a key aide to investigate.[34]

The parks director found himself with few allies. In seeking to professionalize the department, he had hired the best people he could find. Several of these were from out of state, which rankled both those interested in patronage and parochial Washingtonians who resented outsiders getting state jobs. Having hired qualified professionals, Anderson left them alone to do their assigned tasks. Their loyalties remained where they had been before Anderson hired them—to their professions. Neither they nor the state's Republican party offered significant support as Anderson faced his critics. In the highly politicized environment of Olympia, he stood alone—and expendable.[35]

On 14 August newspapers reported that Clayton Anderson was to be ousted as head of Washington's parks. The *Bremerton Sun* reported that Rosellini had called the parks director on the carpet that morning. Anderson, it went on, was "mad as a hornet," believing that he had simply moved too fast and stepped on too many toes. An Anderson supporter was more blunt: too many park employees were Rosellini's "political appointees . . . who won't jump when Anderson cracks the whip." Others tended to support Elmer Anderson's accusations, saying that the director insisted on making all decisions, "chewed out" people publicly, and frequently countermanded the orders staff members received from their supervisors. The *Seattle Times* added that Rosellini had called a closed-door meeting of the parks commission for 16 August where he would insist on "whatever changes are necessary." It seemed clear that Rosellini could obtain Anderson's dismissal if he wished it. As the *Sun* noted, the parks commission was divided, with three members opposed to Anderson and three not, but there was a vacancy on the commission that Rosellini could fill any time he wanted a majority. In acknowledging publicly for the first time that Anderson had not been his first choice for the directorship, Rosellini gave the impression that he was indeed preparing to oust him.[36]

If Anderson had any chance of retaining his position, it probably vanished on 15 August. On that day the *Seattle Times* once more turned its lead editorial to the subject of parks. "Rosellini," it argued, "has had ample time and authority to put an end to the squabbles within the park system . . . [but] things have gone from bad to worse" under Anderson. "A fresh start both in personnel and delineation of policy is now imperative."

On the same day a long column appeared in the Eugene, Oregon, *Register-Guard* outlining the shortcomings of Washington's parks system. It did not amount to much and never would, the paper predicted, until Washington "cleans the politics and favoritism out of its department." No Oregon governor, the paper observed, could politicize the state's parks system the way it was regularly done in Washington. The source of the information was clear to any insider reading the article: Clayton Anderson. During a recent visit to his former hometown, Anderson had dined with an acquaintance from the *Register-Guard* and laid out his problems to him. Anderson said he had not thought of their discussion as grist for a newspaper article, but simply as a conversation between old friends. Rosellini, reading the piece, was outraged. Anderson had committed the unforgivable sin of political disloyalty.[37]

Unaware that Anderson's fate was already sealed, S. P. Carey, president of the Washington State Parks Association, urged Rosellini not to dismiss so valuable a man, especially with the bond issue pending. He reminded the governor that Anderson had been a strong supporter of the youth conservation corps and of Rosellini's legislative package. Anderson himself wrote asking to be judged on the accomplishments of the department during the eighteen months he had headed it. He added, "I wish, Governor, that you could take the time to visit our department and talk to our employees. I think that you would find that morale is good as I have claimed." The pleas fell on deaf ears. Some have suggested that Anderson was guilty of social improprieties in Olympia that were the last straw for Rosellini, but whether there was any truth to those stories is irrelevant. It was already clear that Anderson had to go or the administration's entire outdoor recreation program would be endangered. To those who knew Rosellini well, it was equally clear that Anderson's responsibility for the damning piece in the *Register-Guard* would neither be overlooked nor forgiven.[38]

On 16 August Anderson announced that he had tendered his resignation "in the best interests of harmony and continued progress of the State Parks Department." For the first time he admitted openly that there were morale problems in the department. The commission voted to keep Anderson on for sixty days while they conducted a search for a new director.[39]

The reaction to Anderson's ouster was comparatively mild. G. R. Tuttle wrote to complain that parks had become "a political football" and blamed Rosellini. Ex-commissioner Joseph Whiting, on the other hand, pointed to Washington's system of an independent park commission only nominally controlled by the governor as the basic source of difficulties. "It simply is not realistic in our form of government," he wrote, "to remove control from elected officials." The *Kitsap County Herald* decried the firing as "an admirable example of why statesmanship is hard to come by in the State of Washington." Anderson, it argued, had sought to professionalize the department and in the process had angered time-servers and politicians. In order to survive in office, the *Herald* feared, Anderson's successor would "concentrate more on keeping his head down than on getting things done."[40]

But the tide had already turned. On 6 November 1963, Rosellini announced that Charles H. Odegaard had been selected to succeed Anderson. Odegaard, the thirty-five-year-old Pacific Northwestern representative of the National Recreation Association, was a personable, trained professional with a knack for promoting himself. He had volunteered to help select a successor to Anderson, only to wind up with the position himself. Odegaard later insisted that he had not sought the job, but was flattered when it was offered; Anderson suggested that Odegaard had been maneuvering toward that goal for some time. Be that as it may, Odegaard quickly proved himself a skillful administrator with a touch with personnel, the press, and politicians that Anderson had lacked. Tranquility and order came to the parks department at last, and a period of rapid progress followed. With Rosellini's support, Odegaard increased acquisitions and facilities, especially on Puget Sound and the Pacific Coast. Odegaard stayed on after Republican Daniel Evans replaced Rosellini as governor in 1965, and the progress—if not the tranquility—continued. By 1970 the state's park system had come so far that it earned the Sport Foundation's Golden Medal Award for excellence in park and recreation management, and the following year Odegaard received an Outstanding Achievement Award from the National Conference on State Parks.[41]

Yet not all the credit for the progress that finally came to Washington's state parks can be laid at Odegaard's door. Albert Rosellini deserves a full measure. A politician's politician, Rosellini had at first sought to use parks to advance his party. But the governor's interest in outdoor recreation was as genuine as his devotion to the Democratic party, and when he eventually came to see that neither was being well served by partisanship, Rosellini abandoned his political approach to parks and allowed Odegaard to make decisions on professional grounds. Although Odegaard was himself a Democrat, he later recalled that Rosellini never asked him to do a partisan act or to give money to the party.

What he was able to accomplish, Odegaard confessed, would probably not have been possible earlier. He had inherited a staff of trained professionals and a solid—if often ignored—administration handbook from Clayton Anderson.[42] More important, John Vanderzicht, John Chambers, Sam Long, Ed Putnam, and Elmer and Clayton Anderson had paved the way by making clear the price of politicizing the state parks system. It was a hard-learned lesson. Whether later leaders of the state will profit from Rosellini's experience or have to learn it anew only time will tell, but the fact that Odegaard himself ran afoul first of Governor Evans and then of Governor Dixy Lee Ray, who forced him from office in 1979, is not cause for optimism.[43]

For his part, Rosellini reflected the times. Like Idaho's Governor Smylie, he realized that parks were important to tourism and to local residents, who were increasingly interested in scenery preservation and access to recreational facilities. He also came to recognize, as Smylie had from the beginning, that a modern, broad-based parks system required professional direction. And the system Rosellini wanted was broad indeed—encompassing a youth conservation corps, historical and geological sites, water-based recreation facilities, and stands of roadside timber, as well as scenic sites. In the end, Rosellini seems to have had little more success than Smylie in turning public interest in parks into political support, but the fact that they both thought that such support might be marshalled is revealing. The country had come a long way from the days of Robert Sawyer, when it was more effective to work surreptitiously to save scenery. Environmental concern was growing, and Rosellini and Smylie were both its beneficiaries and its champions.

Chapter 9

To Save A River

Robert Straub, Karl Onthank, Tom McCall, and the Willamette Greenway

On 19 July 1966, Oregon's State Treasurer Robert W. Straub, the Democratic candidate for governor, unveiled a plan for "a family recreation corridor" stretching along the Willamette River from Portland to the Eugene-Springfield metropolitan area. This proposal for a 200-mile-long parkway in the heart of the most densely populated portion of the state might well be "one of the most important conservation-recreation ideas in our state's history," Straub said. He was right, but it was also soon to become one of the most controversial.[1]

Response to Straub's proposal was almost immediate. The Republican-leaning *Portland Oregonian*, no supporter of Straub, suggested the plan was the ploy of a candidate grasping for issues and, in any case, would be unattainable. The more independent *Eugene Register-Guard*, however, announced its support. On 21 July, the unorthodox and outdoor-oriented Republican candidate for governor, Tom Lawson McCall, proclaimed that he too supported the idea. Support soon came from other quarters as well. A major campaign to save the state's largest internal river for scenic and recreational purposes was under way. It led to the largest single project in which Oregon's state parks system ever engaged.[2]

The times were ripe for such an effort. In Washington, D.C.,

President Lyndon Johnson, Secretary of the Interior Stewart Udall, and various congressmen were hammering out legislation to halt environmental degradation and insure the availability of resources for generations to come. This "third wave" of the conservation movement, as it has been labelled, differed from the approach during the Roosevelt presidencies. While this new movement displayed much of the Progressive Era's faith in planning and something less of the New Deal's concern with the economic implications of conservation, it was marked by greater concern for aesthetic considerations and quality of life and stronger fear of what modern science, technology, and industry might bring if left largely unrestrained.[3]

Scenic and recreational use of waterways were among the subjects to which attention had turned in Washington, D.C. In 1960 the Senate Select Committee on National Water Resources endorsed the National Park Service's recommendation that "certain streams be preserved in their free-flowing condition." In 1962 the Outdoor Recreation Resources Review Commission, chaired by Laurence Rockefeller, repeated the recommendation. Out of these and related developments came a drive that was to culminate in the Wild and Scenic Rivers Act of 1968.[4]

The political process in Washington, D.C., reflected a growing concern across the land over the damming, channelizing, and polluting of the nation's rivers and their increasing inaccessibility for recreation because of industrial and residential developments and the growing tendency of private landowners to bar public access. Across the nation, action was under way to save key streams in their wild state. In Maine there was a campaign to save the Allagash from development. In California, the American was the object of protectionist activity; in Wisconsin, it was the lower Nemakagon; in Montana, the Middle Fork of the Flathead; in Arkansas, the Buffalo; and in New York, the Hudson. The pattern varied from state to state and from river to river, but all showed the same basic concern with protecting valued scenic and recreational resources.[5]

Even before Straub's proposal, such concerns had been manifest in Oregon. In the 1950s Oregonians had debated proposals for hydroelectric power development in the Snake River's Hells Canyon (frequently, if not entirely accurately, billed as the nation's deepest chasm). Much of the debate focused on rival plans for dams by federal and private interests, but concern for the wild character of the river itself and for the salmon and steelhead runs that it supported also surfaced.[6]

Such concerns had been evident in Oregon as early as 1949, when a variety of conservation and sportsmen's groups sought to prevent construction of Pelton Dam on the Deschutes River, famed for its trout and steelhead fishing. State authorities ruled against the project, but their decision was overturned in federal court and the dam built. Not long after the controversy over Pelton Dam, the publicly owned Eugene Water and Electric Board proposed building a hydroelectric power plant at Beaver Marsh, thereby altering the scenic and popular upper McKenzie River. The issue became a storm center in local politics. In the end voters rejected the project in spite of EWEB's claim that construction would insure continuation of some of the lowest electric rates in the nation and create a slackwater impoundment more useful for recreation than existing natural conditions. Next, the Forest Service proposed building a road up the Minam River in northeastern Oregon to tap the timber stands of its drainage. Nearby residents were conspicuous among opponents during hearings on the proposal, even though the local economy desperately needed the jobs that sawmills supplied. Obviously, many Oregonians valued their streams for more than the immediate economic returns they could bring.[7]

River pollution was also drawing attention, especially to the Willamette. In 1926–27 the City of Portland began testing to determine the level of pollution in the city's river harbor. Two years later researchers at the new Engineering Experiment Station of Oregon State College published their first bulletin, "Preliminary Report on the Control of Stream Pollution in Oregon." In 1937 the state legislature passed a pollution control bill, but Governor Charles H. Martin, a conservative Democrat, vetoed it out of fear of its economic impact. Undeterred, the champions of regulation pushed ahead. In 1939 they prevailed upon the State Sanitary Authority to establish water quality standards and, using initiative procedures, got a veto-proof antipollution bill passed.

The push to clean up the Willamette promptly resumed following World War II, urged on by publication of another report from OSC's experiment station, "1945 Progress Report on the Pollution of Oregon Streams." By 1957 all cities on the river had primary sewage treatment plants in operation and sportsmen's clubs were pushing the paper and pulp industry to clean up its discharges into the stream. By 1960 municipalities along the river were required to have secondary sewage treatment plants, but a great deal remained to be done and pressure was arising to do it. Tom McCall's award-winning television documentary, "Pollution in Paradise," appeared in 1962, and new legislation required paper and pulp plants, a prime source of pollution, to have systems for treating their discharges operating by 1964. Water quality did improve, and recreational use of the river climbed rapidly. The Willamette cleanup was a harbinger of the commitment to environmental quality that was soon to become the recognized hallmark of Oregon.[8]

Under the circumstances, it is not surprising that President Johnson, who was campaigning against Barry Goldwater, chose Portland as the place to spell out his conservation program and voice support for a national system of wild and scenic rivers. On 17 September 1964 he made what the *Oregonian* labeled "a major policy statement on conservation." Johnson reiterated these ideas in his policy paper, "Conservation of Natural Resources," and incorporated them in his State of the Union message the following January.[9]

Thus, when Robert Straub issued his call for a parkway along the Willamette, he could anticipate support from both inside and outside the state. Indeed, such things were so much in the air that it is impossible to determine where Straub first got the idea. His own recollection is that it came from two sources. First, on a visit to Washington, D.C., in 1964, Secretary of the Interior Udall showed him what was being done along the Potomac. Impressed, Straub asked Udall to send him a copy of the project's plans. Second, Straub credited A. B. Guthrie's novel *The Way West*, a work to which he was led by the filming of a movie version near Eugene in 1964. Straub noted that Guthrie's pioneers on the Overland Trail had spoken of their destination not as "Oregon," but as "the Willamette." The contrast between what the river had been and the polluted, frequently ignored entity that it had become set Straub to dreaming of its restoration. Not inappropriately, he was to label the group he later helped to organize "The Willamette River Rediscovered."[10]

Tom McCall attributed the idea of a parkway along the Willamette to a different source: Karl W. Onthank, longtime Dean of Men at the University of Oregon and an avid outdoorsman and conservationist. McCall said Onthank had proposed a Willamette parkway in letters to Straub and McCall; both had liked the idea, but Straub had been the first to go public with it. Solid evidence to support McCall's claim has not been located, but it seems to contain at least a seed of truth, for McCall wrote Onthank as early as 2 July 1965, "Your hint about the more imaginative use of Oregon's riverbanks for parks has an intriguing ring and I certainly do want to talk to you about it at your early convenience."[11]

Other origins have been suggested. State Park Administrator David G. Talbot remembers a trip he and Glenn Jackson, chairman of the State Highway Commission, made in 1965. Seated by the airplane window as they flew south toward Eugene, Talbot was watching the Willamette pass below and noted to his companion that it was one of the three great scenic attributes of the state—along with the Cascades and the ocean coast—but that the river alone was largely unprotected. Jackson was noncommittal at the time, but he clearly had listened. When he rose to address a local civic group after their arrival in Eugene, he called for action to protect the scenic and recreational potential of the stream. Talbot considers Jackson's call the real beginning of the campaign for the Willamette River Greenway. Certainly, as chairman of the State Parks and Recreation Advisory Committee and of the State Highway Commission, Jackson was in a position to turn rhetoric into reality.[12]

The idea of a parkway running the length of the Willamette Valley may have sprung from all these sources and more, for the times were ripe. Regardless, one thing *is* clear. When Robert Straub went public with his plan for a parkway, Karl Onthank had already been quietly working toward that end for months.

Born in Vineland, New Jersey, in 1890, Onthank came west as a young man. He began his career as a school administrator in Tillamook and then, from 1916 until his retirement in 1956, served in various capacities at the University of Oregon. Always an avid hiker, Onthank gradually became involved in conservation groups. By the 1950s he was a key figure in the fight to prevent the Forest Service from reducing the size of the Three Sisters Wilderness Area; in the campaign to limit development around Waldo Lake; in the struggle to prevent the building of electric power facilities at Beaver Marsh; and in the battles to get congressional approval of the proposed Oregon Dunes National Seashore.

Onthank was something of an anachronism. He had joined a small and undistinguished university at a time when society expected it to play a paternal role with its students. He fit comfortably into that environment, but failed to change with the university and the times. Remembered fondly by many older alumni, Onthank was merely tolerated by most undergraduates who had contact with him in the 1950s. He often visited the local chapter of his college fraternity, where he gave uplifting speeches to "the boys"; his talks were dreaded as longwinded, boring, and platitudinous.[13] But in the woods, Onthank took on a different character. Young people who knew him there found him dedicated and inspiring; he instilled in Michael McCloskey and many another young outdoorsman a lifelong commitment to conservation. Years later, after McCloskey had become head of the Sierra Club, he recalled that "as a young man association with Karl was particularly exciting because he knew everyone in conservation in the West. He introduced me to the important people who were doing things and passed on the background about what they had done and how they were operating. I derived my whole conceptual understanding of conservation from him more than any other individual."

Onthank was, McCloskey had noted earlier, "a truly catholic conservationist." He was primarily interested in parks and wilderness, but also "deeply involved in problems of water, reclamation, and forestry."[14]

Onthank's breadth of knowledge, his judiciousness, his dedication, and his ability to work effectively on committees and through bureaucratic red tape—skills honed during his years in university administration—won him the respect of many in positions of authority. He served as president of the Western Federation of Outdoor Clubs, vice-president of the Oregon County Parks Association, chairman of the Oregon State Water Resources Board, and as a member of the Columbia Basin Inter-Agency Committee and the Lane County Parks and Recreation Advisory Committee. He was an organizer and officer of the Friends of the Three Sisters Wilderness and of the Save the McKenzie River Association.

Like most outdoor activists during the 1950s, Onthank generally focused on the problems of alpine areas, especially wilderness. Yet he also supported the Oregon Roadside Council and spent considerable time working for local and state parks. He joined central Oregonians in pushing for state park status for Smith Rocks, near Redmond. He praised the priorities of Sam Boardman, who "in the '30s hounded the then commission into getting land," and complained that under Boardman's successor, Chester H. Armstrong, all the money was going to development and "little provision is being made for the future." Onthank made the same complaint, less bluntly, to Armstrong himself.[15]

The idea of a Willamette River Greenway gradually took shape in Onthank's mind during the early 1960s. His efforts to save the McKenzie and Minam rivers from development do not seem to have contributed significantly. Both were white-water, mountain streams; Onthank's desire to preserve their pristine character was connected to his interest in mountain areas and wilderness. The Willamette was different—a quiet river flowing through a long-occupied area of farms and urban centers. His concern for protecting and developing its scenic and recreational potential seems to have stemmed primarily from his experience with the Lane County Parks and Recreation Commission and, to a lesser extent, from his work with the Columbia Basin Inter-Agency Committee, especially its Willamette River Basin Survey, and the Upper Willamette Resource and Conservation Development Project.[16]

Onthank had shown an interest as early as 1956 in appraising the "outdoor and scenic resources of this State, [looking] particularly toward their future development." His faith in planning grew as time passed. By 1961, he had joined in efforts to create a major new metropolitan park along the north bank of the Willamette in the Eugene-Springfield area. Talked about for at least a decade, the park at last seemed close to realization. The process was complicated, for the proposed park stretched across a variety of jurisdictions and funding depended on still more. Clearly, success could come only through careful planning and coordinated effort. Onthank's experience with North Bank Park seems to have opened his eyes to the potential for large-scale, regional recreational undertakings. By 1961 he was talking of the need for study of the recreational use of water resources throughout the upper Willamette Valley, and by 1965 advocating extending plans for the North Bank Park to include the entire area from Dexter Dam reservoir to the confluence of the Willamette and McKenzie rivers, a distance of some thirty miles.[17]

Other things also encouraged the development of Onthank's ideas. The Corps of Engineers and the Columbia Basin Inter-Agency Committee had undertaken a survey of water resources in the

Willamette Basin. As a member of the committee, Onthank made sure that recreational considerations received attention, for he recognized both the value of the planning involved and the leverage that such a study could provide for those seeking careful recreational development.[18]

At about the same time, Congress passed the Land and Water Conservation Act, which set up a program of federal aid for state and local conservation projects. In January 1965, in his role as president of the Oregon County Parks Association, Onthank appointed a committee to study how to proceed in tapping the Land and Water Conservation Fund and allocating the proceeds. Onthank saw that the fund could underwrite the sort of major projects that he was by now contemplating. He anticipated using the same cooperative approach that had already proven successful in advancing North Bank Park.[19]

In October 1964 *Sunset* magazine carried an article entitled "How the American River was 'Saved'." Interagency cooperation and citizen participation had resulted in the American River Greenstrip— a twenty-three-mile-long, 5,000-acre parkway along the historic American River near Sacramento. The greenstrip was an even greater undertaking than North Bank Park, but it demonstrated the practicality of the sort of interagency cooperation that Onthank and his allies had been using in behalf of the Eugene-Springfield park.[20]

Onthank sprang into action. He wrote Elmer Aldrich at the California Division of Parks and Recreation for information and arranged for Mervyn L. Filipponi of Sacramento to lecture at the University of Oregon on how the greenstrip had been brought into being. Onthank then sent copies of Filipponi's talk and the article from *Sunset* to members of the Willamette River Basin Survey's Recreational Committee.[21]

Onthank had long been moving toward a program to save the entire Willamette, but his letter to Aldrich on 14 December 1964 is the first known occasion on which he openly articulated the idea. He wrote that California was planning recreational "development along the whole length of the Sacramento. . . . That's something of the idea we have in mind for the Willamette, except we can have a crack at the whole basin [via the Corps of Engineers' Willamette Basin Review] and not just the main stem river and its banks."

Onthank apparently began lobbying at once. Three weeks before Filipponi's speech, Tom McCall was writing to acknowledge his

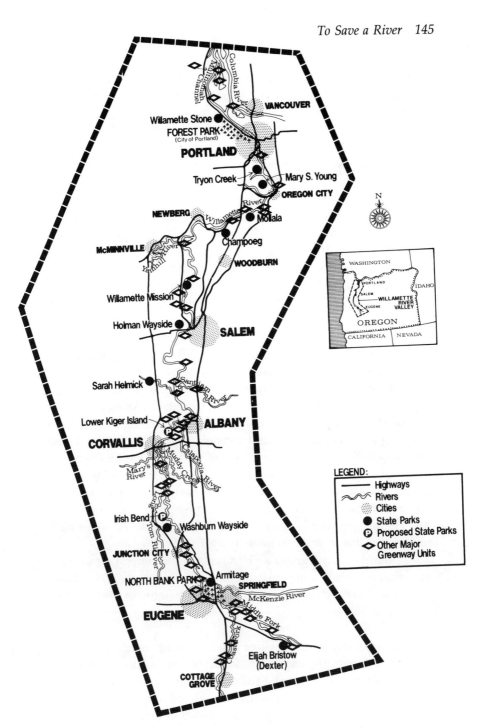

Willamette River Greenway

interest in Onthank's "hint about the more imaginative use of Oregon's riverbanks for parks." Onthank probably contacted Robert Straub at this point too. The two knew one another well. Straub had served on the Lane County Commission when Onthank had been active on the county's parks advisory board and while the North Bank Park campaign was at its height. Straub was receptive to imaginative programs, had been active in various conservation causes, and, as State Treasurer, was in a most influential position.[22]

Events proceeded apace. On 13 December, the Recreation Committee of the Willamette River Basin Survey filed a report in which it listed major recreational resources not being used to a significant degree and announced its intention of studying them more fully. Included on the list was "the Willamette recreation Green Strip from Eugene to Portland." On 22 April, Onthank called the attention of the Oregon Outdoor Recreation Council to the potential of the Willamette and McKenzie rivers and the need for additional acquisition and development along them. On 26 May, Paul R. Beistel, superintendent of parks and recreation for Lane County and a longtime associate of Onthank, presented a staff report, "Willamette River Open-Space Ribbon and Park Proposal," to the Lane County Parks and Recreation Advisory Committee. The committee expressed strong interest, asked to be kept informed, and told Beistel to work with the County Planning Office so the advisory committee "could lend its support to the proposal." Onthank and his allies were moving toward an Oregon equivalent of the broad-based coalition that had been so successful in Sacramento County in bringing protection to the American. There, Filipponi had said, "a river is being saved—and all but the *United Nations* seems to have a hand in it."[23]

Onthank was delighted with the course of events. Late in July he noted that the time "seems exceptionally favorable" for conservation. Two weeks later, he wrote Mark J. Pike, a key figure in the Willamette River Basin Survey,

> the Willamette parkway idea is taking hold amazingly, and not just because various candidates are making political capital out of it—though I suppose that is significant too. As recently as the last election it wouldn't have been considered very highly . . . [but] public opinion is moving into a much better recognition of outdoor recreation and enjoy-

ment of the outdoor scene—there's been a big change even while your committee has been working, and that's all to the good.[24]

To publicize the greenway plan, supporters organized a float trip down the Willamette from Eugene in the fall of 1966. Oddly, Onthank was not invited. He was in poor health, however, and told Pike that he would not have been able to go anyway. Onthank noted that he had not "been much below Eugene on the Willamette for many years—[although I] used to canoe to Corvallis and Albany rather often" and added that he understood "the views from and on the river have changed surprisingly little." Participants on the float trip confirmed Onthank's impression. "Strange how the sense of being far from civilization sets in almost as soon as you are on the river," said one.[25]

Straub continued to push the greenway during his gubernatorial campaign. He helped establish the Willamette River Rediscovered organization, based in Portland, and addressed civic and government groups on its behalf. He also urged Forest Service authorities to protect the McKenzie, the most important of the Willamette's tributaries. Onthank applauded, telling Straub on 12 August that "you are getting more widespread and serious support than anyone would have thought possible even a few months ago. Which is grand. More power to you." Early in October, Jonathan Newman of the prestigious Portland law firm of Cake, Jaureguy, Hardy, Butler & McEwin prepared a seven-page position paper outlining for Straub "points you might wish to make now regarding a recreation plan for the Willamette River area"; he incorporated suggestions from Onthank.[26]

Meanwhile McCall courted Onthank's political support, but without success. By this time Onthank was not only working for the greenway, but also expressing concern for the impact on scenery and the environment of planned rerouting of the Coast Highway. In this he took a position closer to Straub than to McCall, which may explain why he apparently supported Straub in spite of McCall's outspoken advocacy of a Willamette greenway and his solid overall stand on environmental issues. In any case, Onthank would have been able to lend little more than his name to either campaign. When Vera Springer sought to get Onthank to head a Lane County arm of Willamette River Rediscovered, he demurred, saying that while he would be glad to be a member, "I am the worst bottle neck in the business just now and couldn't deliver what the job needs." In fact, his health was too poor for him to take on the task.[27]

In spite of all Straub and Onthank had done, the public was beginning to view the greenway as McCall's idea. As Straub later observed somewhat ruefully, "once Tom wrapped his big arms around an idea, it was his forever."[28] Indeed, McCall's appeal was such that it came as no surprise when he won election as governor in November. Robert Straub stayed on as state treasurer. Karl Onthank continued working for a Willamette greenway through the Willamette River Basin Survey and other groups to which he belonged.

With a popular, dynamic governor who supported the greenway concept and with increasing public interest in protecting Oregon's quality of life, chances of winning protection for the Willamette seemed good. McCall publicized the greenway idea by arranging for another float trip down the river. Although McCall only went part way with the group, his participation received extensive news coverage, cementing his connection with the greenway in the eyes of the public. But turning the greenway into reality would require more than this. Unlike Straub, who had presented a fairly concrete plan, McCall, typically, had offered nothing specific.[29] He faced the challenge of turning platitudes into reality—and of doing it in a way that would not redound too much to the credit of his erstwhile Democratic rival, for Straub was expected to run again in the next gubernatorial election.

Onthank and his allies did not wait. During November and December, while McCall was busy organizing his administration, they continued to work for a greenway. They set up a steering committee to coordinate their support groups in Portland and Eugene and to block out a tentative program. They also worked to gain endorsement of the greenway concept by the recreational subcommittee of the Willamette River Basin Survey Committee. Toward that end, Paul Beistel wrote a ten-page position paper spelling out the need for a greenway, assessing its recreational potential, and listing the uses to which it could be put. Meanwhile Onthank prepared an analysis of problems faced by parks in the Willamette Valley, noting potential pitfalls for those working for a greenway, and a study of the role of county parks in the Willamette Basin. In the latter, he recommended to the Willamette River Basin Survey Committee "a Willamette River Parkway the whole length of the mainstream of the river" and a coordinating agency "to assist local government in planning, promoting, and financing this project . . . [and] seeking federal aid for planning and arousing public interest." In the meantime, James Mount, an advertising executive who was a key figure in the Portland group, kept McCall apprised of developments.[30]

On 30 November the survey's recreational subcommittee adopted the greenway idea "as the central theme of its recommendations on recreation." Beistel's position paper became Appendix K of its final report. However, at Onthank's suggestion, it called the project not the Willamette River Greenway but the Willamette River Recreational Waterway, a title which Onthank believed would be less frightening to those concerned with the program's cost and its impact on property rights. Onthank was pleased, but realistic. As he told McCall, much more needs to be done "to present a clear (and unalarming!) picture of just what is intended—the idea is still pretty new and vague to most people."[31]

Onthank had reason to be concerned. The greenway would be costly. A comprehensive preliminary survey would be needed, and as Onthank looked around, he saw no state agency with the funding and expertise to carry one out. "The nearest," he noted, "would be the State Parks Department but . . . [it] is presently spread thin handling the statewide recreation plan required of it by BOR [the federal Bureau of Outdoor Recreation, which allocated Land and Water Conservation Act funds to the states] and the local projects that have to clear through it." Onthank thought a special Willamette River Commission would be needed to bring the greenway to fruition.[32]

In an attempt to avoid an impasse, Onthank approached Fred Overly, regional director of BOR, for help. He outlined what was being done and the problems faced. Noting that the BOR had done a study of the Hudson River and how to protect its recreational potential, Onthank asked if the agency could do the same for the Willamette. Nor did he stop there; "there is an opportunity to do a job on the Willamette not possible elsewhere," he wrote, for "there isn't a river in the country of similar magnitude which is still so free of development of the wrong kind and so completely available for the right kind. . . . Indeed, the opportunity to demonstrate what can be done with a river to bring maximum enjoyment to people seems so exceptional that we wonder if it might not qualify for special aid as a demonstration project."[33] In time the BOR was to provide much of the money with which the greenway was initiated, but for the time being events turned attention in other directions.

Onthank was farsighted in many ways, but he underestimated the ability of Oregon's parks department to meet the challenge of the Willamette—or perhaps he simply overlooked Glenn Jackson, who not only wielded great influence but also was a man who liked to tackle difficult projects. In any case, in December Jackson proposed to McCall that he name a task force to formulate a program for action. The governor responded, calling a meeting of the heads of state agencies and political leaders interested in establishing a greenway. Onthank was kept away by a family wedding, but he recommended that Paul Beistel and Charles Duncan, chairman of the informal parkway group in Eugene, attend in his place.[34]

The group agreed that a small task force should be formed to spell out the concept in detail and recommend legislation to implement it. Beistel was selected as a member and placed in charge of carrying out its study.[35] He was a logical choice. He had been a central figure in the long fight for North Bank Park, had worked on the Willamette Basin Review Study and with Onthank and others in the drive for a parkway, and was a competent administrator. McCall arranged with the Lane County Commissioners for Beistel's release from his duties as county parks superintendent in order to handle the study, and Jackson persuaded the State Highway Department to pay for the time and expenses of task force members.[36]

Planning was soon under way. In his inaugural address on 9 January 1967 McCall reasserted his support for a greenway and announced that he hoped to have a plan to submit to the legislature by 1 March. Beistel reported on 12 January that the task force had consulted with recreation and planning officials in all eight counties touched by the river, that the information was being compiled into a plan covering the river from Dexter Dam to the Columbia, and that his goal was to have a preliminary report ready by 3 February, when a host of important people were to meet in Salem with the governor and his task force to preview the plan. Appraisal of the cost of the program would follow.[37]

Thanks to support from many sources, a report was ready for the meeting on 3 February. McCall addressed the group, emphasizing that the report was a working document not yet ready for public perusal and that his goal was to have a long-range plan usable for years to come, a plan that could be implemented bit by bit as conditions allowed. He then signed an executive order creating the Willamette Recreational and Greenway Committee, replacing the extralegal task force. Discussion that followed emphasized that the greenway was to be the product of interagency cooperation and that parts would be under different jurisdictions. Still, it was evident that the state parks department, the sole state agency with the scope and expertise that implementing such a plan required, would play a key role.[38]

The new greenway committee met for the first time on 16 February. Differences surfaced almost at once. The task force was evenly divided between those who wanted bold, aggressive action and those who desired "a more subtle, soft sell approach" out of fear of driving conservatives and the farming community into opposition before the program was off the ground. The immediate issue was Glenn Jackson's offer to have the Highway Department pay the costs of the committee's work, just as it had those of the informal task force that preceded it. One group favored accepting the offer, while the other (which included Robert Straub) wanted to seek a special appropriation from the legislature. Such funding, they contended, would put their committee in a stronger position. Their pragmatic opponents responded that the legislature might well deny funds, endangering the program from the outset.[39]

Eager to have a formal proposal in two weeks, McCall intervened, siding with the pragmatists. The impasse broken, the committee forged ahead. At its meeting on 22 February, it asked the parks department to prepare a brief resume of the committee's forthcoming report for general distribution and to aid Orval Etter in drafting legislation to implement it; it also formally adopted the name Willamette River Greenway.[40]

As McCall had promised, a plan was ready for the legislature and public on 1 March. What they received was a general outline rather than a program of specifics. It was a proposal remarkably similar to what Onthank had been urging for some time and considerably less than what Straub had wanted. "The basic objective," the plan stated, shall be "the preservation and enhancement of the river's natural environment while at the same time developing the widest possible recreational opportunities." Such a goal was achievable, its authors added, through "imaginative yet wise planning and with the cooperation of both citizenry and government. . . . We must be astute enough to see that preservation is far easier than correction, perceptive enough to realize that in the Willamette River we still have more to preserve than to correct." Care was taken to make it clear that the plan would not be immensely costly, remove vast tracts from the tax rolls, or unduly disrupt established land use patterns.

Six elements were to be combined in the greenway. There would be a system of camps located at intervals along the river (some accessible only by the river or trails), a series of recreation areas and boat launching sites to guarantee public access to the river, a network of recreational trails along the waterway, a system of scenic drives along portions of the river, a number of large tracts to serve as major centers of varied recreational activity, and a scenic conservation easement system to protect the beauty of the riverbanks in places where the land itself was not needed for recreational development. Toward these ends, the report called for enabling legislation, but no major appropriations.[41]

McCall did his utmost to insure a positive reception for the plan. He arranged for its unveiling at a major press conference, followed by a large dinner at the Hilton hotel in Portland. Out of the latter, it was planned, a formal support group would emerge to help make the parkway a reality. To add a bipartisan air, Robert Straub was present at the dinner to explain the plan. Throughout, McCall worded his statements carefully so as to disarm fiscal conservatives and those fearful for property rights, and he drew upon knowledge and contacts acquired during a long career as a journalist to win press support.[42]

These efforts did not go unrewarded. The plan was well received both at the dinner and in the press. The *Oregon City Enterprise-Courier* was especially effusive:

> The Willamette Greenway taxes the imagination unless you are one who has lived on and in it from childhood and have dreamed of preserving the beauty and recreational values of this great valley stream for beneficial use of all the people into eternity. It behooves us as individuals and as communities to support this project wholeheartedly and without stint. It is worth any effort its successful completion demands.

The following day James Mount and Carlton Whitehead, assistant to the president of Reed College, called a press conference to announce creation of the Willamette River Greenway Association, the voluntary support group that grew out of the dinner. Straub endorsed the organization, as well he might, for in many ways it was an outgrowth of his own group, Willamette River Rediscovered. He argued that the new body would do much to muster public support, indeed, that not much could be done without such a body. The plan seemed well launched.[43]

Things may have appeared under control in early March, but that did not long remain the case. Circumstances became increasingly difficult as the legislative session proceeded. Lawmakers introduced a host of environmental bills, clouding the issue for greenway advocates. The latter's essential proposal was House Bill 1770, which would establish the greenway and make an initial appropriation of $800,000. Two other proposals were nearly as important: House Bill 1581 provided for the use of the scenic easements called for in the plan; Senate Joint Resolution 33 called for a public referendum on a $10 million bond issue to finance land acquisition for the greenway.[44]

All three proposals generated problems. SJR 33 was especially troublesome, for it reopened the divisions within the greenway committee. Straub had insisted upon it, but several members thought it premature despite estimates that the greenway would eventually cost some $15 million. As before, the more cautious members argued that seeking major funding at such an early stage would stir unnecessary opposition to the entire project and might well kill it. Onthank was among those who thought the referendum unwise. In its place, he suggested earmarking a one-cent-per-gallon increase in the gasoline tax for the greenway—an approach that would raise as much money without alienating so many people. In addition, Onthank feared that the cost of the greenway might jeopardize future acquisitions for parks along the coast and elsewhere.[45]

HB 1581 generated even more opposition than the proposed bond issue. Willamette Valley farmers led a chorus protesting that scenic easements and the accompanying restrictions would infringe upon their property rights and undermine legitimate, long-established agricultural uses.

HB 1770, the basic greenway bill, also came in for attack. The Eugene Chamber of Commerce's Highway Committee feared that highway funds would be diverted to the greenway. Howard Fujii, lobbyist for the powerful Oregon Farm Bureau, worried about the cost of the greenway, the withdrawal of land from agriculture, and other effects that it would have on farmers along the river. The Highway Committee's opposition was based on misunderstanding and thus had little permanent effect, but Fujii's concern was merely the opening salvo of a long-continued drumfire of criticism by farmers and their representatives against the greenway.

Not all attacks were as reasoned as Fujii's. Some rural conservatives professed to see in the bill's proviso for a trail system a danger of long-haired, marijuana-smoking hippies backpacking over their land, stealing as they went. The inclusion of an $800,000 appropriation, spokesmen for such views argued, meant that anyone who refused to sell or grant easements to land for the parkway would simply be forced from it through condemnation or the exercise of eminent domain. Assurances that only about 7,500 additional acres were needed to complete the greenway failed to calm these fears.[46]

Letters flooded the committee—and legislators. The Highway Department arranged for staff and an informational brochure to answer the correspondence; at the same time Jackson, Talbot, and others worked to persuade legislators and critics that the fears were unwarranted and overblown. Fred Overly indicated the BOR's enthusiastic support, which implied that aid would be forthcoming from the federal Land and Water Conservation Fund. Meanwhile, the Willamette River Greenway Association lobbied for the bills and did all it could to generate public support—including helping to organize the well-publicized post-election float trip down the river. But legislators from rural constituencies, or of conservative outlook, were not easily placated. In the end major concessions were necessary to get the needed legislation.[47]

The Ways and Means subcommittee that considered the bill thought that $800,000 was too large an appropriation, but the state parks office made it clear that cities and counties along the greenway already had plans that could use more than that amount. In its final form HB 1770 contained $800,000 for use during the coming biennium in matching the contributions of local governments to acquire land for the greenway. However, a proviso had been added that none of the funds could be used to acquire property through condemnation or the exercise of eminent domain. Authorization for a trail system was stricken from the bill, and to erase the image of an interconnected parkway the name was changed from Willamette River Greenway to Willamette River Parks System.[48]

H.B. 1581 also passed after amendment. Like the land itself, scenic easements could be acquired only if the landowner was willing to sell. There was to be no acquisition of easements through eminent domain. SJR 33 failed to pass at all.[49]

McCall, a political realist, professed to be satisfied. The legislature had been generally tightfisted. To get so much represented real interest on its part—and a significant victory for the governor. The legislation, he told the greenway committee, represented "more than just getting the camel's nose under the tent." Straub was less happy. He implied that McCall had settled for less than he should have.[50]

Karl Onthank's feelings about the legislation are unknown. During the final battles in Salem, he was in Eugene, hospitalized and failing rapidly. Vera Springer, a longtime supporter, wrote to him: "You rest now—because you did the most important thing of all— you had the idea." Soon after, Karl Onthank was dead, survived by the greenway he had done so much to create.[51]

The legislative battles of 1967 were a beginning as much as a culmination. McCall's greenway committee continued to oversee the program, and early in 1968 George Churchill, a longtime employee of the Forest Service, was named program director. Jackson urged all concerned to emphasize getting land into public ownership as quickly as possible "to prove to a doubting legislature that the program should be continued in 1969." Meanwhile, Talbot and his staff at state parks surveyed potential recreational sites along the river and met with local representatives to elicit their ideas and support. With a director in place and $800,000 of state matching funds available, the committee moved rapidly to review applications from local governmental units that wanted help with riverfront park projects.[52]

The initial spurt of activity soon slowed. Most municipal and county governments lacked the money for their 50 percent share of costs. Hope rose when Secretary of the Interior Stewart Udall, impressed with the greenway's potential, earmarked money from his discretionary fund to match contributions from Oregon. This meant that local governments would have to contribute only 25 percent of the total cost, but even this generated few new applications, and it began to look as if part of the federal grant would go unused.[53]

Straub, ever impatient, began to complain about a lack of progress, and the Willamette Greenway Association also began to express dissatisfaction. McCall replied that "Straub's analysis is entirely wrong. I think we have made tremendous headway. It [the greenway] has gone farther than any new program we have ever seen." By early 1969, a spokesman for the governor noted, 103 miles of Willamette River frontage were in public hands, which demonstrated that "we have come along quite splendidly." But these assurances failed to alleviate the growing fear among greenway supporters that the program was about to founder. Something more seemed necessary.[54]

Glenn Jackson had an answer. Early in 1969 he suggested that the parks department seek sites for new state parks along the river, one per county. These, he said, would complement, not replace, the county and local parks previously emphasized and would "take the heat off." The parks staff had soon identified five sites, "very fine pieces of land and large enough to be adequate for all needs." This new tack demonstrated to the 1969 legislature, among others, that there was still life in the Willamette River Parks System. Acquisition was soon under way.[55]

But more was needed. Local activity had come to a virtual standstill for lack of funds, negotiations for the five new state parks progressed at a snail's pace, and the system of scenic easements authorized in 1967 had gone nowhere. Easements had proved almost impossible to obtain, for the machinery for getting them was cumbersome and land owners remained suspicious. One staff member called them "nothing but trouble," but George Churchill continued to "have faith in the easement procedure and hope [that] one day we will make a breakthrough." It was a vain hope. Since the state was barred from using eminent domain to obtain easements, the law authorizing them was for all practical purposes a dead letter.[56]

McCall hoped to get revisions in the law from the 1969 legislature. He failed, but sufficient progress had been made during the greenway's first biennium to block those who would kill it altogether. The legislature appropriated another $800,000 for the next biennium, but directed that $150,000 come from unspent funds remaining from the first appropriation. Straub was outraged. "The legislature," he protested, "has taken a magnificent $10 million plan and reduced it to a $800,000 sop." Still, the legislators had given its advocates two more years to prove the worth of the program.[57]

The Oregon Scenic Waterways Act, passed as an initiative measure in 1970, appeared to some to be a way of strengthening the greenway. This act allowed qualifying streams to be classified as scenic waterways, restricted development along them, and prohibited land sales that threatened to bring undesirable new patterns of growth. If other solutions could not be worked out, the state was obliged to buy threatened tracts along classified streams in order to insure their protection. The law had been designed with wild rivers in mind, but Churchill, the Portland chapter of the Izaak Walton League, and others pushed to have the more natural sections of the Willamette incorporated into the system. More cautious souls demurred, fearing the possible costs and administrative difficulties for the already complex greenway system. McCall himself finally ruled against inclusion.[58]

The Scenic Waterways debate was a brief diversion. Jackson and other greenway supporters brought the focus back to the main issue in 1971 when they proposed what came to be known as the Greenway Corridor Program. They suggested that the state acquire long, narrow stretches of land along the river to complement existing state and local parks and take the place of the stalled easements program. This program would protect tracts neither large nor impressive enough to become state parks, and it would bring better balance to the greenway program by concentrating on rural areas (unlike the parks of county and local governments which had received matching funds, nearly all in or near municipalities). The corridor proposal gave fresh impetus to the entire greenway program.[59]

Pleased with progress in Oregon, Udall approved a $5 million matching grant to aid in implementing the corridor plan. Oregon now had to find $5 million dollars of its own for the strips. Chances of obtaining either an appropriation or approval of a bond issue from the legislature were slim, but again Jackson had a solution. The State Highway Commission, he noted, had standing authority to issue up to $5 million in highway bonds. Since parks were under the commission, it could issue the bonds without legislative approval and use the proceeds to purchase the strips. Because the Corridor Program was complementary to but technically separate from the greenway, such an approach was legal.[60]

Beginning in January 1972, the state dispatched highway right-of-way agents to contact owners of riverfront property about selling strips for the corridor. Few were interested. Jackson was frustrated, for he wanted desperately to get key areas "before they are lost to the public forever." At his urging, the greenway committee decided to threaten condemnation proceedings against owners who refused to sell. The state had this power under regular state park law, he pointed out, and it was this, not the 1967 greenway law, under which the strips were being acquired. The committee hesitated, but finally agreed. George Churchill urged that the decision be kept confidential, but Jackson thought the public could be persuaded of the need for this departure. "Let's expose ourselves," he said, "and try to get support for the program."

Jackson was wrong. No condemnation proceedings were actually instituted, but the threat was alone sufficient to generate a storm of protest. To threaten the use of condemnation after the legislature had specifically deleted that power from the greenway bills seemed to many a blatant abuse of authority.

The State Emergency Board intervened, freezing acquisition funds and chastizing Jackson for attempting to circumvent the legislature's intent. He defended his actions, saying that the program could never be accomplished without condemnation and, in any case, it was more a lever to bring owners to negotiate than a weapon that would be used with any frequency. In the end, the board agreed to restore the budget for acquisition, but only after Jackson promised that no farm land would be condemned before the 1973 legislature had a chance to consider the entire program.[61]

Jackson's ploy also led landowners to form the Willamette River Frontage Owners Association, which flooded legislators and the press with protests. Some who had been negotiating with the state to sell land for the five state river parks drew back. One, Liz Van Leeuwen, became a leading lobbyist for revision of the greenway law when the legislature next met. State Representative Norma Paulus, R-Salem, another spokesman for the association, became a prime mover in the legislature in the drive for a new law. Many seized the occasion to call for abolishing the greenway altogether.

McCall and other greenway advocates had to pull out all stops to head off disaster. HB 2497 was, in the words of George Churchill, "written by and for farmers," but a series of amendments and compromises gradually removed the most damaging parts. Under the final version, cities could use condemnation for parks along the Willamette, but the state could do so only for the five river parks. Farming was declared compatible with the greenway; scenic easements were proclaimed sufficient to protect the natural and scenic qualities along the river in most cases, and the power of eminent domain was extended for use in connection with them; and the Department of Transportation was directed to complete a greenway plan by 4 October 1974. All this hardly constituted a great victory for champions of the greenway—Straub denounced it as the work "of a few farmers"—but under the circumstances far worse could have befallen them.[62]

Responding to the legislature's directives, those in charge of the greenway hired a consulting firm to aid in planning, held a series of public meetings, and formed a Greenway Planners Technical Committee (made up of planners from affected governments) to improve communication and reduce interagency frictions. At the same time, Talbot and his allies continued to reassure fearful landholders and to seek wider public acceptance for saving the river. They were only partially successful. Old fears, exacerbated by Jackson's threat of condemnation, died with excruciating slowness.[63]

Indeed, the greenway was soon swept up in a new round of controversy. At the urging of McCall, the 1973 legislature had created the Land Conservation and Development Commission to bring careful, rational land use to Oregon through the state's regulatory powers. Among other things, it was to aid in planning for the greenway. The campaign for SB 100, the bill creating the Land Conservation and Development Commission, heightened landowners' concerns about infringements on their property rights. As a result, McCall was forced to compromise on this legislation too.

The law was not clear as to what role the LCDC would play in drawing up the greenway plan—its authors seem to have assumed its role would be restricted to review and approval—but, regardless of how it did its work, the fact that fears had been increased by debate over the bill did not augur well for the greenway's future.

Soon after the LCDC went into operation it clashed with the Department of Transportation over its Willamette Greenway Plan. State parks had carried out a recreational survey in 1972–73 that went well beyond the preliminary survey of 1969, but neither parks nor any other division in the DOT had the manpower and expertise to prepare the type of plan envisioned under the greenway law of 1973. A consulting firm from San Francisco—Royston, Hanamoto, Beck, & Abey—was selected for the task. But when the DOT presented the firm's plan to LCDC in the fall of 1974, the latter rejected it, charging that public participation in planning had been inadequate. Churchill protested that a "very serious and honest effort has been made . . . to involve the local government officials. . . . Our consultants have gone far beyond contractual requirements." But LCDC was adamant, insisting on additional citizen participation before it would consider approval.[64]

Just what was behind LCDC's action is unclear. Churchill admitted there had been breakdowns in communication, but DOT's record during the planning process had on the whole been good. LCDC may simply have been reflecting an ideological commitment to participatory democracy on the part of L. B. Day, named by McCall to head the agency, and by key members of his staff. Day had been intimately involved in writing the version of SB 100 that had passed the legislature. It called for "widespread citizen involvement and input in all phases of the [planning] process." Day had hailed the act as instituting "planning that comes from the bottom up, not from the top down." But Day may simply have been seeking to demonstrate that LCDC was to be an active agency, that even the powerful DOT was not beyond its purview.[65]

In any case, to meet the statutory requirement that a plan be published by 4 October, LCDC agreed to let the version it had rejected be printed as a "preliminary" plan. Moreover, LCDC personnel unofficially informed DOT that, following additional public hearings and perhaps some relatively minor alterations, the plan would be approved. The final plan was to be ready by 31 January 1975. But in November 1974 Robert Straub was elected governor, replacing McCall, who had reached the constitutional two-term limit in the office. Quickly the situation changed.

For years Straub had been pushing for a stronger greenway program. The DOT's plan, like the rest of what had been done during the McCall years, seemed too weak to him. Straub wanted greater state and less local authority, the power of condemnation, less emphasis on the use of scenic easements (which, he noted, "cost nearly as much as ownership and can't be used by hikers"), and some method to prevent farmers from intensifying their land use along the river without first obtaining permission. He directed Jackson to have the plan amended before resubmitting it to LCDC. McCall, knowing the risks of delay, urged the governor-elect to let the existing plan go through with the understanding that it would be amended later. For his part, Talbot sought to persuade Straub that the plan was the best that could be obtained, that farmers and others suspicious of the greenway had only reluctantly accepted the consultants' plan and would not yield further. But Straub was adamant. Convinced of widespread public support, he intended to wring a strengthened greenway law from the legislature; a stronger plan would be a natural adjunct of such a law. Talbot, Churchill, and the others responsible for producing a plan would simply have to go back to public hearings to win approval for the changes that Straub wanted.[66]

What followed was even worse than McCall and Talbot had feared. Straub's revisions eliminated references to local participation in planning, to the emphasis on scenic easements, and to LCDC's role in planning. Central control was strengthened by enlarging the role of the Department of Transportation at the expense of local governments and LCDC. At public hearings on the new version, farmers and others assailed the DOT bitterly for the changes. They charged that the new version was contrary to earlier understandings and ignored previous protests. LCDC joined in the assault. L. B. Day himself attended some of the hearings and heaped scorn on the revisions and the way they had been handled. Day may simply have been angered by the distrust of the public and of his agency that he thought he detected in the changes, but some suspected he opposed the greenway because as a Teamster's union official he feared it would harm Willamette Valley farmers and the trucking businesses they supported. In time Straub became convinced that Day was indeed engaged in an effort to undermine the greenway. He removed him as head of LCDC, but the damage had already been done.[67]

So heated were the protests that in the end the DOT plan was scrapped, Straub's effort to get a stronger greenway bill through the legislature failed, and LCDC was left to draw up a greenway plan of its own to replace it. Additional public hearings and revision followed. What emerged was described by Robert K. Potter (who replaced Churchill in charge of the greenway program after the latter's retirement in February 1975) as "more than anything else a planning corridor in which local government should consider natural, scenic, recreational and historical values along the river in making future land use decisions." Interspersed along this corridor were state and local parks and the state's riverfront strips. This was a far cry from what Karl Onthank had originally envisioned and equally distant from what Robert Straub had hoped for when in 1974 he had insisted on revising the DOT's plan. Straub had lost ground because of what McCall called his "bull-in-the-china-shop approach." Talbot's assessment was similar. Straub's "heart was always in the right place," he said, "but when it came to getting things done, he was a Mr. Bumble."[68]

During the interminable battles over planning, the greenway remained stalled; not until 1979 was Talbot able to announce that the DOT was at last turning its main attention from planning to making the greenway an on-the-ground reality. But all this made little difference. Oregon's economy fell on extraordinarily hard times beginning in the mid-seventies, when skyrocketing interest rates drove home buyers from the market and led to a collapse in demand for lumber. By the time Straub took over as governor, financial exigencies ruled out the massive state expenditures on the greenway that he had long advocated. Federal funds too largely dried up. For the time being, completion of the Willamette Greenway was impossible.

In time many Oregonians came to blame the environmental legislation of the 1960s for the state's economic woes, although the real source of difficulties lay outside the state. One result of the more conservative new mood was that in 1980 the parks department was stripped of its privileged position of being able to use DOT funds, including those from gasoline taxes, rather than having to seek appropriations from the legislature. Parks and the state police, it was charged, frittered away money that should be used for roads. With education, public services, and much else being cut back, with taxes rising, and with unemployment rates among the highest of any state, chances of getting appropriations to complete the greenway were nonexistent.[69]

But the greenway remained, incomplete though it was, and the concept was still alive, if not universally popular. Tom McCall had told his greenway task force that he wanted a plan that could last for fifty years, a plan that could be completed over time. That he got such a plan was even more important than he realized at the time. As the President's Council on Environmental Quality observed in 1973:

> The original concept of the Greenway was visionary—an entire river bordered by a natural parkway. That concept has been altered to fit more modest goals. In the longer view, however, the initial vision may not be misplaced. Within 50 years, a strip city is projected to run the length of the valley. A parkway of the original scale would be an invaluable asset at that time.

A decade later Dave Talbot was still expressing such views, calling the greenway one of the grandest dreams in the history of state parks.[70] In view of Oregon's long commitment to its parks, it seems likely that eventually the greenway will move toward completion once more— and that there will be dedicated leaders around to aid it in doing so.

But regardless of what becomes of the greenway in the long run, the battles to build it during the 1960s and '70s marked a major step in the history of state parks in the Pacific Northwest. Early parks advocates had sought to keep their efforts out of the public and legislative limelight. Later Robert Smylie and Albert Rosellini had tried to make political capital of the need for parks, but with little success. By the late 1960s the winds of environmentalism were strong, and both Tom McCall and Robert Straub were markedly successful in using environmental concerns—including the green-way—to win public support.

Moreover, the planning, interagency coordination, and combi-nation of federal, state, and local funding that were hallmarks of the greenway effort represented the full flowering of tendencies that, though they traced back to some of the central ideas of the Progres-sive Era, had first impinged on parks management in a major way during the New Deal. This development promised major changes in the parks movement. Hitherto individual activists—in and out of government—had dominated. This would change in the new order. People with Karl Onthank's combination of administrative and bu-reaucratic experience, persuasive power, and environmental commit-ment are few indeed. Even he would have had little impact, one suspects, if his ideas had not been picked up by McCall and Straub, who recognized not only their merit, but also their political value. Group action seems destined to dominate from this point forward. The Willamette Greenway thus stands both as the harbinger of things to come and as the last great campaign of a series of individual park builders who had carved out a legacy of parks for future citizens of Oregon, Washington, and Idaho.

Chapter 10

Parks and Their Builders
in Perspective

From the days of Robert Moran and Weldon Heyburn to Karl Onthank and Robert Smylie, Northwesterners fought to save the scenery of their region. While state parks were never the sole vehicle used for this purpose, they were one of those most frequently drawn upon. The battles varied in intensity from state to state, developments in each being shaped by local circumstances. But for all their variation, a basic pattern was present. In the beginning the state parks movement was a campaign of and by private citizens. By the 1970s—perhaps even by the 1950s—it no longer was.

The state parks movement grew out of and was a part of the Progressive crusade—albeit a generally overlooked one. The nature of the leadership, its methods and goals, and its basic conceptions of society all combined to make it so.

Like the people who gathered in Des Moines in 1921 to found the National Conference on State Parks, early champions of state parks in Oregon, Washington, and Idaho were almost all educated professionals from towns and cities. Newspaper editors, attorneys, and engineers were prominent among them. Most were in comfortable economic circumstances, and some few were wealthy by anyone's standards. Activists turned repeatedly for support to local chambers of commerce and civic groups, to garden, automobile and women's clubs, and to others among the middle-class, professional organizations that proliferated during the early decades of the twentieth century. A person of modest means could work with and through

such organizations without the wealth that underwrote the philan-
thropies of affluent allies, thus helping to make wealth less important
than education and persuasiveness in the region's parks movement.

Political figures who supported parks tended to come from
backgrounds similar to those of the leading activists or, at least, to
represent constituencies where such leaders were numerous or
influential. All in all, the Northwest's early champions of state parks
had backgrounds remarkably similar to those of progressive leaders
with other interests.[1]

But more than a similarity of leadership is needed to justify
classifying the state parks movement as a progressive crusade. After
all, conservative leadership had a similar profile to that of progressives; both groups depended on middle-class professionals for the
bulk of their leaders. Perhaps in the American political system, no
other leadership was ever a real possibility.

An even more important justification for labeling the parks
movement a progressive crusade was the fact that its advocates saw
themselves as working in behalf of "the people," preserving scenery
for both present and future generations. They believed that through
their actions they would raise the quality of life for all. Moreover, if
their actions would not enlarge the middle class, at least they would
add to the number of those who shared their own middle-class
patterns of utilizing and appreciating nature. On other levels, progressives championed participatory democracy; through parks they
would increase participation in the enjoyment of the outdoors. A later
generation of conservationists might worry about the impact of
throngs of visitors on natural settings, but in the early twentieth
century the emphasis was quite the opposite; a host of new publications sought to convince Americans of the value not just of preserving
but also of visiting and savoring unsullied nature, and much time was
spent working for the highways, lodges, and other means of access
that would make such visits possible. The back-to-nature movement,
pervasive in middle-class America at the time, added force to their
efforts.[2]

As middle-class businessmen, a large number of the Northwest's
early champions of parks also saw them as a means of furthering the
economic fortunes of the region by attracting increased numbers of
tourists. This should neither come as a surprise nor be seen as
somehow in conflict with other espoused goals. Progressives were

never opposed to business and economic growth; they were simply opposed to exploitive and irresponsible economic activities that harmed long-range public interests. Parks seemed to encourage the sort of steady, conflict-free economic development that they idealized. Certainly, there was little in their words or deeds to suggest that they were striving to eliminate some sort of psychic guilt for industrial-urban despoliation. As Western boosters, they tended perhaps even more than most progressives to see urban development and economic growth as "progress."

Although the state parks movement had middle-class leadership and was shot through with middle-class values, opposition did not come primarily from the working class or its champions. Unlike city parks, which were accessible to people of all classes and thus worth battling over, state parks were long beyond the reach—and outside the interests—of most laborers.[3] The state parks movement grew with and was tied to the automobile revolution, and automobile ownership was long the almost-exclusive prerogative of people of middle- and upper-class standing. Instead of from laborers, opposition to the efforts of state parks activists came largely from inertia and stand-pat politicians—fiscal conservatives who opposed the expenditures involved.

Leaders in the parks movement advocated typical progressive means to the ends they sought. They called for active use of government to preserve and manage selected tracts, protecting them from those who would destroy their scenic values for economic gain. Compared with the work of a later generation of parks planners, their programs hardly seem to reflect the emphasis on planning, efficiency, and technocracy that were so much in evidence in other progressive campaigns, including many within the larger field of conservation.[4] Still, compared with the haphazard erection of stands, signs, tourist camps, and the like that the advent of the automobile age was bringing to more and more scenic sites, their approach to development was planned and careful indeed.

If the early parks movement in the Northwest was imbued with the spirit of progressivism—as it was—then it should come as no surprise that it prospered best in Oregon, for progressivism blossomed more fully and had a more lasting impact in Oregon than in Washington or Idaho. In the name of participatory democracy, Oregon's progressives virtually destroyed party machinery in the state, creating conditions in which in 1910 Democrat Oswald West was elected governor by a comfortable margin even though Republicans had an overwhelming edge in registered voters. The situation changed little over the years. Politicians courted success by building personal networks of supporters while virtually ignoring the party organization. The position of state party chairman was so weak that at times no one with ability would take it; and Wayne Morse, elected to the United States Senate as a Republican, had little difficulty winning reelection as a Democrat only shortly after changing his registration. The "Oregon story" that Tom McCall did so much to champion in the 1960s and 1970s was little more than progressivism in modern dress, as McCall himself recognized.[5] Considering the strength of the progressive tradition in the state, it should come as no surprise that, from the time of Ben Olcott to that of Karl Onthank, Oregon's champions of parks worked to form citizens' action groups as a primary means to the ends they sought.

Idaho was another matter. It was poorer, its citizenry less educated than Oregon's. With its smaller urban centers, it had fewer middle-class professionals, the backbone of the progressive movement. Moreover, its conservative political traditions undermined the chances of proposals requiring positive action by the state's government. Populism and labor radicalism prospered in this environment, largely in rejection of the status quo, but progressivism did not. The editor of the *Coeur d'Alene Evening Press* revealed the common outlook when, referring to Oregon on 9 January 1911, he ran the headline "Freak State to Have More Laws"; Oregon's legislature, the accompanying article noted, was preparing to meet, but it seemed unlikely that it would be as radical as the voters themselves had been through the use of the initiative in the state's general elections the preceding November. When reform movements did begin to gain force in Idaho late in the Progressive Era, the emotional issue of Mormonism repeatedly divided its supporters and turned attention in other directions.[6]

To be sure, there was some parks activity in Idaho during the Progressive Era. Thomas Davis's donation of land along the Boise River for use as a park, the Boise *Idaho Daily Statesman*'s support of the City Beautiful movement, and the call by the state's newspaper editors for a park at Payette Lake all came from the type of people who dominated progressivism and provided most of its parks promoters. Even Weldon Heyburn, an attorney by profession, came from such a background, although he was far from progressive and championed a park at Lake Chatcolet more as a regional booster than anything else. Yet even if one includes Heyburn State Park, the list of parks efforts in Idaho during the first decades of the twentieth century is short indeed when compared to the campaigns in Oregon and Washington during the same period. On the whole, the attitude of Idahoans toward conservation and parks was more akin to that of their neighbors in the Mountain states.[7] Not until the days of Robert Smylie did state parks begin to prosper in Idaho. Even then, progress came in the face of general indifference among the state's citizens. Indeed, Smylie worked not just to create a professional parks system in the state, but in a larger sense to reorient the state's dominant political traditions. Idaho's political orientation in subsequent years—influenced by the increasing political influence of the conservative Mormon community—would suggest that Smylie's victories in the latter realm, if not the former, may have been largely transitory.

Washington occupied an intermediate position. The activities of Robert Moran, Asahel Curtis, Herbert Evison, and their allies reflected the progressive outlook at least as well as the work of parks advocates in Oregon, but as time passed the effectiveness of these men and their successors dwindled sharply.

Class and regional divisions seem to have been more deeply etched in Washington than in Oregon, lending a level of rancor to the political scene and a strength to political parties that were seldom seen south of the Columbia after the turn of the century. Perhaps for this reason progressivism never took as firm a hold there. Obscured to a degree during the progressive period, these divisions soon reasserted themselves. Citizen activists were increasingly frustrated after Roland Hartley became governor, and state parks activity soon languished. When it was revived during the administration of Albert Rosellini, it came not primarily as a citizen's movement but as a product of Rosellini's political ambitions. Insofar as there was a legacy of progressivism at work, it was embodied in the campaigns to expand the state's civil service system and free professionals in the parks department from political control, rather than in a campaign for state parks per se—and even these campaigns were more a reaction to the excesses of the Rosellini administration than a manifestation of a lingering progressive spirit.[8]

The old state parks movement in Washington, the movement that *had* been tied to progressivism, died in the 1930s. The futile battle to extend Mather Memorial Parkway was its last major effort. W. A. Weigle kept state parks alive in Washington during the 1930s and even managed to expand the system, but he was an administrator shaped by his earlier experiences in the Forest Service—an agency which, in spite of protestations to the contrary, tended to keep the public at arm's length—not a Sam Boardman who used his position to encourage citizen participation in park building.

The progressive parks movement died elsewhere in the Northwest too. Vestiges persisted in Oregon after Sam Boardman's retirement, but as an important force, the movement came to an end when Chester Armstrong took over as superintendent. Never strong in Idaho, any hint of a state park movement had disappeared by the end of the 1930s.

The general decay of progressivism and the corrosive effects of the Great Depression contributed to the demise of the old parks movement, but other things were at work too. Perhaps most important was the growing ascendancy of technicians, planners, and administrators, not just in the realm of state parks but in all areas of government. The sort of personal campaigns that Robert Moran had waged outside and Samuel Boardman inside of government became less and less common—and less and less successful when they were attempted.

Rare private citizens such as Karl Onthank knew how to work within the ever-more-complex bureaucratic maze of committees, commissions, and departments for ends that oldtime parks advocates would surely have applauded, but most who shared Onthank's views lacked his skills. Parks became the responsibility of administrators like Charles Odegaard and David Talbot, men who, often in spite of personal views and inclinations, were relatively insulated from the public. They were so dependent upon planners, public relations experts, and technicians that Sam Boardman, for one, would have viewed their situation with horror.

Reflecting the change, in 1965 the National Conference on State Parks merged with the American Institute of Park Executives to form the National Recreation and Park Association. Weakened by fiscal problems during the Great Depression and further undermined by suspension of its annual meetings for the duration of World War II, the organization had gradually lost much of the citizen support that had been an important source of strength during its early years. The merger completed the transition. Far from the combination of activists in and out of government that the NCSP had been, the new organization was dominated by parks professionals. Another new organization, the National Association of Parks Directors, also handled much once done by the NCSP and was even more thoroughly professional in its orientation.[9]

Activists outside of government could only hope for success if they adopted the weapons of the age. They had to develop their own network of planners, technicians, and other specialists to gain through interminable hearings and court actions what an earlier generation had gained through personal appeals and moralistic argument. But they seldom used their new weapons in behalf of state parks. They continued to be concerned with the preservation of scenic beauty, but they had turned their attention from the lowlands, where most state parks were located, to alpine areas, which were largely administered by federal authorities. Battles over the Wilderness bill, clearcutting and other policies of the Forest Service, and the construction of dams on wild rivers directed their attention to the nation's capital and necessitated new protest and lobbying techniques. Even Ben Olcott, Robert Sawyer, and Herbert Evison—each of whom had devoted much effort to getting legislation favorable to their causes passed—would probably have felt out of place in this new order.

Technological changes played a major part in ushering in the new emphases. High-speed automobiles and improved techniques of highway construction led to the relocation of many of the early highways—leaving behind many of the timbered strips that earlier campaigners had struggled to save. Freeways whisked motorists past the tiny roadside parks of early days and made them largely obsolete. Only sizable parks with major recreational facilities, parks that could serve as destinations rather than waystops, seemed sufficiently alluring to be of much interest or use. At the same time, the growth in the number of motor homes and recreational power boats called for shifts in the types and location of facilities. The sort of restorative communion with nature that Sam Boardman had sought to insure through his parks became less and less possible in those of his successors. The person seeking spiritual rejuvenation was now more apt to journey to the high mountains than to state parks; as such people turned their attention to alpine areas, parks were left increasingly to the planners and technicians on the one hand and the recreation-seeking masses on the other.

The shift had class overtones. Thanks in large part to the now-ubiquitous automobile, state parks had come to play the sort of role in mass recreation that champions of the working class had envisioned for city parks early in the twentieth century. Driven from dominance in the making of state parks policy, just as they had earlier been driven from control of city parks, middle-class and elite spokesmen found in the high country a last bastion where genteel communion with nature and spiritual uplift could be found. However often denied, charges that the wilderness movement was a campaign by an elite seeking to preserve tracts for its own enjoyment had much truth to them. Wilderness advocates cast their arguments in democratic, as well as time-honored romantic terms, but the bulk of them were clearly neither of the masses nor for the values that the masses held. In time, the backpacking boom and related developments would introduce such hordes into all but the farthest reaches of the mountains that even these were threatened with inundation by a flood of ordinary citizens with ordinary values, but that is another story—one impinging little on state parks.[10]

Thanks in part to these national trends in which they have shared, the approaches of Oregon, Washington, and Idaho to parks—so distinct from one another in the early days—gradually converged. By the 1970s their problems and methods were so similar as to be almost indistinguishable. Idaho's difficulties as it has developed Harriman State Park have been paralleled by Oregon's with its Willamette River Greenway and Washington's with its system of water-oriented parks centered on Puget Sound. In all three, the central problems have been those of planning, budget, and personnel. All three have been plagued by constricting financial resources. In short, all three reflect the now-dominant national pattern.

Politics had once been in evidence primarily in Washington. Now it intruded in parks in all three states. The opposition to Robert Smylie's plans for a park department in Idaho sprang in large part from political motives. Even Oregon, which long stood out for its success in keeping politics out of parks, was no longer immune from such influence. The Willamette Greenway was enmeshed in politics from the beginning; the use of gas-tax revenues for parks came under political attack soon thereafter. Though less important in the long run, a revealing harbinger of things to come occurred in 1962 when Governor Mark Hatfield removed Mark Astrup from his position as parks superintendent for personal and political reasons.[11] Parks had become a major operation of state governments throughout the country. As such, there was no reason for them to remain outside the political process, and by the 1960s they no longer were in any of the Pacific Northwestern states.

By the 1980s if any of the three states could be called the most typical, ironically it would be Idaho. Oregon's Willamette River Greenway is a grandiose project whose very size has tended to distort the overall picture by diverting attention and resources from the rest of the state's park system.[12] Its scope and its intimate connections with the larger questions of land-use planning and the protection of overall environmental quality make the project especially controversial. Puget Sound, the focal point of much of Washington's recent parks activity, is atypical in the variety and scope of recreational opportunities it offers in the heart of the most densely populated part of the state. Each has presented unique challenges. But Idaho's experiences with Harriman State Park could have been repeated in almost any state. A fine new park became available; resourceful state authorities moved to take advantage of the opportunity, drawing upon experts for help and planning, holding public hearings, and lobbying for legislation and funds. Continuing demand for money for parks in other, frequently more heavily populated parts of the state, hampered their efforts. So did turnover in personnel and associated internal frictions and struggles for power. And all this took place in the midst of growing political conservatism and fiscal stringency.[13]

The opening of Harriman State Park to the public in July 1982 was the fruition of efforts with which park executives all across the country could identify. The planning had been unusually slow and deliberate, because the area involved was pristine and extremely fragile ecologically, but in nearly every other way Harriman Park could serve as the archetype of major park additions across the land. At the same time, the differences between the efforts that brought Harriman into being and those behind the creation of Moran and other early parks demonstrate clearly how far society has come from the old progressive parks movement.

Yet just because state parks in the Pacific Northwest more closely parallel national trends today than they once did, one should not assume that the region used to be a leader in the parks movement, but is no longer. In fact, it has never been much of a pioneer in parks building. In the early years, the emphasis on the preservation of roadside timber was stronger in the Northwest than perhaps anywhere else in the country, and Robert Sawyer and Charles McNary played a leading role when they pushed for legislation that would allow federal-private exchanges to save roadside stands. Sam Boardman's approach to saving the Oregon Coast was also distinct from that used elsewhere at the time. But on the whole Northwesterners followed rather than led. They were not significant contributors to the creation of the National Conference on State Parks and drew upon outsiders such as Stephen Mather and Madison Grant more than they contributed to them. Leaders in such states as New York and Indiana were long more important in the nationwide movement for state parks. Herbert Evison was the only representative from the region at the NCSP meeting in Des Moines in 1921; David Whitcomb was the sole representative at the following year's meetings in New York.[14] Even after Tom McCall had risen to national prominence as a conservation figure, the Northwest could still hardly be considered a pioneer in the field of parks. The Willamette River Greenway was inspired by forerunners in Connecticut, New York, California, and the District of Columbia. The impressive, water-oriented system of parks that Charles Odegaard and others developed around Puget Sound was equally derivative. And Idaho's Harriman State Park was a gift of New Yorkers who were following eastern—and family— precedents from over fifty years before.

But if Northwesterners were not pioneers, they were nonetheless dedicated and perservering, representative of the best of the mainstream of the state parks movement. It is this as much as anything that makes their activities of more than passing, regional interest. Through them one can gain a better understanding of the dynamics of the parks and conservation movements, of the methods used and pitfalls confronted, not just in the Pacific Northwest but wherever conservation activity was carried out at the state and local levels.

Some years ago Donald Swain demonstrated that conservation made significant progress at the federal level between the presidencies of Theodore and Franklin Roosevelt in spite of the absence of dynamic presidential support. These gains, he argued, came in large part because of dedicated professionals, many of whom had been attracted into federal service by Gifford Pinchot and Stephen Mather and who gradually rose through the civil service ranks. Working at the bureau chief level and below, these men made solid if often overlooked contributions.[15]

But as this study shows, far more than just federal activity was under way during the period. Across the country, especially in that tier of states extending from New England to South Dakota and on the Pacific Coast, conservationists were at work, in and out of government, seeking to save scenic and other resources. These activists provided grassroots support that helped to make possible the gains won at the federal level at the time and that later provided a springboard for New Deal conservation programs when there was once again a president in the White House who shared their concerns.

In the same way, some two decades later, John F. Kennedy and Lyndon Johnson were to find the prospects for their conservation programs strengthened by the presence at the state and local levels of people like Smylie, McCall, Onthank, and Rosellini as well as a growing number of conservation organizations. In a democratic, federal system, a student of government and policy-making ignores developments at the grassroots at his own peril.

Conservation activity, including campaigns for state parks, may have varied from place to place in intensity and longevity, but it was clearly widespread during and even after the 1920s. Taken altogether it provides a striking demonstration that the progressive impulse did not come to an abrupt end with World War I or with the advent of Warren G. Harding in the White House. The Women's Suffrage and Prohibition amendments hardly seem isolated last gasps of progressivism when considered in the light of advances in conservation during the postwar period.[16]

The parks movement in the Northwest also demonstrates that, however much a local movement might reflect national trends and concerns, it still is shaped by the purely local. Even in Oregon, Washington, and Idaho—lumped though they usually are as a single region—activity took different routes and showed differing levels of intensity and continuity because of variations in tradition and outlook in the three states. Famed Dutch scholar Johan Huizinga once observed that the historian should be the guardian of the particular.[17] It is an observation that seems especially apropos in considering conservation activity in the Pacific Northwest.

In the end, the story of state parks in the Pacific Northwest is not just the story of men working in the markedly different sociopolitical contexts of three states but of men who themselves were different—for all that they shared. Harvard educated and cautious, Robert Sawyer was as different from tobacco-chewing, impulsive, romantic Sam Boardman as any two contemporary professionals in the same society are ever apt to be. And it was the impact of these two men, conditioned as it was by their values and personalities, that shaped Oregon's parks as much as it was local values and traditions of government. The same thing could be said of Smylie, Curtis, Rosellini, and Odegaard: though they were limited in what they could accomplish by the context within which they operated, their contributions in the final analysis were different as much because they themselves differed as because of anything else. *They*, not their states or even their class, were the park builders.

Notes

ABBREVIATIONS USED IN THE NOTES

ACP	Asahel Curtis Papers
ARP	Albert D. Rosellini Papers
BOP	Ben Olcott Papers
EMP	Edmond Meany Papers
HCM	Oregon State Highway Commission minute books
HDP	Oregon State Highway Department general files
IORC	Inter-Agency Outdoor Recreation Commission
JFH	*Journal of Forest History*
KOP	Karl Onthank Papers
LCPRC	Lane County Parks and Recreation Commission
MRNPP	Mount Rainier National Park Papers
NCSP	National Conference on State Parks
NCSPP	National Conference on State Parks Papers
NPSSPP	National Park Service Records, State Parks Papers
OGC	old Greenway committee files
OHQ	*Oregon Historical Quarterly*
ORS	New Outdoor Recreation Study file
PCS	Papers of Commissioner Sawyer (Oregon State Highway Commission)
PNQ	*Pacific Northwest Quarterly*
PRC	Parks and Recreation Commission files (Washington State)
PRCP	Parks and Recreation Commission Papers (Washington State)
PRDP	Oregon Parks and Recreation Commission, main office files
RMP	Robert Moran Papers
RNPAB	Rainier National Park Advisory Board
RSP	Robert Sawyer Papers
WRBS	Willamette River Basin Survey
WRG	Willamette River Greenway files
WRGP	Willamette River Greenway Papers

1.   THE NORTHWEST AND THE NATION: *A Parks Movement in the Making*

1. Robert Shankland, *Steve Mather of the National Parks* (New York: Alfred A. Knopf, 1951), pp. 185–88; Freeman Tilden, *The State Parks: Their Meaning in American Life* (New York: Alfred A. Knopf, 1962), pp. 3–5; Beatrice Ward Nelson, "A Brief History of State Recreation Areas," in Herbert Evison, ed., *A State Park Anthology* (Washington, D.C.: National Conference on State Parks, 1930), pp. 31–32; W. O. Tilley, "Brief Report on Park Conference at Des Moines, January 10–12, 1921," typescript, Society of American Foresters Papers (Forest History Society, Durham, N.C.), box 72, state parks. The conference can be followed in some detail in the *Des Moines Register*, 9–13 Jan. 1921. Its official proceedings were never published, although those of the three subsequent meetings were.

2. *Des Moines Register*, 10 Jan. 1921; Shankland, *Steve Mather*, pp. 184–200; John Ise, *Our National Park Policy* (Baltimore: Johns Hopkins University Press, 1961), pp. 185–95, 296–300; Donald C. Swain, *Federal Conservation Policy, 1921–1933* (Berkeley: University of California Press, 1963), pp. 123–43; Conrad Wirth, *Parks, Politics, and the People* (Norman: University of Oklahoma Press, 1980), p. 39; Tilley, "Brief Report"; memo for Mather, 23 May 1924, and Arno Cammerer to W. T. Grant, 3 Oct. 1929, National Conference on State Parks Papers, Records of the National Park Service, Record Group 79, Central Classified Files, 0–33 (National Archives, Washington, D.C. [hereafter NCSPP]): Herbert Evison to Horace Albright, 31 Oct. 1929, ibid. See, also: Mather's comments in National Conference on State Parks [hereafter NCSP], *Proceedings of the Fourth National Conference on State Parks* (Washington, D.C.: NCSP, c. 1925), pp. 61–62.

3. Tilden, *State Parks*, pp. 101–104; J.P Kinney, *The Development of Forest Law in America* (New York: John Wiley & Sons, 1917), p. 61; Nelson, "Brief History," p. 28; David C. Smith, *A History of Lumbering in Maine, 1861–1960* (Orono: University of Maine Press, 1972), pp. 313–314; John W. Hakola, *Legacy of a Lifetime: The Story of Baxter State Park* (Woolrich, Maine: TBW Books for Baxter State Park Authority, 1981). Even Mt. Greylock was not *called* a state park; the first site in Massachusetts actually so designated was Tri-State Park, acquisition for which began in 1924. On Boston Commons and other manifestations of the early concern for open space, see: Thomas R. Cox, Robert S. Maxwell, Phillip Drennon Thomas, and Joseph J. Malone, *This Well-Wooded Land: Americans and Their Forests from Colonial Times to the Present* (Lincoln: University of Nebraska Press, 1985), pp. 42–43.

4. Tilden, *State Parks*, pp. 47–52; Gurth Whipple, *A History of Half a Century of the Management of the Natural Resources of the Empire State, 1885–1935* (Albany, N.Y.: New York Conservation Department and New York State College of Forestry, 1935), pp. 17–23, 67–76, 157–72; Alfred Runte, "Beyond the Spectacular: The Niagara Falls Preservation Campaign," *New-York Historical Society Quarterly* 57 (1973): 30–50: Frank Graham, Jr., *The Adirondack Park:*

A Political History (New York: Alfred A. Knopf, 1978), pp. 65–132. Some insist that the Adirondack tract is a "preserve," not a "park," but the latter term is generic, having such broad and varied application that it can certainly be used here. For a discussion of the issue, see: Thomas R. Cox, "From Hot Springs to Gateway: The Evolving Concept of Public Parks, 1832–1976," *Environmental Review* 5 (1981): esp. 14–17. California's Anza-Borrego Desert State Park (490,336 acres) has been called the largest state park, but this is done by not considering Adirondack as a park. See Diana Elaine Lindsay, *Our Historic Desert: The Story of Anza-Borrego Desert, the Largest State Park in the United States of America*, ed. Richard Pourade (San Diego, Calif.: Copley Books, 1974).

5. Keith R. Widder, *Mackinac National Park, 1875–1895* ([Lansing, Mich.]: Mackinac Island State Park Commission, 1975); Hans Huth, *Nature and the American: Three Centuries of Changing Attitudes* (Berkeley: University of California Press, 1957), pp. 143–52; C. Raymond Clar, *California Government and Forestry from Spanish Days until the Creation of the Department of Natural Resources in 1927* (Sacramento: California State Division of Forestry, 1959), pp. 69–70; William E. Colby, "Yosemite and the Sierra Club," *Sierra Club Bulletin* 23 (April 1938); 11–19; Harlean James, *Land Planning in the United States for City, State and Nation* (New York: Macmillan Co., 1926), pp. 362–63; James Willard Hurst, *Law and Economic Growth: The Legal History of the Lumber Industry in Wisconsin, 1836–1915* (Cambridge, Mass.: Belknap Press of Harvard University Press, 1964), pp. 101–2.

6. "State Parks Win Public Favor," *Conservation* 15 (1909): 360–69; James, *Land Planning*, pp. 362–63; Nelson, "Brief History," pp. 30–31: Raymond J. O'Brien, *American Sublime: Landscape and Scenery of the Lower Hudson Valley* (New York: Columbia University Press, 1981), pp. 237–59. See, also: John Nolen, ed., *City Planning*, 2nd ed. (New York: D. Appleton & Co., 1929), pp. 159–80; Charles E. Doell and Gerald B. Fitzgerald, *A Brief History of Parks and Recreation Areas in the United States* (Chicago: Athletic Institute, 1954), esp. pp. 36–39, 82–83.

7. Idaho's first, Heyburn State Park, was obtained by purchase from the federal government; Washington's Larrabee and Oregon's Helmick parks came via donations. Heyburn park is discussed at length in Chapter Two.

8. John Minto, "Autobiography," chapter XIII, typescript account, John Minto Papers (Oregon Historical Society, Portland), box 3; *Mazama: A Record of Mountaineering*, 1 (1897): 279–80; L. Byrd Mock, "The Lucerne of America," *Overland Monthly* 57 (1911): 1–10; Thomas R. Cox, "Weldon Heyburn, Lake Chatcolet, and the Evolving Concept of Public Parks," *Idaho Yesterdays* 24 (Summer 1980): 3–4.

9. *Portland Oregonian*, 19 Aug. 1854, 12 June 1894; Tolmie to Minto, 1 Oct. 1885, Minto Papers, box 2; Fred H. McNeil, *Wy'east, 'The Mountain': A Chronicle of Mount Hood* (Portland: Metropolitan Press, 1937), pp. 35–51, 58, 61, 94–99 ; Aubrey L. Haines, *Mountain Fever: Historic Conquests of Rainier* (Portland: Oregon Historical Society, 1962), pp. 3–57; Edmond S. Meany, ed., *Mount Rainier: A Record of Exploration* (New York: Macmillan, 1916), pp.

6–12, 94–131; William Gladstone Steel, *The Mountains of Oregon* (Portland: D. Steel, 1890), pp. 67–81; *Mazama* 1 (1896): 12–20; *Oregon Out of Doors* 1 (1920): 27–30; Lawrence Rakestraw, "Before McNary: The Northwest Conservationist, 1889–1913," *Pacific Northwest Quarterly* [hereafter *PNQ*] 51 (1960): 50; John D. Scott, *We Climb High: A Thumbnail Chronology of the Mazamas, 1894–1964* (Portland: Mazamas, 1969), p. 1.

10. Earl Pomeroy, *In Search of the Golden West: The Tourist in Western America* (New York: Alfred A. Knopf, 1957), pp. 114–18.

11. W. A. Langille, "Sodaville Mineral Springs, Oregon's First Dedicated Public Park, May 4, 1871" (mimeographed; [Salem, Ore.], n.d.); E. Walton and Charles Whittam, "Sodaville State Park: Linn County," (mimeographed; [Salem], 1967), copies of both are in Oregon Parks and Recreation Division, main office files (Parks and Recreation Division, Salem [hereafter PRDP]). Summers's quotation is from Langille, p. 2. In the 1890s the State Board of Control assumed jurisdiction over the site. Occasional appropriations for it were forthcoming from the state legislature in the years that followed, but not until 1947 did Sodaville Park offically become a part of the state park system. In 1975 the state deeded the site back to the community.

12. *Idaho Statesman*, 27 July 1876, 1 Sept. 1898.

13. Haines, *Mountain Fever*, pp. 186–200; *Mazama* 1 (1896): 58; *Steel Points* 1 (Jan. 1907): 37–39, 68–74; *Oregon Out of Doors* 1 (1922): 10–18, 96, 104–6; Howard and Marian T. Place, *The Story of Crater Lake National Park* (Caldwell, Idaho: Caxton Printers, 1974); Rakestraw, "Before McNary," pp. 49–56. For an example of early press coverage of "Lake Majesty," see: *West Shore* 1 (1876): 2.

14. Jean Conley Smith, "In God's Own Country: The Proposed Sawtooth National Park in Idaho"; Smith, "What is There of National Interest in the Proposed Sawtooth National Park?" Jean Conley Smith Papers (Idaho State Historical Society, Boise); Ralph E. Woods, "The Proposed Sawtooth National Park," *New West Magazine* 7 (May 1916): 7–11; Enos Mills, "Proposed Sawtooth National Park," ibid. (Oct. 1916): 18–22. No study of the Sawtooth campaign has been done. Although the area never received park status, in 1939 it was set aside by the Forest Service as a primitive area and in the 1960s was changed to wilderness and recreational areas.

15. So great was the popularity of the Columbia Gorge by the mid-1890s that William Gladstone Steel complained in his report of 1894 as president of the Mazamas: "Many tourists have gazed on the grandeur and beauty of the scenery of the Columbia river, and have marvelled at the scene; its praises have been sung by poets and its beauties painted by artists; yet within the limits of Oregon I have seen twenty miles of unbroken scenery, the poorest portion of which is equal to the best of the Columbia river." One of the objects of the Mazamas, he noted, was to find and publicize "these gems of nature." *Mazama* 1 (1896): 21–22. Victor's poem appeared in *West Shore* 1 (March 1876): 12.

16. On the boom of the 1880s, see: Dorothy O. Johansen and Charles M. Gates, *Empire of the Columbia: A History of the Pacific Northwest*, rev. ed. (New

York: Harper & Bros., 1967), pp. 316–32, and the articles in *Oregon Historical Quarterly* [hereafter *OHQ*] 67 (1966): 101–78.

17. See: Thomas R. Cox, "Trade, Development, and Environmental Change: The Utilization of North America's Pacific Coast Forests to 1914 and Its Consequences," in Richard P. Tucker and J. F. Richards, eds., *Global Deforestation and the Nineteenth-Century World Economy* (Durham, N.C.: Duke University Press, 1983), esp. pp. 16, 18–19, 22.

18. Bowles, *Across the Continent: A Summer's Journey to the Rocky Mountains, the Mormons, and the Pacific States with Speaker Colfax* (Springfield, Mass.: S. Bowles & Co., 1865), p. 183; *West Shore* 11 (1885): 61–62; 13 (1887): 103; 14 (1888): 239; 16 (1890): 356. Harvey Scott of the Portland *Oregonian* displayed similarly mixed feelings. See, also: Lancaster Pollard, "The Pacific Northwest," in Merrill Jensen, ed., *Regionalism in America* (Madison: University of Wisconsin Press, 1965), pp. 191–93.

19. Dorothy O. Johansen, "The Oregon Steam Navigation Company: An Example of Capitalism on the Frontier," *Pacific Historical Review* 10 (1941): 179–88; Johansen, "A Working Hypothesis for the Study of Migration," ibid. 36 (1967): 1–12; Arthur L. Throckmorton, *Oregon Argonauts: Merchant Adventurers on the Western Frontier* (Portland: Oregon Historical Society, 1961), pp. 224–25, 276, 309–15; Pollard, "Pacific Northwest," pp. 196–98, 210–11; David Sarasohn, "Regionalism, Tending Toward Sectionalism," in William G. Robbins, Robert J. Frank, and Richard E. Ross, eds., *Regionalism and the Pacific Northwest* (Corvallis: Oregon State University Press, 1983), pp. 223–36; *Olympia Columbian*, 10 Dec. 1853; *Olympia Pioneer and Democrat*, 10 June 1854; *Seattle Intelligencer*, 11, 17, 21 Oct. 1876, 16 and 30 May 1877. Cf. Gene M. Gressley, "Colonialism: A Western Complaint," *PNQ* 44 (1963): 1–8.

20. F. Ross Peterson and W. Darrell Gertsch, "The Creation of Idaho's Lifeblood: The Politics of Irrigation," *Rendezvous* 11 (Fall 1976): 53–61; Merle W. Wells, "Idaho and the Civil War," ibid., pp. 9–26; Wells, *Anti-Mormonism in Idaho, 1872–92* (Provo, Utah: Brigham Young University Press, 1978); Pollard, "Pacific Northwest," p. 198. See, also: Judith Austin, "Desert, Sagebrush, and the Northwest," in Robbins, Frank, and Ross, *Regionalism and the Pacific Northwest*, pp. 129–47.

21. *Argus* 27 (11 Dec. 1920): 44–46; Seattle Board of Park Commissioners, *Parks, Playgrounds and Boulevards of Seattle, Washington* (Seattle: Pacific Press, 1909); J. M. Neil, "Paris or New York? The Shaping of Downtown Seattle, 1903–1914," *PNQ* 75 (1984): 22–33; Padraic Burke, "The City Beautiful Movement in Seattle" (M.A. thesis, University of Washington, 1973); Spokane Board of Park Commissioners, *Report . . .* (Spokane: Spokane American Engaving Co., 1913); *Oregonian*, 4 Feb., 8 and 23 April, 16 July, 26 May 1911; E. Kimbark MacColl, *The Shaping of a City: Business and Politics in Portland, Oregon, 1885 to 1915* (Portland: Georgian Press, 1976), pp. 14–16; Nolen, *City Planning*, pp. 160–61; John Fahey, "A. L. White, Champion of Urban Beauty," *PNQ* 72 (1981): 170–79.

22. *Idaho Statesman*, 23 and 24 Nov. 1907, 22 Aug. 1943; Salem *Oregon*

Statesman, 24 Feb. 1907; Marjorie O'Harra, *Ashland, The First 130 Years* (Jacksonville: Southern Oregon Historical Society, 1981), pp. 77–78, 88.

23. Samuel Christopher Lancaster, *The Columbia, America's Great Highway through the Cascade Mountains to the Sea* (3rd ed.; Portland: J. K. Gill Co., 1926), pp. 100–24; Lancaster, photo book on the Columbia River highway, Ronald J. Fahl private collection (Santa Cruz, Calif.), pp. 8, 20, 25, 37, 43, 50; Fahl, "S. C. Lancaster and the Columbia River Highway: Engineer as Conservationist," *OHQ* 74 (1973): 101–44; Alice Benson Allen, *Simon Benson: Northwest Lumber King* (Portland: Binfords and Mort, 1971), pp. 110–29.

24. Theodore Roosevelt, "The People of the Pacific Coast," *Outlook* 99 (11 Sept. 1911): 159–62.

25. On the City Beautiful Movement, see: Jon A. Peterson, "The City Beautiful Movement: Forgotten Origins and Lost Meanings," *Journal of Urban History* 2 (1976): 419–27; William H. Wilson, "J. Horace McFarland and the City Beautiful Movement," ibid. 7 (1981): 320–30. On the urban parks movement, see: Geoffrey Blodgett, "Frederick Law Olmsted: Landscape Architect as Conservative Reformer," *Journal of American History* 62 (1975): 869–89; Robert A. J. McDonald, "'Holy Retreat' or 'Practical Breathing Spot'?: Class Perception's of Vancouver's Stanley Park, 1910–1913" *Canadian Historical Review* 65 (1984): 127–53; Galen Cranz, *The Politics of Park Design: A History of Urban Parks in America* (Cambridge, Mass.: Harvard University Press, 1982), ch. 2.

26. See: Hugh Myron Hoyt, Jr., "The Good Roads Movement in Oregon, 1900–1920" (Ph.D. diss., University of Oregon, 1966); John Chynoweth Burnham, "The Gasoline Tax and the Automobile Revolution," *Mississippi Valley Historical Review* 48 (1961): 435–59; Frederic L. Paxson, "The Highway Movement," *American Historical Review* 51 (1946): 236–53; Pomeroy, *In Search of the Golden West,* pp. 125–30, 146–51, 210–11; Huth, *Nature and the American,* pp. 188, 201–3. There is no full treatment of the impact of truck logging; however, see: Clyde S. Webb, "Truck Hauling in the Inland Empire," *Timberman* 38 (March 1937): 120–22; "Beginning of Western Truck Logging," ibid., (Oct. 1949): 168–70; "Billion Feet of Logs by Motor Truck," ibid., pp. 172–80, 228.

27. Peter J. Schmitt, *Back to Nature: The Arcadian Myth in Urban America* (New York: Oxford University Press, 1969).

28. For explication of this interpretation of the conservation movement, see: Samuel P. Hays, *Conservation and the Gospel of Efficiency: The Progressive Conservation Movement, 1890–1920,* reprint ed. (New York: Atheneum, 1969), esp. pp. 261–76. Cf. J. Leonard Bates, "Fulfilling American Democracy: The Conservation Movement, 1907–1921," *Mississippi Valley Historical Review* 44 (1957): 29–57; J. Ronald Engel, "Social Democracy, the Roots of Ecology, and the Preservation of the Indiana Dunes," *Journal of Forest History* [hereafter *JFH*] 28 (1984): 4–13.

29. The attendance list for the Des Moines meeting is incomplete, but sufficient to show that it was basically the same group as at subsequent meetings. See, also: John S. Rath, "Regional Participation and Influences in

the Conservation Movement in the United States: A Statistical Study" (M.A. thesis, San Diego State University, 1976); Tilden, *State Parks*, pp. 5–7.

30. Studies of state parks in the Rocky Mountain–Intermountain Basin states and in the South focus on individual parks and states. However, for a list of parks that clearly reveals the weakness of the movement in the two areas during the period under review, see: NCSP, *Proceedings, Fourth Conference*, following p. 128. Reports to this conference from individual states reinforce this conclusion. Similarly, in 1927 Beatrice Ward noted that Arizona, Colorado, Delaware, Georgia, Maryland, Mississippi, Montana, Nevada, New Mexico, Oklahoma, Rhode Island, South Carolina, Utah, and Virginia all lacked state parks. Ward to Isabelle Story, 15 July 1927, NCSPP.

31. On the "worthless lands" thesis, see: Alfred Runte, *National Parks: The American Experience* (Lincoln: University of Nebraska Press, 1979), esp. chapters 3 and 4, and the forum thereon in *JFH* 27 (1983): 130–45.

32. Illustrative of the lack of national stature among the advocates of state parks is the fact that, except for those working in the New York area or those involved in national affairs, such as Senator Peter Norbeck of South Dakota, they go almost totally unmentioned in the *New York Times*. Even Norbeck, when mentioned, was discussed for his other activities, not his parks work.

2. WELDON B. HEYBURN AND ROBERT MORAN: *Two Men and Two Parks*

1. On Heyburn, see: R. G. Cook, "Senator Heyburn's War Against the Forest Service," *Idaho Yesterdays* 14 (Winter 1970–71): 12–15; *National Cyclopedia of American Biography* (New York: James T. White & Co., 1891–   ), 13: 101; Merrill D. Beal and Merle W. Wells, *History of Idaho* (2 vols.; New York: Lewis Publishing Co., 1959), 2: 201, 205. On Moran, see: Lancaster Pollard, *A History of the State of Washington* (4 vols.; New York: American Historical Association, 1937), 4: 529; Moran to Edmond S. Meany, 15 Nov. 1911, Edmond S. Meany Papers (University of Washington Library, Seattle [hereafter EMP]), box 27, file 4; Moran to Meany, 22 Oct. 1926, ibid., 41–42; Moran to Meany, 25 May 1912, Robert Moran Papers (University of Washington Library, Seattle [hereafter RMP]), box 2, file 1.

2. Two years earlier Idaho's legislature had set aside state lands on Payette Lake as a "state park," but they provided no funds or machinery for the improvement or management of the tract. The lands there remained under the State Board of Land Commissioners, which proceeded to lease out summer home sites on the tract and in general manage it so as to bring a profit to the state. Lava Hot Springs, transferred to Idaho by the federal government in 1902, was not declared a state park until 1913. Washington did not acquire its first major state park until 1915, Oregon not until the 1920s.

3. *Congressional Record*, 60th Cong., 1st Sess., p. 3378. When Senator Henry M. Teller of Colorado replied that, though Heyburn might want a

national park for Idaho, Teller certainly did not want one for Colorado, Heyburn curtly reminded him that Colorado already had one, Mesa Verde.

4. Act of 21 June 1906, 34 *Stat.* 335; Jack Dozier, "The Coeur d'Alene Land Rush, 1909–10," *PNQ* 53 (1962): 145–50; Commissioner of Indian Affairs, *Report, 1906* (Washington, D.C.: GPO, 1907), p. 74; ibid., *1908*, p. 61; *St. Maries Gazette*, 1 Feb. 1907; *Coeur d'Alene Press*, 26 Jan. 1907.

5. There is some indication that settlement on, or despoliation of the site was already under way when Heyburn moved into action. See: *Congressional Record*, 59th Cong., 2nd Sess., p. 3972; 62nd Cong., 2nd Sess., p. 2703; *Coeur d'Alene Evening Press*, 17 Nov. 1906.

6. *Congressional Record*, 59th Cong., 2nd Sess., pp. 2265, 3715, 3831. The *Coeur d'Alene Press*, 2 Mar. 1907, mistakenly reported the park "secured" when the bill passed the Senate. Moreover, it gave credit for the bill to Idaho's other Senator, Fred T. Dubois.

7. Ibid., p. 3972.

8. Ibid., pp. 4591–92.

9. On the activities of Washington Water Power Company, see: Lucile F. Fargo, *Spokane Story* (New York: Columbia University Press, 1950), pp. 200–10. Newspapers suggest that the area around Lake Chatcolet had been a favorite excursion spot and campground for white residents of the vicinity since the 1890s. *St. Maries Gazette*, 15 June, 27 July, 21 Dec. 1906, 31 Jan., 21 Feb., 24 April 1908; *Coeur d'Alene Evening Press*, 27 Jan., 8 Feb., 6 April 1908.

10. *Congressional Record*, 59th Cong., 2nd Sess., p. 4592.

11. Shankland, *Steve Mather*, pp. 184–85 and passim; Marion Clawson, *Man and Land in the United States* (Lincoln: University of Nebraska Press, 1964), p. 85; United States Department of the Interior, *Reports, 1909* (2 vols; Washington: Government Printing Office, 1910), 1: 507–9, 511–15, 517–31; memorandum for Mather, 23 May 1924, NCSPP; NCSP, *Proceedings, Fourth Conference*, pp. 61–62, 100; David Harmon, "Sullys Hill and the Development of National Park Standards," *North Dakota History* 53 (Spring 1986): 2–9.

12. *Congressional Record*, 59th Cong., 2nd Sess., pp. 2265, 3831, 4592.

13. Ibid., 60th Cong., 1st Sess., pp. 137, 2658.

14. Ibid., pp. 2111, 2531.

15. Ibid., 59th Cong., 2nd Sess., p. 3715; U. S. Congress, Senate, Committee on Indian Affairs, *Senate Report 251*, 60th Cong., 1st Sess., 18 Feb. 1908.

16. *Congressional Record*, 60th Cong., 1st Sess., p. 2627. Representative French introduced a companion bill (H.R. 17054). Sent to the Committee on Indian Affairs, this bill also was never reported out. See: ibid., 2014. French was coming in for sharp criticism from independent *Coeur d'Alene Evening Press* for failure to get the bill through the House at previous session of Congress. See: 8 Feb. and 6 April 1908.

17. *Congressional Record*, 60th Cong., 1st Sess., p. 2658.

18. There had apparently been some latent sentiment for this all along. See: ibid., 59th Cong., 2nd Sess., p. 4592.

19. Ibid., 60th Cong., 1st Sess., pp. 3253, 3378. The *St. Maries Gazette*

gave Heyburn, "who is ever watchfull [sic] of the interests of his home state," responsibility for the shift to a state park. See: 1 May 1908.

20. Chief Peter Moctelme had long lived near the park; his claim would no doubt impinge on it. In 1908 he led a delegation to Washington, D.C., in connection with the termination. Jack Dozier suggests that their concern was over the size of allotments, but information on that subject was available without traveling to Washington. Moctelme was later compensated for certain of his land that had been within the tract withdrawn for the park. One reason for the trip to Washington may well have been to secure assurances from Senator Heyburn that he would introduce a private bill calling for the payment to Moctelme. See: Dozier, "Coeur d'Alene Land Rush," p. 146; *Congressional Record,* 61st Cong., 3rd Sess., p. 477; 62nd Cong., 2nd Sess., p. 2703; *Coeur d'Alene Evening Press,* 8 Feb. and 4 Apr. 1908; Thomas R. Cox, "Tribal Leadership in Transition: Chief Peter Moctelme of the Coeur d'Alenes," *Idaho Yesterdays* 20 (1979): 2–9, 25–31.

21. *Congressional Record,* 60th Cong., 1st Sess., p. 3378. As Heyburn put it at the time, "The question of whether this is to be a national park or a state park is an important question." He made it clear he preferred the former.

22. Ibid., pp. 4979, 5020, 5563.

23. For their coverage of Heyburn's efforts, see: Boise *Idaho Daily Statesman,* 3 Dec. 1907; 10, 19, and 25 Feb. 1908; *St. Maries Gazette,* 31 Jan., 21 Feb., 24 Apr., 1 May 1908, 3 Feb. 1911; *Coeur d'Alene Press,* 2 Mar. 1907; *Coeur d'Alene Evening Press,* 27 Jan., 8 Feb., 6 Apr. 1908, 2 Mar. 1909, 31 Jan., 8 Feb. 1911. Although newspapers from northern Idaho were often in error, their coverage was the fullest, as one might expect.

24. Boise *Idaho Daily Statesman,* 23 and 24 Nov. 1907. The newspapers that most fully reported on Heyburn's efforts also gave coverage to the city beautiful and national parks movements. See: *St. Maries Gazette,* 14 and 21 Sept., 5 Oct. 1906; *Coeur d'Alene Evening Press,* 5 Feb. 1908.

25. Idaho, House of Representatives, *Journal . . . Ninth Session,* pp. 271–73; ibid., *Tenth Session,* pp. 213 and passim; Idaho, Senate, *Journal . . . Ninth Session,* p. 184; ibid., *Tenth Session,* pp. 209 and passim; Act of 13 Mar. 1909, *Idaho Session Laws,* 1909, 145; Lardo (Idaho) *Long Valley Advocate,* 21 June, 2 Aug., 27 Sept., 25 Oct., 29 Nov. 1906, 17 and 31 Jan., 7 Feb., 14 Mar. 1907; Boise *Idaho Daily Statesman,* 7 Mar. 1907.

26. Act of 16 Mar. 1909, *Idaho Session Laws, 1909,* p. 338; Act of 7 Feb. 1911, *Idaho Session Laws, 1911,* p. 334.

27. *Fourth Biennial Report of the Fish and Game Warden* (Boise, 1912, pp. 49–50; O. H. Barber to John M. Haines, 12 July 1913, Haines Papers (Idaho State Archives, Boise); J. B. Gowen, report to State Board of Examiners, 15 Dec. 1914, copy in Department of Parks and Recreation, Heyburn State Park Papers (Idaho State Historical Society, Boise); F. G. Miller and Henry Schmitz, "A Report on Heyburn Park," ibid., box 2, pp. 16–20: timber sale file, ibid.; *Idaho Fish and Game* 1 (Feb. 1914): 6.

28. Cook, "Heyburn's War Against the Forest Service," pp. 12–15; Gifford Pinchot, comp., *Forest Reserves in Idaho,* U.S. Forest Service Bulletin

no. 67 (Washington: Government Printing Office, 1905); Elmo R. Richardson, *The Politics of Conservation: Crusades and Controversies, 1897–1913* (Berkeley: University of California Press, 1962), pp. 31–33, 75, 98–99, 108; *Congressional Record*, 62nd Cong., 1st Sess., p. 5728; *St. Maries Gazette*, 13 April 1906; *Coeur d'Alene Press*, 5 Feb. 1907.

29. *Congressional Record*, 62nd Cong., 2nd Sess., pp. 8037–39.

30. Ibid., 60th Cong., 1st Sess., pp. 3253, 5020.

31. Boise *Evening Capital News*, 13 June 1912. A copy of the deed is also available in Departmental Files—Land, 1970, Attorney-General's files (Idaho State Archives, Boise). Although Heyburn professed to see no possible reason for federal authorities reserving control over the waters of the lake, this proviso probably resulted from the construction of facilities by the Washington Water Power Company at Post Falls. The dam and associated flooding had already become a hotly contested issue. Among other issues was that of whether federal or state authority was to rule in this case. See: *Coeur d'Alene Evening Press*, 8 Jan. 1908; *St. Maries Gazette*, 10 Jan., 29 May 1908, 5, 12, and 19 Mar. 1909, 23 Dec. 1910, 13 Jan., 10 Feb. 1911, 21 June 1912; correspondence re. Washington Water Power Co., Heyburn Park Papers, folder 35.

32. *Congressional Record*, 62nd Cong., 2nd Sess., pp. 8037–39.

33. The granting of leaseholds at the park to private individuals, a practice begun early in the park's history led in the 1970s to litigation in which it was charged that leasing constituted a breach of the conditions in the deed. See Chapter Seven.

34. Heyburn's only other known activity in behalf of parks occurred in 1912, when he introduced an amendment appropriating $250,000 for roads in Yellowstone Park "in order to permit the use of automobiles therein." See *Congressional Record*, 62nd Cong., 2nd Sess., p. 4904.

35. Gordon Newell, ed., *The H.W. McCurdy Marine History of the Pacific Northwest . . .* (Seattle: Superior Publishing Co., 1966), pp. 21, 27, 34, 61, 90, 104–5, 112, 122, and 480; Pollard, *History of Washington*, 4: 529.

36. Moran to Meany, 22 Oct. 1926, EMP, 41–24.

37. Meany to Moran, 3 March 1912, RMP, 2–1; ibid., 22 Aug., 1912, RMP, 2–2. Floor plans, photographs, and descriptions of Rosario are in RMP, box 1. See also: Fred John Splitstone, *Orcas, Gem of the San Juans'* (Sedro-Woolley, Wash.: Courier-Times Press, 1946), pp. 94–98. The Mountaineers were founded in 1907. See: *Mazama* 3 (1907): 61–62.

38. Moran to Meany, 13 Oct. 1910, EMP, 26–3.

39. Ibid., 23 Feb. 1912, RMP, 2–1.

40. Meany to Moran, 3 Mar. 1912, ibid.

41. Ibid., 26 Mar., 28 and 29 Aug. 1912, RMP 2–1 and 2–3; Meany to university party members, 21 Aug. 1912, RMP, 2–3; [Meany] to Moran, 20 Jan. 1913, EMP, 28–12.

42. Meany to Moran, 28 Jan. 1913, RMP, 2–5. See also: Moran to Nichols, 27 and 30 Jan, 6 Feb. 1913, RMP, 2–7; Moran to Meany, 28 Jan. 1913, RMP, 2–4.

43. Moran to Meany, 30 Jan. 1913, RMP, 2–5.

44. Ibid., 14 Feb. 1913, RMP, 2–6.

45. Moran to Bone, 3 Feb. 1913, RMP, 2–8.

46. Moran to Meany, 3 and 14 Feb. 1913, EMP, 28–13; Meany to Moran, 7 Feb. 1913, RMP, 2–6.

47. Capron to Moran, 17 Feb., 3 and 21 Mar. 1913, RMP, 2–8. Quotation from 17 Feb. See also: Meany to Moran, 27 Apr. 1913; Moran to Meany, 29 Apr. 1913, RMP, 2–6; Everett C. Griggs to Moran, 29 Nov. 1919, RMP, 2–21; State Parks Committee, *Washington State Parks, A Recreational Resource* ([Olympia?], 1941).

48. Moran to Meany, 1 Sept. 1913, EMP, 28–26. See also: Moran to Bone, 4 April 1913, RMP, 2–8.

49. Blaine was apparently appointed as an unpaid commissioner to work under the State Park Board that had been created in 1913. As the three members of the board were all elected officials with more pressing duties, the only way parks were apt to get attention was if these ex officio members were aided by someone specially designated to give them attention. There is no evidence that Governor Lister had this in mind when he appointed Blaine, but it seems reasonable to assume as much.

50. Blaine to Moran, 23 Oct. 1913, RMP, 2–9; Moran to Blaine, 25 Oct. 1913, ibid.; Moran to Green, 20 Jan. 1915, RMP, 2–11.

51. Green to Moran, 27 Jan. 1915, RMP, 2–11. On Green, see: Seattle *Post-Intelligencer*, 17 Jan. 1975.

52. Capron to Moran, 9 Feb. 1915, RMP, 2–13; Moran to Capron, 12 Feb. 1915, ibid.; Moran to Blaine, 20 Feb. 1915, ibid.

53. Blaine to Moran, 9 Apr. 1915, RMP, 2–13.

54. Beaton to Moran, 18 Oct. (quotation), 29 Nov., and 7 Dec. 1916, RMP, 2–16.

55. Nash to Moran, 8 Feb. 1917, RMP, 2–13; Moran to Nash, 10 Feb. 1917, ibid.

56. Nash to Moran, 22 Apr. 1917, RMP, 2–13. See also: Moran to Blaine, 10 Feb. 1917, RMP, 2–9.

57. Nash to Moran, 31 Jan. and 10 Feb. 1919, RMP, 2–17; State of Washington, House Bill No. 164, Mr. Nash, first read 6 Feb. 1919 (copy in RMP, 2–17).

58. On Mather and his role in NPS, see: Swain, *Federal Conservation Policy*, pp. 123–43; Shankland, *Steve Mather*, pp. 184–200; Ise, *National Park Policy*, pp. 185–95, 296–300.

59. No full-length biography of Grant is available. For short accounts, see: *Dictionary of American Biography*, Supplement 2: 256; *National Cyclopaedia of American Biography*, 29: 319–20; *New York Times*, 31 May 1937; W. Redmond Cross, "A Tribute to Madison Grant," New York Zoological Society *Bulletin* 40 (1937): 102–4. Consult also: David Spitz, *Patterns of Anti-Democratic Thought* (New York: Macmillan Co., 1949), pp. 10–11, 141–62, 277–78: John Higham, *Strangers in the Land* (corrected ed., New York: Atheneum, 1965), pp. 155–57.

60. Shankland, *Steve Mather*, pp. 78–80, 94–95, 149–51, 184–200. See

also: Tilden, *State Parks,* pp. 3–16; Portland *Oregonian,* 29 Aug. and 28 Nov. 1920; *Ashland* (Oregon) *Weekly Tidings,* 28 Feb. 1922; *Bend* (Oregon) *Bulletin,* 14 Aug. 1919.

61. Shankland, *Steve Mather,* pp. 194–95; Griggs to Moran, 29 Nov. 1919, RMP, 2–21; Moran to Griggs, 4 Dec. 1919, ibid; Grant to Ben Olcott, 27 Sept. 1920, Ben Olcott Papers (University of Oregon Library, Eugene [hereafter BOP]), vol. 3. According to the Natural Parks Association's letterhead, Griggs was the group's president; Moran, Meany, Grant, Savidge, Whitcomb, Suzzalo, Mather, and twenty others were vice presidents; and Evison was secretary.

62. *Argus* 27 (11 Dec. 1920): 44–46; *Park Playgrounds and Boulevards of Seattle, Washington* (Seattle: Board of Park Commissioners, 1909), pp. 7, 73–154.

63. *Natural Parks Bulletin* 1 (Aug. 1920): 1–2; Evison to Moran, 10 Feb. 1921, RMP, 2–2; Tilley, "Brief Report," p. 1; Evison to Asahel Curtis, 10 Feb. 1921, and Curtis to John Culp, 23 Feb. 1921, Asahel Curtis Papers (University of Washington Library, Seattle [hereafter ACP]), box 1, file 35. On earlier interest of the State Federation of Women's Clubs in conservation, see: Elvira Elwood to Meany, 14 Mar. 1903, EMP, 19–28. Copies of the *Natural Parks Bulletin* are in RMP, 2, passim.

64. Moran to Griggs, 12 Jan. 1920, RMP, 2–21.

65. Washington, *House Journal of the Seventeenth Session . . . 1921* (Olympia: State Printer, 1921), pp. 442, 566–67; ibid., *Senate Journal,* p. 543.

66. Evison to Curtis, 19 Mar. 1920, ACP, 1–33; Moran to Allen, 24 June, 22 July, 9 Oct. 1920; Allen to Moran, 22 Jan., 24 Mar., 8 and 16 Apr. 1921, RMP; John Rea to Moran, 18 Apr. 1921, RMP, 2–15; *Tacoma News-Tribune,* 16 Apr. 1921.

67. Moran to Clifford Babcock, 26 July 1921, 13 July 1922, 25 Jan., 23 Oct. 1923, 10 Mar. 1924, and other dates, RMP, 2–25, 29, 30, 43, 53; Moran to Savidge, 13 Jan. 1922, RMP, 2–29; Charles Signer to Moran, 13 Feb. 1922, ibid.; Moran to Nova Langell, 21 Feb. 1922; Moran to James Allen, 8 Sept. 1922, ibid.; Moran to Evison, 4 Oct. 1922, ibid.; Moran to John Murray, 20 Jan. 1923, RMP, 2–31; Murray to Moran, 6 Feb. 1923, ibid.; Capron to Moran, 5 Mar. 1923, RMP, 2–34; Evison to Moran, n.d., RMP, 2–51; *State Recreation* 1 (Mar. 1927): 5.

68. Smaller parks donated during the tenure of the earlier state park board, most notably Larrabee State Park near Bellingham and those roadside parks of five acres or less established by Land Commissioner Savidge beginning in 1919, all predate Moran State Park.

3.   BEN OLCOTT'S CRUSADE TO SAVE OREGON'S SCENERY

1. See: Hays, *Conservation and the Gospel of Efficiency,* pp. 122–27; Swain, *Federal Conservation Policy,* pp. 1–6, 123–43, 169–70; Gifford Pinchot, *Breaking*

New Ground (New York: Harcourt, Brace & Co., 1947), p. 71. Cf. Bates, "Fulfilling American Democracy," pp. 29–57; Rakestraw, "Before McNary," pp. 49–56.

2. Oregon Conservation Commission, *Report* (Nov. 1910), p. 5. See also: ibid., (Nov. 1908), pp. 101–3; (Nov. 1912), pp. 14–15; (Nov. 1914), pp. 9–10.

3. Grant to Olcott, 27 Sept. 1920, BOP, 3.

4. *Bend Bulletin*, 14 Aug. 1919; Portland *Oregonian*, 16 Aug. 1919. On the growth of Bend and its lumber industry, see: Philip Cogswell, Jr., "Deschutes Country Pine Logging," in Thomas Vaughan, ed., *High & Mighty: Select Sketches about the Deschutes Country* (Portland: Oregon Historical Society, 1981), pp. 234–47 and passim.

5. Quoted in *Bend Bulletin*, 14 Aug. 1919. Grant used the Bronx Parkway as "the shining example when he preached preservation of timber along the highways . . ." of Oregon. Mather to Sawyer, 20 Oct. 1925, Oregon State Highway Commission, Papers of Commissioner Sawyer (University of Oregon library, Eugene [hereafter PCS]), box 6.

6. Indeed, the *Bulletin*'s editorial policy so emphasized the benefits that good roads would bring to previously isolated central Oregon that one historian has cited its stance as an example of the pork barrel mentality at work. See: Burnham, "Gasoline Tax and the Automobile Revolution," p. 443, n. 28.

7. *Bend Bulletin*, 16 Aug. 1919. These people had not been entirely silent prior to the Grant-Mather visit. George Palmer Putnam, formerly editor of the *Bulletin* and the man who brought Sawyer into the newspaper business, had, for instance, noted in 1915 that most westerners were "all for turning [trees] into dollars as fast as logging roads and band saws can contrive . . ." but there were also those, like himself, "with a secret dread of the time when the old earth will be divested totally of her timber covering. . . ." George Palmer Putnam, *In the Oregon Country* . . . (New York: G. P. Putnam's Sons, 1915), pp. 93–95. See also reference to this early interest in the *Bend Bulletin*, 18 Nov. 1919.

8. *Bend Bulletin*, 14 Aug. 1919.

9. Sawyer to Horace Albright, 6 Feb. 1953, Robert W. Sawyer Papers (University of Oregon library, Eugene [hereafter RSP]), box 1. In his letter to Albright, Sawyer recalled the visit as having taken place in 1924; however, contextual evidence clearly indicates that he had the 1919 visit in mind.

10. Portland *Oregonian*, 16 Aug. 1919; Lancaster, photo book, pp. 8, 20, 37, 50; Fahl, "Lancaster and the Columbia River Highway," pp. 100–44.

11. Quoted in Portland *Oregonian*, 5 Sept. 1920. See, also: 16 Aug. 1919.

12. Grant to Olcott, 28 Sept. 1920, BOP, 3. On Cornwall, see: Gage McKinney, "'A Man Among You, Taking Notes': George M. Cornwall and the *Timberman*," *JFH* 26 (1982): 76–83.

13. Portland *Oregonian*, 17 Aug. 1919. In fact local Forest Service officials had already been moving in that direction. See: Henry S. Graves, journal of

trip to Alaska in 1915, entries for July 18–20, Graves Papers (Sterling Memorial Library, Yale University, New Haven, Conn.), box 2.

14. Grant to Olcott, 27 Sept. 1920, BOP, 3; Shankland, *Steve Mather*, p. 195.

15. *Timberman* 20 (Sept. 1919): 69; Grant to Olcott, 27 Sept. 1920, BOP, 3. Cornwall did, however, give the Save-the-Redwoods League a favorable press. See: *Timberman* 21 (June 1920): 30; 22 (June 1921): 74; 23 (Apr. 1922): 25; 23 (Aug. 1922): 85; 24 (Jan. 1923): 33.

16. Portland *Oregonian*, 17 Aug. 1919.

17. Grant to Sawyer, 9 Dec. 1919, RSP, 9.

18. *Bend Bulletin*, 14 Aug. 1919.

19. See the biographical sketches of Sawyer written for the *Bulletin* by Phil F. Brogan at the time of Sawyer's retirement, *Bend Bulletin*, 1 Oct. 1953, and in the *Oregon Voter* 62 (19 July 1930): 14–20, when a minor Sawyer-for-governor movement was under way. See also: Sawyer to C. C. Chapman, 8 July 1930, PCS, 1.

20. *Bend Bulletin*, 1 Oct. 1953. King, Populist candidate for governor in 1898, returned to the Democratic Party fold, served on the state Supreme Court from 1907 to 1911, and was a member of the Oregon Conservation Commission. At the time of Sawyer's attempt at poetry he was chief counsel for the U.S. Reclamation Service.

21. *Bend Bulletin*, 16 and 19 Nov. 1919; Portland *Oregonian*, 24 Feb. 1924; Sawyer to Grant, 25 Nov. 1919, RSP, 9; Sawyer to Samuel H. Boardman, 18 Mar. 1924, RSP, 3; Grant to Olcott, 27 Sept. 1920, BOP, 3; Cogswell, "Deschutes Country Pine Logging," pp. 242–43.

22. Sawyer to Grant, 25 Nov. 1919, Grant to Sawyer, 3 Dec. 1919, RSP, 28. Both Sawyer and Grant felt that the canyon should eventually be made a national monument or, as Sawyer suggested, included in the proposed Three Sisters National Park. See: Grant to Sawyer, 17 Dec. 1919, RSP, 9; Sawyer to Mather, 24 Dec. 1919, RSP, 11.

23. Since Sawyer's early efforts to get Brooks-Scanlon to follow the Shevlin-Hixon lead were done through personal contact, no written records exist. The story must be pieced together from references in the correspondence that ensued after Olcott entered the picture, cited below n. 27.

24. Olcott to Johnson, 19 Aug. 1920, BOP, 3; Olcott, address to preliminary meeting Scenic Preservation Society, Portland, 25 Apr. 1922, typescript copy, BOP, 6; Portland *Oregonian*, 26, 27, and 29 Aug. and 4 Sept. 1920.

25. Olcott to Sawyer, 18 Oct., 8 Nov. 1920, 25 Aug., 9 Nov. 1921; Sawyer to Olcott, 11 Nov. 1920; Olcott to Brooks, 12 Nov. 1920; Brooks to Olcott, 4 Nov. 1920, 19 Aug. 1921; George H. Cecil to Olcott, 2 Feb. 1922; McNary to Olcott, 23 Nov. 1921, RSP, 13; Olcott to Manager Brooks-Scanlon Lumber Co., 18 Oct. 1920, BOP, 3 (another copy, RSP, 13); Sawyer to Boardman, 18 Mar. 1924, RSP, 3; Portland *Oregonian*, 19 Oct. 1920 and 24 Feb. 1924; Olcott, press release dated 10 Nov. 1921, BOP, 5. The Sawyer letter to Olcott of 15 Oct. 1920, which triggered the entire correspondence and which is referred to in Olcott to Sawyer, 18 Oct. is not in either collection.

26. For biographical accounts of Olcott see: Portland *Oregonian,* 22 and 23 July 1952, 16 Feb. 1959; *Oregon Voter* 5 (13 May 1916): 35–38; Olcott, speech to Portland Chamber of Commerce, 1 Apr. 1922, BOP, 6. As the *Oregon Voter* put it, Olcott "doesn't go into exclamatory raptures over scenery, but he loves the rocks and hills of his native country like an Indian loves his hunting ground."

27. Undated typescript account and typescript account dated 4 May 1921, BOP, 2. One of Olcott's companions on this trip was Herbert Nunn, a state highway official who was later to play a role in the preservation and development of state parks in Oregon.

28. Olcott, account of his appointment, in Olcott to F. P. Burgett, 2 May 1911, BOP, 7; *Oregon Voter* 5 (13 May 1916): 35–37.

29. Olcott, press releases dated 12 and 27 Aug. 1920, BOP, 3.

30. Olcott, *Special Message to the Thirty-First Legislative Assembly . . .* (Salem: State Printer, 1921), p. 4; Portland *Oregonian,* 4 Sept., 17 Oct. 1920. Olcott gives a different list of committee members than does the *Oregonian.* The discrepancy apparently results from the latter's failure to distinguish between actual committee members and those called in as consultants. Olcott's list is no doubt correct.

31. Olcott, address to preliminary meeting of Scenic Preservation Society, 25 Apr. 1922, BOP, 6; Portland *Oregonian,* 27 Aug., 12 Sept. 1920.

32. Portland *Oregonian,* 26 Aug., 5 Sept. 1920. The *Oregonian* had anticipated the governor's call to action when, on 29 July, it observed editorially: "It is difficult to escape the notion that something should be done—something *is* in California where strips of forest have been preserved to roadways, and it ought not to be regarded as impossible in Oregon."

33. Booth to Olcott, 23 Aug. 1920, BOP, 3.

34. Benson to Olcott, 23 Aug. 1920, BOP, 3. Benson, a Portland logging magnate, claimed to have spent $200,000 of his own money on parks, roads, and roadside beautification. He was a leading figure in the building of the Columbia Gorge Highway. See: Fred Lockley, *History of the Columbia River Valley from The Dalles to the Sea* (3 vols., Chicago: S. J. Clarke Co., 1928), 1: 630, 832; Lancaster, *Columbia,* pp. 110, 114, 118; Allen, *Simon Benson,* pp. 110–29.

35. Mrs. A. H. Russell to Olcott, 22 and 30 Oct. 1921, BOP, 5.

36. Quoted in Portland *Oregonian,* 5 Sept. 1920.

37. Portland *Oregonian,* 24 Sept. 1920.

38. Ibid., 7 Oct. 1920. See also: Oregon State Highway Commission, *Fourth Biennial Report* (Salem: State Printer, 1920), pp. 71–72.

39. Nunn to Olcott, 19 Oct. 1920, BOP, 3; Olcott, *Special Message,* p. 4. Apparently it was Nunn who first interested West in saving these strips.

40. Mather to Olcott, 15 Nov. 1920, BOP, 3.

41. D. H. Upjohn [secretary to the governor] to H. N. Pratt, 7 Oct. 1920, BOP, 3; Olcott, typed manuscript on saving Oregon forests, BOP, 3. In his manuscript Olcott not only emphasized his roadside program but also his initiation of the use of airplane patrols in forest fire detection.

42. Grant to Olcott, 27 Sept. 1920, BOP, 3.

43. *Forest Patrolman* 1 (19 Sept. 1920): 2. See also: Johnson to Olcott, quoted in Portland *Oregonian*, 27 Aug. 1920.

44. C. S. Chapman to F. A. Elliott [State Forester], 26 Aug. 1920; Chapman to Olcott, 20 Oct. 1910; Elliott, Chapman, and Cecil to W. B. Ayer, 27 Sept. 1920, BOP, 3; *Timberman* 22 (Sept. 1920): 30. Ayer was chairman of the investigating committee appointed by Olcott and president of the Eastern and Western Lumber Co. of Portland; Chapman was secretary of the Western Forestry and Conservation Society, an organization established under the auspices of the Weyerhaeuser Timber Co. A professional forester, he worked for the Forest Service until 1924, then for Weyerhaeuser. See also: *Forest Patrolman* 1 (19 Sept. 1920): 2 and the reply to these arguments in the Portland *Oregonian*, 26 Sept. 1920.

45. Portland *Oregonian*, 29 Aug. 1920. There was windthrow in roadside strips that were set aside, but it was limited. The danger varied with the species, location, and width of strips.

46. *Timberman* 21 (Sept. 1920): 30.

47. Chapman to Olcott, 20 Oct. 1920, BOP, 3.

48. Portland *Oregonian*, 5 Sept. 1920.

49. Chapman to Olcott, 20 Oct. 1920, BOP, 3.

50. Rakestraw, "Before McNary," p. 53. For the classic expose of the timber frauds in Oregon see: Stephen A. D. Puter, *Looters of the Public Domain* (Portland: Portland Printing House, 1908). A scholarly treatment, covering primarily the legal aspects, is John Messing, "Public Lands, Politics, and Progressives: The Oregon Land Fraud Trials, 1903–1910," *Pacific Historical Review* 35 (1966): 35–66.

51. Elliott, Chapman, and Cecil to Ayer, 27 Sept. 1920, BOP, 3; Portland *Oregonian*, 24 Sept., 7 and 17 Oct. 1920; *Timberman* 21 (Oct. 1920): 174. The actual report of the committee has not been located, but other sources make its general content clear.

52. Olcott, *Special Message*; Olcott, press release regarding scenery preservation recommendations, typescript, n.d., BOP, 4.

53. Portland *Oregonian*, 26 Jan. 1921. There is no indication that Governor Tom McCall was aware of the precedent Olcott had provided when he issued his own call to preserve Oregon's livability during the late 1960s. McCall's appeal drew far more national attention than Olcott's, for preserving the quality of life was a major nationwide concern by that time.

54. Olcott, press release regarding scenery preservation recommendations, typescript, n.d., BOP, 4.

55. Quoted in *Ashland Weekly Tidings*, 23 Nov. 1921. See also: *Medford* (Oregon) *Mail-Tribune*, 30 Nov. 1921; Arthur H. Bone, ed., *Oregon Cattleman/ Governor, Congressman: The Memoirs and Times of Walter M. Pierce* (Portland: Oregon Historical Society, 1981), p. 129. It should be kept in mind that Olcott's battle with the Ku Klux Klan was under way and that Senator Thomas was, according to at least one analyst, openly a klansman. See: Eckard Vance Toy, "The Ku Klux Klan in Oregon: Its Character and Program" (M.A. thesis, University of Oregon, Eugene, 1959), p. 75; Malcolm Clark, Jr.,

"The Bigot Disclosed: 90 Years of Nativism," *OHQ* 75 (1974): esp. pp. 161–75; Bone, *Oregon Cattleman/Governor*, pp. 159–80.

56. Oregon Legislative Assembly, *Journals of the Senate and House of the Thirty-First Legislative Assembly . . . 1921* (Salem: State Printer, 1921), pp. 58, 185, 200, 218, 368, 372, 381, 383, 388.

57. Ibid., pp. 147, 214, 230, 244, 484, 515, 530, 571. In the voting on SB 365, "no" votes were cast by senators from Eugene, Burns, Portland, Halsey, Oregon City, Baker, Prineville, and McMinnville. Five of the eight were attorneys. In the House, "no" votes were cast by representatives from Shedd, Brownsville, The Dalles, Beaverton (2), Independence, Portland (2), Enterprise, Salem, Gervais, Amity, Milton, Sixes, and Banks. Even making allowance for the rural bias of apportionment, the generally rural nature of the opposition is clear.

58. Ibid., p. 214.

59. Ibid., pp. 58, 185, 206, 368, 372, 382, 389.

60. Olcott, address to meeting of county judges and commissioners, Portland, 14 Dec. 1921, longhand copy, BOP, 6. See also: Olcott, address to preliminary meeting of Scenic Preservation Society, 25 Apr. 1922, BOP, 6.

61. Olcott, address to county judges and commisioners, 14 Dec. 1921; address to preliminary meeting Scenic Preservation Society, 25 Apr. 1922, BOP, 6; Olcott to Sawyer, 25 Aug. 1921, RSP, 13. In the last-named source two of these individuals are identified; they were Herbert Nunn of the Highway Department and John Yeon, prominent Portland logging magnate and—with Simon Benson—a driving force behind the construction of the Columbia River Highway.

62. *Medford Mail-Tribune*, 26 and 30 Nov. 1922; Portland *Oregonian*, 26 Jan. 1921; *Ashland Weekly Tidings*, 14 Sept. 1921; Olcott, address to preliminary meeting of the Scenic Preservation Society, 25 Apr. 1922, BOP, 6.

63. Olcott, address to county judges and commissioners, 14 Dec. 1921; address to preliminary meeting of Scenic Preservation Society, 25 Apr. 1922; address to meeting of Portland Federation of Women's Clubs, Portland, 24 Jan. 1922, BOP, 6; *Medford Mail-Tribune*, 12 Sept. 1921.

64. Portland *Oregonian*, 17 Sept. 1922; Olcott, address to preliminary meeting Scenic Preservation Society, 25 Apr. 1922. For a complete listing of county directors of the society, see typescript list, BOP, 5.

65. Quoted in *Ashland Weekly Tidings*, 23 Nov. 1921.

66. Ibid.; *Medford Mail-Tribune*, 30 Nov. 1921.

67. Portland *Oregonian*, 17 Sept. 1922.

68. Bone, *Oregon Cattleman/Governor*, pp. 142–77; Hoyt, "Good Roads Movement in Oregon," pp. 11, 43, 161–206, 230–41; Gerald Schwartz, "Walter M. Pierce and the Tradition of Progressive Reform: A Study of Eastern Oregon's Great Democrat" (Ph.D. diss., Washington State University, 1969), pp. 51–52, 59, 61, 65, 71–73, 77–78.

69. For analyses of the election, see: Toy, "The Ku Klux Klan in Oregon," 91–108; Lawrence J. Saalfeld, "Forces of Prejudice in Oregon, 1920–1925," (M.A. thesis, Catholic Univ. of America, Washington, D.C., 1950, microfilm

copy, Univ. of Oregon library, Eugene), pp. 52–64, 88–97, 113–16; Malcolm E. Clark, "The Bigot Disclosed," pp. 161–75; Robert E. Burton, *Democrats of Oregon: The Pattern of Minority Politics, 1900–1956* (Eugene: University of Oregon Books, 1970), pp. 47–50; Bone, *Oregon Cattleman/Governor,* pp. 144–80; Schwartz, "Pierce and the Tradition of Progressive Reform," pp. 58–63.

70. Portland *Oregonian,* 24 Feb., 2, 5, 6, 13, and 27 Apr. 1924; Boardman to Sawyer, 22 Oct. 1927; Sawyer to Boardman, 27 Oct. 1927, PCS, 3; Boardman to C. W. Wanzer, 12 Nov. 1927, Boardman to H. G. Smith, 9 Nov. 1927, PCS, 1; Boardman, "Oregon State Park System: A Brief History," *OHQ* 55 (1954): 226–29; National Council for the Protection of Roadside Beauty, *The Roadsides of Oregon* (Washington, D.C.: National Council for the Protection of Roadside Beauty, n.d.), pp. 29–31; Sawyer to H. B. Glaisyer, 20 June 1952, RSP, 9.

71. Scenery preservation is not even mentioned in the "Platform of Ben W. Olcott, Candidate for Republican Nomination for Governor, Primary Election, 19 May 1922," (mimeographed copy, BOP, 9), in the pre-general election analyses of the campaign issues in the *Oregonian,* 5 Nov. 1922, in the *Oregon Voter* 31 (14 Oct. 1922): 7, and (28 Oct. 1922): 3, 8–10, nor in the Republican party campaign analysis [*Oregon Voter* 31 (28 Oct. 1922): 27–31].

72. Portland *Oregonian,* 24 and 25 Dec. 1924, 21 June 1925; Chester H. Armstrong, *History of the Oregon State Parks* (Salem: Oregon State Highway Department, 1965), pp. 6–7, 13–14, 33; Oregon State Highway Commission, *Sixth Biennial Report* (Salem: State Printer, 1924), pp. 85–86.

73. Sawyer to Albright, 6 Feb. 1953, RSP, 1.

4.   CONSERVATION BY SUBTERFUGE: *Robert W. Sawyer and the Birth of the Oregon State Parks*

1. Swain, *Federal Conservation Policy,* pp. 5–6, 126, 166, 169–70 (quotation p. 170).

2. Swain credits rising interest in scenery preservation in the 1920s largely to Mather and his supporters at the national level. See: ibid., pp. 123–43. Differences were most visible when Senator Charles McNary proposed federal aid to state parks; NPS leaders opposed, fearing diversion of funds from their programs. See: Herbert Klein to Sawyer, 16 Oct. 1929; Sawyer to Klein, 19 Oct. 1929, PCS, 4; Arno B. Cammerer, speech to NCSP, Linville, N.C., 19 June 1930; Horace Albright to Newton Drury, 21 Dec. 1931; NCSP, minutes, board of directors meeting, 19 Dec. 1931, NCSPP.

3. Beatrice Ward to R. A. Klein, 27 Aug. 1927; C. G. Sauers to J. C. Ainsworth, 5 Nov. 1927, Oregon State Highway Department, general files (Department of Transportation, Salem [hereafter HDP]), file 112–9C; Evison, *State Park Anthology,* p. 195; Armstrong, *History of the Oregon Parks,* p. 14; *State Recreation* 1 (Oct. 1927): 2–3. Sauers was chief of the Division of Lands and Waters, Indiana Department of Conservation.

4. Shankland, *Steve Mather,* pp. 184–200; Tilden, *State Parks,* pp. 3–5; Nelson, *State Recreation,* pp. 5–7, 16–17; Evison to Albright, 31 Oct. 1929, NCSPP.

5. Nelson, *State Recreation*, pp. 5, 7–8, and *passim; State Recreation* 1 (Mar. 1927): 4; (May 1927): 4; Clar, *California Government and Forestry*, pp. 517–20, 601–3; New York State Conservation Department, *Report*, No. 17 (Albany: State Printer, 1929): 17–18, 35, 67–68.

6. Chapter Three. See also: Rakestraw, "Before McNary," pp. 49–56; Scott, *We Climb High*, pp. 1–34.

7. C. J. Buck to Klein, 21 Oct. 1927, HDP, 112–9C; Herbert Cuthbert to H. B. Van Duzer, 7 Nov. 1927; Outdoor Recreation Committee, Portland Chamber of Commerce, minutes of meeting, 25 Oct. 1927, PCS, 3.

8. Van Duzer to Sawyer, [8 or 9 Nov. 1927], PCS, 1. See also: Sawyer to Van Duzer, 11 Nov. 1927, PCS, 3; *Four L Lumber News* 12 (Dec. 1931): 2.

9. Armstrong, *History of Oregon Parks*, pp. 1–6. See also: John B. Rae, *The Road and the Car in American Life* (Cambridge, Mass.: MIT Press, 1971), pp. 71–72, 137–44.

10. *Bend Bulletin*, 31 Mar. and 8 Sept. 1926, 16 Mar. 1927, 3 Apr. 1928; Sawyer to Wanzer, 7 Jan. and 30 Sept. 1926, RSP, 20; Sawyer to Albright, 6 Feb. 1953, RSP, 1; Oregon State Highway Commission, "State Park Land Acquisitions Prior to 1930" (mimeographed; [Salem], n.d.). See also, Chapter Three.

11. Bone, *Oregon Cattleman/Governor*, pp. 144–80; Schwartz, "Pierce and the Tradition of Progressive Reform," pp. 71–75, 85–86; Isaac L. Patterson, *Message to the Thirty-fifth Legislative Assembly* (Salem: State Printer, 1929), pp. 1–4, 22–23. In his first message to the legislature, Pierce denounced both spending money to encourage tourism and the amount being spent by the Highway Commission. The sentiments were widely shared. However, Pierce did contribute in a major way to highway construction, for he allowed one of the Highway Department's division engineers, R. H. Baldock, to experiment with road surfacing using crushed rock bound with asphaltic oil. The experiments resulted in greatly reduced costs for all-weather highways at a time when the state's rising number of motor vehicles made such roads essential. See: Walter M. Pierce, *Regular Message to the Thirty-Second Legislative Assembly* (Salem: State Printer, 1923), pp. 5, 7; Bone, *Oregon Cattleman/Governor*, pp. 233–34, 240–42.

12. Sawyer to Van Duzer, 24 Aug. and 10 Nov. 1927, PCS, 3. Others had similar fears. As Albert M. Turner of Connecticut put it, in his state "you couldn't go after parks with a brass band." Quoted in *State Recreation* 6 (July-Oct. 1932): 28.

13. Burnham, "Gasoline Tax and the Automobile Revolution," pp. 435–59; Hoyt, "The Good Roads Movement in Oregon," esp. pp. 230–39.

14. Evison, *State Park Anthology*, p. 88; Nelson, *State Recreation*, pp. 258–61, 276–78, 420–22; Tilley, "Brief Report," p. 1; NCSP, *Proceedings, Fourth Conference*, pp. 28, 34–43, 81–83, 103–4; Washington State Parks Committee, *Washington State Parks: A Recreational Resource* (n.p., n.d.); Herbert Evison, *The State Parks of Washington* (Seattle: Washington Natural Parks Association, 1923).

15. Sawyer to Van Duzer, 3 May 1928; Van Duzer to Sawyer, 7 May 1928, PCS, 3; Sawyer to Patterson, 18 May 1928, PCS, 2; Mather to members of

Oregon State Editorial Association, 28 June 1928; Sawyer to Mather, 13 July 1928; Ward to Sawyer, 20 July 1928, PCS, 3.

16. Sawyer to Van Duzer, 24 Aug. 1927, PCS, 1; Sawyer to Chapman, 8 July 1930, PCS, 7; Sawyer to Boardman, 13 Feb. 1952, RSP, 3; Sawyer to Albright, 6 Feb. 1953, RSP, 1.

17. Oregon State Highway Commission, minutes of meeting, 13 June 1921, Highway Commission minutes books (Oregon State Highway Department, Salem [hereafter HCM]), 6: 1034; Oregon State Parks Commission, Oregon State Planning Commission, and National Parks Service, *A Study of Parks, Parkways and Recreation Areas of Oregon* (2 vols.; [Portland], 1938), 1: 39–51; Samuel H. Boardman, "Owyhee, A Recreation Area of Promise" (mimeographed; [Salem], 1952), p. 1. See also: Wanzer correspondence, various dates, PCS, 3, and RSP, 20.

18. Sawyer to Van Duzer, 24 Aug. 1927, PCS, 1.

19. HCM, 13 Aug., 1 and 20 Sept. 1920, 6: 1044, 1052, 1071; Cheney to Klein, 16 July 1921; Cheney to Booth, 31 Aug. 1921; J. C. Ainsworth to Booth, 15 Sept. 1921, HDP, 151.

20. Chapter One. See also: Portland *Oregonian,* 4 Feb. 1911, 17 Aug. 1919; Lancaster, *The Columbia,* p. 118; Lockley, *A History of the Columbia River Valley,* 1: 630, 832.

21. Ainsworth to Booth, 25 May 1921, HDP, 151.

22. Cheney to Klein, 16 July 1921; Cheney to Booth, 31 Aug. 1921, HDP, 151. Failing to win a position with the state, Cheney soon left for California where he was active in planning development at Palos Verdes and in working for state parks. Earlier he had done similar work in Kansas City. See: Cheney to J. B. Yeon, 12 Feb. 1923; Cheney to Klein, 21 Feb. 1923, HDP, 151; Cheney to Newton Drury, 25 Aug. 1926, NCSPP.

23. HCM, 1 and 20 Sept. 1921, 6: 1052, 1071; N. J. Drew to Natural Parks Association of Washington, 6 Mar. 1922, HDP, 151. See also: Drew to Herbert Nunn, 14 Feb. 1922, HDP, 151.

24. Van Duzer to Sawyer, 13 Dec. 1927, PCS, 3; Sawyer to Boardman, 18 May 1939, 13 Feb. 1952, RSP, 3. Officially called the Advisory Committee on Roadside Planting until August 1928, when it became the Highway Parks and Recreation Committee, the group was referred to, even in its own minutes, by various titles. Commissioner William Duby referred to it as "the Parks Board, so called." See: Advisory Committee on Roadside Planting, reports of meetings, various dates; Duby to Highway Department, 28 June 1926, HDP, 112–9C.

25. Portland *Oregonian,* 24 and 25 Dec. 1924, 21 June 1925; Armstrong, *History of Oregon Parks,* pp. 6–11, 14, 33; Oregon State Highway Commission, *Sixth Biennial Report* (Salem: State Printer, 1924), pp. 85–86; Advisory Committee, report of meeting, 26–27 March 1926; Klein to Raymond H. Torrey, 28 June 1926, HDP, 112–9C.

26. Van Duzer to Sawyer, 13 Dec. 1927, PCS, 1; Advisory Committee, reports of meetings, 11–12 May and 3 Aug. 1928, HDP, 112–9C; Armstrong, *History of Oregon Parks,* pp. 7, 8–10.

27. Sawyer to Van Duzer, 27 July 1928, PCS, 3; Advisory Committee, report of meeting, 3 Aug. 1928, HDP, 112–9C. Additional correspondence regarding Sawyer's work for a park in the fossil beds is in PCS and RSP, *passim*.

28. Sawyer to Van Duzer, 10 Nov. 1927; Van Duzer to Sawyer, 11 Nov. 1927, PCS, 1.

29. Cuthbert to Van Duzer, 7 Nov. 1927; Outdoor Recreation Committee, Portland Chamber of Commerce, minutes of meeting, 25 Oct. 1927, PCS, 1; Buck to Klein, 21 Oct. 1927, HDP, 112–9C. Van Duzer's influence with the Chamber of Commerce partially stemmed from the fact that he was a former president of the organization.

30. Sawyer to Van Duzer, 10 Nov. 1927, PCS, 1. Sawyer had doubts that a volunteer group would prove viable in Oregon, but John C. Merriam pushed the idea with enthusiasm and Sawyer cooperated. See: Merriam to Sawyer, 19 Aug. 1928, PCS, 2; Sawyer to Van Duzer, 6 July and 28 Aug. 1928; Van Duzer to Sawyer, 7 July 1928, PCS, 3.

31. Cuthbert to Thomsen, 3 Feb. 1929, PCS, 2.

32. Van Duzer to Sawyer, 5 Nov. 1927, PCS, 3; Klein to Highway Commission, 10 Nov. 1927, PCS, 2. Beatrice Ward Nelson, the executive secretary of the National Conference on State Parks, remained skeptical of the efficacy of Oregon's approach. See: Nelson, *State Recreation*, p. 8.

33. Sawyer to Patterson, 3 Oct. 1928, PCS, 2.

34. Patterson to Sawyer, 9 Oct. 1929, PCS, 3; Patterson, *Message to the Thirty-Fifth Legislative Assembly.* See also: Advisory Committee, report of meeting, 3 Aug. 1928, HDP, 112–9C. Stephen Mather had attended the NCSP meetings in California. As Newton Drury later recalled, he "was the dominant leader and tremendous impetus was given to our California State Park program thereby." Sawyer does not seem to have mentioned Mather's influence on him at this point, but, active as he was by this time in pushing for state parks, he surely welcomed renewed contact with the Park Service director. Drury to Harlean James, 9 Sept. 1946, NCSPP.

35. Patterson to Sawyer, 6 July 1929, PCS, 2; Sawyer to H. B. Glaisyer, 20 June 1952; Glaisyer to Sawyer, 8 Aug. 1952, RSP, 9; HCM, 22 May 1929, 12: 2514; Samuel H. Boardman, "Oregon's State Parks and Roadside Timber Program," *Commonwealth Review*, New Series, 21 (1939): 140; Oregon, Secretary of State, *Oregon Blue Book, 1929–1930* (Salem: State Printer, 1929), p. 12; Armstrong, *History of Oregon Parks,* pp. 10–11, 33.

36. Booth to Olcott, 23 Aug. 1920, BOP, 3; Boardman to C. H. Reynolds, 13 Feb. 1952, PRDP, Boardman files, 1950–51; Armstrong, *History of Oregon Parks,* p. 15; Sawyer to Bernard Mainwaring, 11 July 1927, PCS, 3; Bone, *Oregon Cattleman/Governor,* pp. 233–34.

37. Klein to E. D. Merrill, 4 Sept. 1929; Ray Conway to Klein, 28 Aug. 1929, HDP, 112–9C; Oregon State Parks Commission, minutes of meeting, 24 July 1929, PRDP, Boardman files; Glaisyer to Sawyer, 8 Aug. 1952, RSP, 28; C. E. Greider, "The Parks, Parkways and Recreation Areas Study," *Commonwealth Review* New Series, 20 (1938): 532. That Patterson's interest in parks

was genuine is made clear by correspondence in PCS, 3. Until his death in late 1929, Patterson took an active interest in the Highway Commission's parks work.

38. Jean Ewen to Klein, 23 July 1929; William Maskell to Klein, 27 July 1929; A. L. Olmsted to Klein, 31 July 1929; Mark Astrup to Klein, 3 Aug. 1929, HDP, 112–9C.

39. Klein to Astrup, 9 Aug. 1929, PRDP, main office files; Klein to A. L. Peck, 9 Aug. 1929; Klein to Ewen, 9 Aug. 1929, HDP, 112–9C. Years later Astrup did become Parks Superintendent, serving in that position from January 1961 to July 1962. See: Armstrong, *History of Oregon Parks,* p. 76; Oakridge (Oregon) *Telegram,* 3 Dec. 1968.

40. Sawyer, undated memo; Boardman to Sawyer, 2 June 1930, PCS, 3; Van Duzer to Sawyer, 17 July 1930, PCS, 4; Sawyer to Chapman, 8 July 1930, PCS, 1. For reactions to Sawyer's ouster, see, RSP, 14 and PCS, 1, commissioner file.

41. *Bend Bulletin,* 1 Oct. 1953; Charles A. Sprague to author, 20 Sept. 1968, Thomas R. Cox, personal correspondence, San Diego, Calif.

42. Boardman to Sawyer, 19 Feb. 1952, RSP, 3.

5.   ASAHEL CURTIS, HERBERT EVISON, AND THE PARKS AND ROADSIDE TIMBER OF WASHINGTON STATE

1. James, *Land Planning,* pp. 197–98. One product of these rising concerns was the Washington State Conservation Society, organized in 1926 as the Washington State Society for the Conservation of Wildflowers. See: Mrs. Alexander F. McEwan, undated typescript account, Washington State Conservation Society Papers (University of Washington Library, Seattle), box 5, file 9.

2. See: Susan R. Schrepfer, *The Fight to Save the Redwoods: A History of Environmental Reform, 1917–1978* (Madison: University of Wisconsin Press, 1983).

3. Pollard, *History of Washington,* 4: 726–27; *Seattle Times,* 8 Mar. 1941; *Seattle Post-Intelligencer,* 10 Mar. 1941; Archie Satterfield, *Seattle: An Asahel Curtis Portfolio* (San Francisco: Chronicle Books, 1985), pp. 118–28.

4. See: [Asahel Curtis], *Rainier National Park, Washington* ([Seattle, c. 1913]); David Sucher, ed., *The Asahel Curtis Sampler: Photographs of Puget Sound Past* (Seattle: Puget Sound Access, 1973); Richard Frederick and Jeanne Engerman, eds., *Asahel Curtis: Photographs of the Great Northwest* (Tacoma: Washington State Historical Society, 1983); Richard Frederick, "Photographer Asahel Curtis: Chronicler of the Northwest," *American West* 17 (Nov.–Dec. 1980): 26–40; G. Thomas Edwards, "Irrigation in Eastern Washington: The Promotional Photographs of Asahel Curtis," *PNQ* 72 (1981): 112–20.

5. *Seattle Times,* 8 Mar. 1941; *The Mountaineer,* 35 (Apr. 1941), 1.

6. T. H. Martin, "Proceedings from Several Meetings," Tacoma, 18 Mar. 1912, ACP, Mt. Rainier Scrapbook No. 2.

7. Arthur D. Martinson, "Mount Rainier National Park: First Years," *Forest History* 10 (Oct. 1966): 28–29. For a full discussion of the controversy over the name, see: Martinson, "Mountain in the Sky: A History of Mount Rainier National Park" (Ph.D. diss., Washington State University, 1966), pp. 120–37.

8. Asahel Curtis and T. H. Martin to Walter L. Fisher, 15 Apr. 1912, Mount Rainier National Park Papers (Mount Rainier National Park Headquarters, Longmire, Washington [archive no. 350.03 N1; hereafter MRNPP]), box 201, file 011.

9. Samuel Christopher Lancaster, "Report to Seattle-Tacoma Rainier National Park Committee," 22 Apr. 1913, ibid.; Martinson, "Mount Rainier National Park," pp. 31–33; Arthur D. Martinson, *Wilderness above the Sound* (Flagstaff, Ariz.: Northland Press, 1986), pp. 55–59.

10. On the founding of NPA, see: Shankland, *Steve Mather*, p. 195; Everett G. Griggs to Robert Moran, 29 Nov. 1919, RMP, 2–21. The quotation is from Herbert Evison, "Sixty Miles Nearer to Mount Rainier," Seattle *Town Crier* 12 (24 Jan. 1920): 17.

11. Curtis was a natural person to invite. His photographs of Mount Rainier and other scenic sites were already well known in the state, and he had been active in the Seattle-Tacoma joint committee. The vice-presidents included leading lumber industry, university, community, and government figures. See: Griggs to Moran, 29 Nov. 1919, RMP, 2–21.

12. Evison, "Sixty Miles Nearer," p. 17. On the Carbon River route, see: Martinson, "Mountain in the Sky," pp. 14–19.

13. *Natural Parks Bulletin* 2 (Jan. 1922): 2; Horace Albright to Curtis, 16 Dec. 1929; Curtis to O. A. Tomlinson, 6 Mar. 1930, Rainier National Park Advisory Board [hereafter RNPAB], minutes, 8 Jan. 1931, MRNPP, A1615, 1929–41. No complete file of the *Bulletin* seems to be extant; individual copies are found in the papers of Moran, Curtis, and other conservationists of the period as well as in those of the National Conference on State Parks.

14. Herbert Witherspoon to Moran, 1 July 1921, RMP, 2–23; Whitcomb to Meany, 25 July 1921, EMP, 36–27; *Proceedings of the Second National Conference on State Parks* ([Washington, D.C.: National Conference on State Parks], 1923), pp. 121–22, 154–57.

15. Witherspoon to Moran, 19 Sept. 1922, RMP, 2–29; Evison to [Moran], n.d., RMP, 2–51.

16. Quoted in *Natural Parks Bulletin* 2 (Oct. 1921): 1–3.

17. Ibid. 1 (Aug. 1920): 1–2; 2 (Oct. 1921): 1; 3 (Nov. 1922): 1.

18. Evison to Moran, 2 Sept. 1920, RMP, 2–20.

19. Ibid., 10 Feb. 1921; Evison to Curtis, 10 Feb. 1921, ACP, 1–35; Allen to Moran, 24 March 1921, RMP, 2–18; Washington, *House Journal of the Seventeenth Session . . . 1921* (Olympia: State Printer, 1921), pp. 442, 566–67; ibid., *Senate Journal*, p. 543.

20. Evison to Curtis, 19 Mar. [1921 misdated 1920], ACP, 1–33.

21. Curtis to Culp, 23 Feb. 1921, ACP, 1–35.

22. Ibid.; *Natural Parks Bulletin* 2 (Jan. 1922): 1.

23. Evison to Curtis, 12 Dec. 1922, ACP, 2–8.

24. Curtis to Evison, 18 Dec. 1922, ibid.

25. Moran to Clifford Babcock, 25 Jan. 1923, RMP, 2–30.

26. Virgil Frits to Moran, 21 Jan. 1923, RMP, 2–39.

27. *Natural Parks Bulletin* 2 (Jan. 1922): 1. Moran and Savidge shared Donovan's view that parks were a natural adjunct of highways. Moran wrote somewhat later, "Mr. Savidge expressed himself of the mind that the whole State Park business should be administered by the Highway Department to which I agree as I look on a State Park as simply a turnout on a highway." Moran to Curtis, 19 Sept. 1925, ACP, 2–40.

28. Ibid. 3 (Nov. 1922): 1; (Apr. 1923): 1.

29. Evison to Moran, 19 Jan. 1923, RMP, 2–19; Mabel I. Miller to Moran, 3 Feb. 1923, RMP, 2–3; V. J. Capron to Moran, 5 Mar. 1923, RMP, 2–34; NCSP, *Proceedings, Fourth Conference,* pp. 103–4.

30. *Natural Parks Bulletin* 3 (July 1923): 1; Evison to Moran, 13 Apr. 1923, RMP, 2–19.

31. NCSP, *Proceedings, Fourth Conference,* p. 104; Seattle *Post-Intelligencer,* 13 and 14 Mar. 1924.

32. *Natural Parks Bulletin* 4 (Sept. 1924): 1.

33. W. H. Peters to George E. Goodwin, n.d., ACP, 2–8.

34. *Natural Parks Bulletin* 4 (Sept. 1924): 1; Moran to Evison, 18 Sept. 1924, RMP, 2–46; Babcock to Moran, 2 Jan. 1925, RMP, 2–52; Evison to [Moran], n.d., RMP, 2–51.

35. *Natural Parks Bulletin* 4 (Sept. 1924): 1; National Conference on Outdoor Recreation, "A Report . . .", Senate Document 158, 70th Cong., 1st Sess. (Washington: GPO, 1928). See, also: Curtis to Chauncey Hamlin, 24 Oct. 1924; L. F. Kneipp to Curtis, 3 Nov. 1924, ACP; James B. Trefethen, "The 1928 'ORRC'," *American Forests* 68 (Mar. 1962): 8, 38–39.

36. For examples of these varying views, see: Henry S. Graves, journal of trip to Alaska in 1915, entries for 18–20 July, Graves Papers, box 2; George H. Cecil to Ben Olcott, 2 Feb. 1922, RSP, 46; R. Y. Stuart to Charles L. McNary, 1 Oct. 1929; Paul Grieder to William C. Duby, 15 Nov. 1929; Grieder to Robert W. Sawyer, 8 Dec. 1934, RSP, 28.

37. On Hartley, see: Albert Frances Gunns, "Roland Hill Hartley and the Politics of Washington State" (M.A. thesis, University of Washington, 1963); Herbert Hunt and Floyd C. Kaylor, *Washington West of the Cascades* (3 vols., Chicago: S. J. Clarke Publishing Co., 1917), 2: 172–77; Robert E. Ficken, *Lumber and Politics: The Career of Mark E. Reed* (Santa Cruz, Calif., and Seattle: Forest History Society and University of Washington Press, 1979), pp. 93–131 and passim; Maude Sweetman, *What Price Politics? The Inside Story of Washington State Politics* (Seattle: White & Hitchcock Corp., 1927), pp. 46–47, 82–83; Gordon Newell, *Rogues, Buffoons, & Statesmen* (Seattle: Hangman Press, 1975), pp. 321–63.

38. Gunns, "Hartley," pp. 38, 54–55, 65, 68–70; Ficken, *Lumber and Politics,* pp. 93, 94, 99; Jonathan Dembo, *Unions and Politics in Washington State, 1885–1935* (New York: Garland Publishing Co., 1983), pp. 115, 371–72;

E. L. French, statement, n.d. (Pacific Northwest Room, Henry Suzzalo Library, University of Washington, Seattle), vertical file, Washington governors—Hartley folder.

39. As quoted in Gunns, "Hartley," p. 77. See, also: Sweetman, *What Price Politics?*, pp. 48–49.

40. Gunns, "Hartley," p. 104. See, also: ibid., 77, 80–81, 100–1, 186.

41. Ibid., 82–133; Dembo, *Unions and Politics*, pp. 390–1, 394–95; Curtis to Christie Thomas, 21 Dec. 1925; Curtis to J. Grant Hinkle, 22 Dec. 1925, ACP, 3–7; Moran to Evison, 16 Dec. 1925, RMP, 2–48; Evison to Moran, 18 Dec. 1925, RMP, 2–47; *State Recreation* 1 (March 1927): 5. See, also: Evison to [Moran], n.d., RMP, 2–51. *State Recreation* was the periodical of the National Conference on State Parks; copies may be found in the NCSP papers.

42. Savidge to George F. Meacham, 20 Apr. 1926, ACP, 3–23.

43. Witherspoon to Moran, 19 Sept. 1922, RMP, 2–29; Evison to Mather, 22 May 1923, NCSPP, 1; *Natural Parks Bulletin* 4 (Sept. 1924): 1; Evison to [Moran], n.d., RMP, 2–51; Charles W. Saunders to Curtis, 27 Apr. 1926, ACP, 3–23; Curtis to Evison, 24 Mar. 1930, ACP, 7–17.

44. Curtis to Evison, 8 June 1925, ACP, 2–36. For all his setbacks, Curtis remained optimistic. He told a Good Roads Association meeting in Wenatchee: "There is going to be considerable doing in State Parks before long." See: Curtis to J. L. Tucker, 4 June 1925, ibid.

45. Curtis to H. Hafenbrack, 22 July 1927, ACP, 4–23.

46. Curtis to Savidge, 22 and 27 July 1927, ACP, 4–23; Beatrice M. Ward to Curtis, 1 Dec. 1927, ACP, 4–33.

47. Savidge to Curtis, 26 July 1927, ACP, 4–23.

48. Curtis to Moran, 12 Nov. 1930, ACP, 8–10; Ward to Curtis, 1 Dec. 1927, ACP, 4–33.

49. Evison to [Moran], n.d., RMP, 2–51. See, also: Rutherford to Moran, 4 Feb. 1925, RMP, 2–49.

50. Moran to Curtis, 15 Nov. 1930, ACP, 8–10; Curtis to Evison, 21 June 1929, ACP, 6–15. In 1931 the State Chamber of Commerce finally began to function in the capacity that Curtis had urged earlier through its Recreation Development Committee. Curtis played a key role. See: Curtis to P. T. Harris, 9 June 1931; Curtis to Douglas Shelor, 10 June 1931, ACP, 8–31 (this file also contains numerous other items dealing with this subject); Curtis to E. A. Smith, 22 July 1932, ACP, 9–32.

51. Gunns, "Hartley," pp. 128, 134–82, 188–220; Ficken, *Lumber and Politics*, pp. 112–31; Dembo, *Unions and Politics*, pp. 424–25, 428–30, 436–37, 441–42, 462–65; Sweetman, *What Price Politics?*, pp. 128–31; Curtis to Harold Stewart, 18 June 1929, ACP, 6–14.

52. Curtis to members RNPAB, 27 Mar. 1929; Curtis to H. R. Nelson, 28 Mar. 1929; Curtis to Savidge, 28 Mar. 1929, ACP, 6–8 (quotation); F. O. Hagie to Curtis, 29 Mar. 1929; Moran to Curtis, 27 Mar. 1930, ACP, 7–17.

53. Savidge to Curtis, 29 Mar. 1929, ACP, 6–8; Evison to Curtis, 8 June 1929, ACP, 6–14. Curtis was by now growing bitter from frustration. He told Evison "the only thing we can do is get things just as bad as we possibly can

with the hope that eventually there will be a revolt and overthrow the whole [Hartley] crowd." Curtis to Evison, 21 June 1929, ACP, 6–15. See, also: Edward W. Allen to Curtis, 8 Sept. 1932, EMP, 48–26.

54. Curtis to Moran, 12 Nov. 1930, ACP, 8–10.

55. Beatrice Ward (later Beatrice Ward Nelson) had served as secretary of NCSP from 1921 to 1929. Evison followed, continuing in that position until 1934 when, short on funds, the NCSP combined its secretariat with that of the American Civic and Planning Association. Harlean James held the joint position for many years thereafter. Evison went to work for the National Park Service in 1934, serving first as liaison with the states on work carried out in state parks by the CCC under NPS direction, later as Associate Regional Director of Region I, and then as Chief of Information.

56. Ward to Curtis, 1 Dec. 1929, ACP, 4–33. See, also: Evison to Curtis, 7 Nov. 1929, ACP, 6–28; ibid., 25 Nov. 1929, 6–29; and Chapter Four.

57. *State Recreation* 1 (Mar. 1927): 5; Cora C. Whitley to Mather, 11 June 1926, NCSPP, 1; "Conservation in Washington," undated typescript report, Washington State Conservation Society Papers, 5–9.

58. Curtis to Hagie, 20 Oct. 1927; T. H. Martin to Curtis, 21 Oct. 1927; Robert Sterling Yard to Curtis, 24 Oct. 1927, ACP, 4–29 (there is additional correspondence on the subject in this file). The tramway was but part of the larger question of how much development should be allowed in the park. Curtis tended to favor development, but apparently took no stand on the tramway proposal. Still, his general position caused some tension with the Mountaineers; its secretary told Curtis pointedly, "we oppose turning the entire park over to automobilists and believe that a well-rounded system includes the preservation of substantial wilderness areas." See: Curtis to Martin, 21 Nov. 1924, ACP, 2–27; J. F. Beede to Curtis, 21 June 1927, ACP, 4–29. The tramway question was not exclusively, or even primarily, focused on Mount Rainier. See: Richard Carter Davis, "Wilderness, Politics, and Bureaucracy: Federal and State Policies in the Administration of San Jacinto Mountain, California, 1920–1968" (Ph.D. diss., University of California, Riverside, 1973); Scott, *We Climb High*, pp. 31, 34, 37; *Mazama* 9 (Jan. 1927): 4–7; (Mar. 1927): 9–10; (Apr. 1927): 4–5; (May 1927): 4–5; (Sept. 1927): 7; 11 (Sept. 1929): 9.

59. Rudo L. Fromme, "Random Recollections Regarding the Old, Original, Opulent, Often Cozy Olympic National Forest, with a Sidetrack for some Siskiyou Swan Songs," typescript, Fromme Papers (Henry Suzzallo Library, University of Washington, Seattle), pp. 112–16; Asahel Curtis to C. M. Grainger, 25 Sept. 1929, ACP, 6–23. Cf. Curtis to Yard, 25 Sept. 1929, ACP, 6–23; Grant to Curtis, 16 July 1932, ACP, 9–32; Curtis, "The Proposed Mount Olympus National Park," *American Forests* 42 (1936): 166–69, 195–96. Curtis's switch of support from the Park Service to the Forest Service put him in an untenable position and led to his resignation as chairman of the RNPAB in 1936. See: Curtis to C. B. Blethen, 29 Aug. 1925, ACP, 2–39; T. A. Stevenson to Curtis, 20 May 1936; Stevenson to Tomlinson, 28 May 1936, MRNPP, A1615, 1929–41; ACP, 10 and 11, passim. For further insights, see:

Elmo Richardson, "Olympic National Park: Twenty Years of Controversy," *Forest History* 12 (Apr. 1969): 6–15; Michael G. Schene, "Only the Squeal Left: Conflict over Establishing Olympic National Park," *Pacific Historian* 27 (1983): 53–61; Ben Whitfield Twight, "The Tenacity of Value Commitment: The Forest Service and Olympic National Park" (Ph.D. diss., University of Washington, 1971).

60. Albright to R. Y. Stuart, 24 July 1930; Wallace W. Atwood to Albright, 10 Sept. 1930; Albright to Walter L. Huber, 15 Oct. 1930, MRNPP, 120–11; Curtis to H. A. Rhoads, 24 Nov. 1930; Tomlinson to Samuel J. Humes, 28 Nov. 1930; Curtis to Tomlinson, 2 Dec. 1930; Humes to Tomlinson, 16 Dec. 1930; Curtis to members RNPAB, 26 Dec. 1930, ibid., 620; RNPAB, minutes, 8 Jan. 1931, ibid., A1615, 1929–41; Martinson, "Mountain in the Sky," pp. 79–81, 104–5.

61. Robert N. McIntyre, *Mather Memorial Parkway: A Brief History* (mimeographed, [Longmire, Wash.: Mount Rainier National Park], 1952), p. 1; Martinson, *Wilderness above the Sound,* pp. 59–60.

62. J. A. McKinnon to Curtis, 8 Nov. 1928; Curtis to McKinnon, 12 Nov. 1928; F. W. Mathias to Curtis, 10 Nov. 1928; Harry M. Myers to Curtis, 12 Nov. 1928, ACP, 5–25; Curtis to McKinnon, 11 Feb. 1929, ACP, 6–2; ibid., 10 March 1932, ACP, 9–18.

63. Evison to Curtis, 7 Feb. 1929, ACP, 6–2; McIntyre, *Mather Memorial Parkway,* p. 1; Shankland, *Steve Mather,* p. 284. After his stroke, Mather's sole continued activity was as a director of the NCSP; its work, an associate explained, was "very close to his heart." Arno Cammerer to W. T. Grant, 3 Oct. 1929, NCSPP.

64. Evison to Curtis, 7 Feb. 1929, ACP, 6–2; Curtis to Evison, 21 Jan. 1930; Evison to Curtis, 5 Feb. 1930, ACP, 7–5; Buck to Forester, 25 Mar. 1930, ACP, 7–17; Curtis to Evison, 18 Mar. 1933, ACP, 10–7 (much additional correspondence on this subject is in ACP, 7 and 8, passim); RNPAB, minutes, 8 Jan. 1931, MRNPP, A1615; Tomlinson to Albright, 9 Jan. 1931, ibid., 120–11; Shankland, *Steve Mather,* pp. 284–91; Donald C. Swain, *Wilderness Defender: Horace M. Albright and Conservation* (Chicago: University of Chicago Press, 1970), pp. 182–83. Regional Forester Buck noted that Curtis was "very insistent" that the parkway be administered by the Forest Service, rather than the Park Service.

65. Copies of the orders are in MRNPP, 120–11. See, also: McIntyre, *Mather Memorial Parkway,* pp. i [sic]-2; Shankland, *Steve Mather,* pp. 287–88.

66. Curtis to T. A. Stevenson, 24 Dec. 1931, ACP, 9–10; Curtis to Chester W. Cleveland, 13 July 1932, ACP, 9–32; McIntyre, *Mather Memorial Parkway,* pp. 2–3. Cf. Sweetman, *What Price Politics?,* pp. 128–35.

67. RNPAB, minutes, 8 Jan. 1931; Curtis to members RNPAB, 12 Aug. and 30 Dec. 1931; Curtis to Buck, n.d. [1931]; Curtis to Tomlinson, 13 Feb. 1931; Tomlinson to Curtis, 17 Feb. 1931, MRNPP, A1615, 1929–41; Allen to Curtis, 8 Sept. 1932, EMP, 48–26; Gunns, "Hartley," pp. 185, 190–98. Hartley continued to be uninterested in state parks as a whole. For a classic example of his manipulation of highway funds, see: Overlook Improvement

Club to Seattle Chamber of Commerce [with enclosure], 26 Dec. 1931, ACP, 9–10.

68. Humes to Curtis, 23 Jan. 1932; Curtis to Humes, 25 Jan. 1932; Curtis to Tomlinson, 25 Jan. 1932, ACP, 9–12; Curtis to McKinnon, 10 Mar. 1932, ACP, 9–18; Curtis to Howard A. Hanson, 9 May 1932, ACP, 9–22; Humes to Curtis, 19 May 1932; Alexander Baillie to Curtis, 20 May 1932; Mark Gray to Curtis, 20 May 1932, ACP, 9–24.

69. Tomlinson, statement at dedication, 2 July 1932; Curtis to Tomlinson, 5 July and 15 Sept. 1932, MRNPP, 608–01; Tomlinson to Albright, 8 July 1932, ibid., 608-Ml; *Rainier National Park News*, 10–17 July 1932, p. 1, copies in ibid. Curtis, Tomlinson, and residents of Yakima all wanted truck traffic banned from the route or regulated so that tourist value would not be harmed.

70. Curtis to Evison, 11 Feb. 1929, ACP, 6–2. See, also: Curtis to McKinnon, 11 Feb. 1929, ibid.

71. Curtis to Hagie, 14 July 1932, ACP, 9–32; Harry M. Myers to Curtis, 8 Feb. 1933, ACP, 10–6; RNPAB to legislature, 16 Jan. 1933; Curtis to Governor C. D. Martin, 9 Mar. 1933; Curtis to Buck, 18 Mar. 1933; Curtis to Franklin Adams, 18 Mar. 1933; Evison to Curtis, 22 Mar. 1933, ACP, 10–7. See, also: McKinnon to Curtis, 8 Nov. 1928; Curtis to McKinnon, 12 Nov. 1928, ACP, 5–25; Curtis to Tomlinson, 29 Apr. 1931, ACP, 8–28.

72. Curtis to Hartley, 30 Jan. 1933, ACP, 10–5.

73. Curtis to Evison, 18 Mar. 1933; Curtis to Buck, 18 Mar. 1933, ACP, 10–7.

74. McIntyre, *Mather Memorial Parkway*, p. 3; Myers to Curtis, 8 Feb. 1933, ACP, 10–6; E. N. Hutchinson to Curtis, 15 Nov. 1933, ACP, 10–17.

75. Asahel Curtis, "Washington's State Parks," *Argus* 41 (15 Dec. 1934): 19; Weigle to Meany, 5 Mar. 1933, EMP, 49–16; Curtis to Savidge, 15 July 1932, ACP, 9–32; Evison to Curtis, 22 Mar. 1933, ACP, 10–7. On Weigle's pre-park years, see: "W. G. Weigle's Early Experiences" (mimeographed; n.p., n.d.), copy in Fromme papers.

76. Curtis, "Washington's State Parks," pp. 18–26 (quotation p. 19).

77. *Seattle Post-Intelligencer*, 8 Mar. 1941.

6. SAMUEL H. BOARDMAN: *The Preservationist as Administrator*

1. Sawyer to H. B. Glaisyer, 12 Aug. 1952, RSP, 9; Boardman to R. H. Baldock, 4 Aug. 1936, PRDP, Boardman file, 1936–38; Van Duzer to Sawyer, n.d., PCS, 1; Boardman to Douglas McKay, 3 July 1953, PRDP, Boardman files, misc. On Klein, see: Portland *Oregonian*, 3 and 4 June 1971.

2. Biographical information on Boardman is scattered. See: "Wayland's Who's Who," *Wayland Greetings* 38 (Dec. 1947): 5–7; Boardman to Lewis A. MacArthur, 9 Mar. 1943, PRDP, Boardman files, 1941–43; Portland *Oregonian*, 10 Nov. 1946, 15 June and 9 July 1950; Portland *Oregon Journal*, 5 and 23 June 1950, 21 Aug. 1962; *Salem Capital Journal*, 29 June 1950.

3. Samuel H. Boardman, "A Narrative of a Tree Born of the Desert" (mimeographed; [Salem], 1952), copy in PRDP, Boardman files. A shorter version appears in Boardman, "Brief History." See, also: *Arlington Bulletin*, 6 Oct. 1939; Tom Lawson McCall, "His Love of Trees Built State Parks," *Oregonian*, 21 May 1939.

4. Armstrong, *History of Oregon Parks*, pp. 15–16; Bone, *Oregon Cattleman/ Governor*, pp. 240–42; Sawyer to Bernard Mainwairing, 11 July 1927, PCS, 3; Boardman to C. H. Reynolds, 13 Feb. 1952, PRDP, Boardman files, 1950–51; Portland *Oregonian*, 2 and 6 Apr. 1924.

5. Boardman, "Brief History," pp. 227–29. See, also: Boardman to J. D. Wood, 4 Mar. 1933, PRDP, Boardman files, personal, 1936–38; Boardman to Charles H. Reynolds, 13 Feb. 1952, ibid., 1950–51.

6. Boardman to Klein, 26 April 1925; Klein to Boardman, 27 Oct. 1927; Boardman to Wanzer, 12 Nov. 1927, HDP, 112–9C; Boardman to Sawyer, 22 Oct. 1927; Boardman to H.G. Smith, 29 Nov. 1927; W. S. Nelson to Oregon State Highway Commission, 16 Nov. 1927, PCS, 2; Boardman to Baldock, 4 Aug. 1936, PRDP, Boardman files, 1936–38; G. L. Hoffman to Julius Meyer, 10 Apr. 1933, ibid., 1941–43; Portland *Oregonian*, 20 Oct. 1927. Sawyer had the program reinstituted when he became a commissioner. See: Sawyer to Boardman, 22 Oct. 1927, PCS, 2; HCM, 27 Mar. 1928, 12: 2316.

7. Samuel H. Boardman, Field Engineer's Weekly Reports, Aug.–Sept. 1929; Armstrong to Glaisyer, 13 Aug. 1952; Grace Chamberlain to Boardman, 30 Aug. 1951, PRDP, Boardman files; Boardman to Sawyer, 31 Aug. 1929; Glaisyer to Sawyer, 8 Aug. 1952; Sawyer to Glaisyer, 12 Aug. 1952, RSP, 9.

8. A full study of the struggle to save roadside timber in the West is needed. For introductions to the effort in Oregon, see: Robert W. Sawyer, "Save Oregon Scenery," *Commonwealth Review of the University of Oregon* New Series, 16 (1936), 14–20; Samuel H. Boardman, "Oregon's State Park and Roadside Timber Program," ibid., pp. 137–41; Oregon State Planning Board, *Preservation of Oregon Roadside Timber* [Salem, 1938], pp. 7–51. Boardman summed up his own views on the preservation of roadside timber in a letter to Sawyer. "What assininity," he wrote, "to construct a road system second to none and then stand by while the very panes of the windows of our souls are shattered in a million pieces." Boardman to Sawyer, 1 June 1932, RSP, 3.

9. Sawyer to Van Duzer, 19 Aug. 1929, PCS, 3.

10. Van Duzer to Sawyer, 24 Oct. 1929, ibid.

11. Sawyer to Boardman, 13 Feb. 1952, RSP, 3. See, also: Sawyer to Boardman, 18 May 1939, ibid.; Sawyer to Albright, 6 Feb. 1953, ibid., 1. Van Duzer's contributions were officially acknowledged in 1939 when, at Boardman's suggestion, a six-mile strip of roadside timber along the Salmon River Highway in the Coast Range was named the Henry B. Van Duzer Forest Corridor. See: *Timberman* 61 (Apr. 1939): 76.

12. Boardman to Sawyer, 19 Feb. 1952, ibid., 3.

13. Conrad Wirth, "Parks for the Millions," *American Forestry* 40 (1932): 531–32; Franklin Delano Roosevelt, "Speech at the Dedication of the Shenandoah National Park," in Edgar B. Nixon, ed., *Franklin D. Roosevelt &*

Conservation (Hyde Park, N.Y.: Franklin D. Roosevelt Library, 1957), 1: 537–39; "A New Defender of the Wilderness," *Nature Magazine* 26 (1935): 178–79; Lena F. Dalton, "Conservation," *Commonwealth Review of the University of Oregon* New Series, 16 (June 1936): 149; Pomeroy, *In Search of the Golden West*, p. 155.

14. Boardman, "Brief History," p. 206; Boardman, "Oregon's Park and Roadside Timber Program," p. 139; Boardman to Marshall Dana, 4 Aug. 1933, PRDP, policy files; Boardman to editor, *Oregon Journal*, 9 Mar. 1936; Boardman to Baldock, 10 June 1937, PRDP, Boardman files, 1936–38; Boardman to Newton B. Drury, 24 Mar. 1941, ibid., 1941–43; Boardman to Redwood Empire Association, 23 Jan. 1945, ibid.

15. Minutes, meeting of 24 July 1929, PRDP, Boardman files, misc.; Armstrong, *History of Oregon Parks*, p. 10 (quotation).

16. Boardman, "Brief History," p. 198. A fuller account is Samuel H. Boardman, "Guy W. Talbot and George Joseph State Parks," (mimeographed; [Salem], 1952), PRDP, Boardman files.

17. Boardman to Sawyer, 17 May 1939, 8 June 1940 (quotations); Boardman to D. H. Peoples, 17 May 1939. Sawyer, his own tastes changing, agreed. As he put it, "I think now that tree planting almost anywhere along the highway is a mistake." He singled out Boardman's earlier plantings as an example: "since the trees are not native and since their presence produces an incongruous effect in the desert setting, they are quite out of place." Sawyer to Boardman, 18 May 1939, RSP, 2.

18. Boardman to Frank A. Kittredge, 25 July 1940; Boardman to Baldock, 27 Nov. 1940, PRDP, Boardman files, 1938–40. See, also: Boardman to Baldock, 26 Nov. 1934, ibid., 1936–38: Boardman to Sam Bellah, 5 Nov. 1934, ibid., 1934–50.

19. Boardman to Frank A. Kittredge, 25 July 1940, PRDP, Boardman files, 1941–43.

20. Boardman to Sawyer, 2 Feb. 1934, RSP, 3. The Salmon River holdings he refers to became the Van Duzer Forest Corridor.

21. Ibid., 14 Mar. and 10 Sept. 1934.

22. Armstrong, *History of Oregon Parks*, pp. 182–83; Boardman, "Brief History," pp. 194–96; Wirth, "Parks for the Millions," pp. 505–7 (first quotation, p. 507); Boardman to Sawyer, 2 Feb. 1934, RSP, 3; Leonard L. Hohl to Eighth Regional Office, 18 Feb. 1936, National Park Service Records, RG 79, Branch of Recreation, Land Planning, and State Cooperation, State Parks Files (National Archives, Washington, D.C. [hereafter NPSSPP]), file 601.03.1, Oregon. One reason for Saddle Mountain's popularity was, as Hohl noted, that the "people of this county are park-minded to an unusual degree. They recognize the fact that logging can not last forever and that outstanding scenic areas are of paramount importance for the day when only the tourist trade (and a little fishing) are left for them." He mentioned especially Judge J. A. Boyington of Astoria and George Henry of Seaside as being "tireless in unending work toward conservation of wooded areas for parks or extension of parks such as Saddle Mountain, Ecola, and Tongue Point."

23. Boardman to Sawyer, 10 Sept. 1934, RSP, 3 (quotation); Boardman to editor, *Oregon Journal*, 9 Mar. 1936.

24. Boardman, "Brief History," pp. 214–15. CCC workers were also instrumental in laying the foundation for state parks systems elsewhere—in New Mexico and Nevada, for examples. See: Elmo R. Richardson, "The Civilian Conservation Corps and the Origins of the New Mexico State Park System," *Natural Resources Journal* 6 (1966): 248–67; David Moore, "Faces of the Valley of Fire," *Nevada* 45 (1985): 6–10; Thomas W. Miller to Harold Fleischhauer, 15 July 1935, Miller Papers (Western History Center, University of Nevada, Reno), box 4; additional material in this collection fills out the Nevada story.

25. Armstrong, *History of Oregon Parks*, pp. 25, 191–94; Boardman, "Brief History," pp. 210–18; Boardman to Baldock, Nov. 1951 (mimeographed recollections of Silver Creek Falls park and demonstration area; copy in PRDP, Boardman files, historical accounts); Hohl to Eighth Regional Office, 18 Feb. 1936; Boardman to Charles L. McNary, 2 Apr. 1938, NPSSPP, 601.03.1, Oregon.

26. Boardman to Sawyer, 29 Aug. 1929, RSP, 3 (quotation); Boardman, "Brief History," pp. 180–83; Boardman to Jessie M. Honeyman, 27 Mar. 1933, PRDP, Boardman files, 1936–38. Boardman returned to this theme again and again.

27. Memo on parks policy, Oct. 1943, PRDP, policy file; Boardman to Sawyer, 1 June 1932, 10 Sept. 1934, RSP, 3; Boardman to Jessie Honeyman, 27 Mar. 1933, PRDP, Boardman personal file, 1936–38; Boardman to Baldock, 22 Mar. 1935, ibid.; Boardman to Honeyman, 6 Oct. 1943, ibid., 1941–43; Boardman to Baldock, 11 Mar. 1941, RSP, 3.

28. Boardman to Sawyer, 18 May 1930, PCS, 1.

29. Boardman to Jessie Honeyman, 27 Mar. 1933, PRDP, Boardman files, 1936–38; Boardman to Baldock, 22 Mar. 1935 and 10 June 1937, ibid.; Boardman to Honeyman, 6 Oct. 1943, ibid., 1941–43; Chester H. Armstrong, interview by author, Salem, Oregon, 6 May 1956.

30. As quoted by Emma Miles, interview, Eugene, Ore., 1 Aug. 1957; Boardman, "Brief History," pp. 208–9; Boardman to Sawyer, 13 Mar. 1933, RSP, 3. Spalding was not alone. Boardman rejoiced that the Highway Department's biennial report to be published in 1933 would be condensed for economy's sake and that expenditures for parks would not be shown. "The 'wolves' are looking for every point of attack," he noted. "Of course," he added with a characteristic mixing of metaphors, "the figures are available for those who seek them, but some bulls are complacent when not flaunted by irritant thoughts." Boardman to Sawyer, 22 Dec. 1932, RSP, 3.

31. Boardman, "Brief History," p. 193. For a fuller account, see: Samuel H. Boardman, "An Unknown Park of Today, A Recreational Paradise of Tomorrow: Henry Newburgh State Park" (mimeographed; [Salem], 1952), copy in PRDP, Boardman files.

32. Boardman, "Brief History," pp. 188, 203, 208, 211–12; Boardman to Sawyer, 2 Feb. 1934, RSP, 3; C. E. Greider, "The Parks, Parkways and

Recreation Areas Study," *Commonwealth Review of the University of Oregon* New Series, 20 (1938): 531–38.

33. Miles, interview; Sawyer to F. L. Stetson, 14 Feb. 1941, RSP, 14; Oregon State Federation of Garden Clubs, minutes of executive board meeting, 1 Mar. 1935, 23 Feb. 1938, Oregon State Federation of Garden Clubs Papers (Oregon Historical Society, Portland); Jessie M. Honeyman to Sawyer, 16 June 1933, PCS, 2; Mrs. J. S. Landers, "Report of the Oregon Roadside Council, 1934 to May 7, 1935," ibid.; Honeyman, "The Present Status of Roadside Beautification Program," *Commonwealth Review of the University of Oregon* New Series, 13 (1931): 176–87; Vina C. Smith, "Oregon Roadside Council: What It Is—What It Does," ibid. 21 (1939): 144–47; Ernestine Moffitt, "Jessie M. Honeyman: Woman of Spirit," *Northwest Magazine*, p. 21, Portland *Sunday Oregonian*, 5 Aug. 1979.

34. HCM, 2 Apr. 1931, 16:2935; S. O. Johnson to Boardman, 19 May 1931; Boardman to Sawyer, 25 May 1931 and 2 Feb. 1934; Sawyer to Boardman, 4 Aug. 1931, 21 Aug. 1936, RSP, 3; Vaughan, *High & Mighty*, p. 43.

35. Sawyer to Charles McNary, 21 Sept. 1929; McNary to Sawyer, 3 Oct. 1929, Robert Y. Stuart to McNary, 1 Oct. 1929, RSP, 11; Boardman to Sawyer, 29 Aug. 1929, 19 June 1931, 1 June 1932 (quotation); Sawyer to Boardman, 4 June 1932, RSP, 3; Oregon State Highway Commission, "Parks Acquisitions Prior to 1930" (mimeographed; [Salem, n.d.]) copies in PRDP, Boardman files, misc. and RSP, 15; *Bend Bulletin*, 11 June 1932. Eventually state holdings on Quartz Mountain reached 311 acres. They were christened Booth Wayside, after former highway commissioner R. A. Booth who donated the first section the state acquired.

36. Boardman to Sawyer, 16 Sept. 1936, RSP, 3. See also Boardman, Weekly Reports, 13 Sept. 1930, PRDP, Boardman files.

37. Boardman to Baldock, 4 Feb., 10 June 1937, PRDP, Boardman files, 1936–38; ibid., 11 Mar. 1941 (quotation), PRDP, Boardman files, 1941–43; Boardman to Sawyer, 16 Sept. 1936, 22 Mar. 1941, RSP, 3. On Ickes, see: Barry Mackintosh, "Harold L. Ickes and the National Park Service," *JFH* 29 (1985): 78–84.

38. Boardman to Baldock, 11 Mar. 1941; Boardman to Drury, 24 Mar. 1941, PRDP, Boardman files, 1941–43. See, also: Drury to Boardman, 13 Aug. 1937 and 17 Apr. 1941, ibid.; Boardman, "Oregon's Park and Roadside Timber Program," p. 139. Boardman frequently exemplified this view by referring to his parks as "sermonettes." See, for example: Boardman to Marshall Dana, 4 Aug. 1933; Boardman to B. F. Irvine, 9 Mar. 1936, RSP, 3.

39. Memo on parks policy, Oct. 1943, PRDP, policy file. See, also: memo dated 12 Mar. 1948, ibid.

40. Boardman to Ainsworth, 30 June 1936; Boardman to Sawyer, 16 Sept. 1936, 22 March 1941; Boardman to Baldock, 11 Mar. 1941, RSP, 3.

41. Frederic Law Olmsted, Jr., *California State Park Survey* (Sacramento: California State Park Commission, 1928), p. 5; New York Conservation Department, *Seventeenth Annual Report* (Albany: J.B. Lyon Co., 1928), pp. 67–68; Ainsworth to Sawyer, 18 June 1936; Boardman to Ainsworth, 30 June,

13 July 1936, RSP, 1; Boardman to Sawyer, 4 July 1936, RSP, 3. Having failed to win a bond issue, Boardman tried to get the Portland Chamber of Commerce to follow the lead of the Save-the-Redwoods League by launching a campaign to match state expenditures on the coast with private funds. This effort also failed. See: Boardman to Sawyer, 9 Aug. 1943, RSP, 3.

42. Leiber to Conrad Wirth, 8 Oct. 1936, NCSPP, 2. See, also Harlean James, "State Parks—A Recognized Land Use" (copy in NCSPP, 2), p. 8; Robert A. Frederick, "Colonel Richard Leiber, Conservationist and Park Builder: The Indiana Years" (Ph.D. diss., Indiana University, 1960). Humbug Mountain park was, according to one authority, "one of the largest and finest of the Oregon Coast parks" and was developed cautiously to insure against harming its beauty. See: Mark H. Astrup to Eighth Regional Office, 13 Feb. 1936, NPSSPP, 601.03.1, Oregon.

43. Boardman, "Brief History," p. 181. Also in Samuel H. Boardman, "Our Scenic Beauty," Portland *Oregon Journal,* 10 Nov. 1947. Boardman's comment about gerrymandering stemmed from his irritation over advertisements from California which implied that Crater Lake and other Oregon sites were among the things tourists could see there.

44. Portland *Oregon Journal,* 24 Feb. 1948; Boardman to Sawyer, 16 Sept. 1936 (quotation), 26 June 1941, RSP, 3; Portland *Oregonian,* 25 Sept. 1951; Earl A. Trager to Regional Officer, Region IV, 30 Nov. 1936, NPSSPP, 601.03.01, Oregon. By 1951 there were 184 parks in the Oregon system, 75 percent of them west of the Cascade Range.

45. Boardman to Sawyer, 10 Apr. 1943, RSP, 3 (quotation); Boardman to Henry F. Cabell, 21 Oct. 1942, PRDP, Boardman files, 1941–43; Boardman to Mark Pike, 11 July 1952, ibid., 1950–51; Armstrong, *History of Oregon Parks,* pp. 205–7; Portland *Oregonian,* 14 Nov. 1973, 21 Mar., 2 May, and 5 Sept. 1976. John Day Fossil Beds National Monument incorporated Painted Hills State Park and other holdings in the area, yet even it fell short of Merriam's original plan, for it was made up of relatively small, separated tracts rather than the giant preserve he had envisioned.

46. Boardman to Brogan, 8 Oct. 1938, RSP, 3; Sawyer to Boardman, 18 May 1939, RSP, 2. Unbeknown to Boardman, Sawyer and Van Duzer had interested Merriam in the idea of a fossil beds park years before, while Sawyer and Brogan were behind Merriam's proposal for the Burnt Ranch site. Sawyer to Van Duzer, 28 Aug. and 20 Nov. 1928, PCS, 3; John P. Buwalda to Van Duzer, 26 Nov. 1928, PCS, 2; Samuel Callaway to Sawyer, 8 Nov. 1928, PCS, 3. See also: Brogan, *East of the Cascades* (Portland: Binfords and Mort, 1964), pp. 5–9, 288–90, and passim; Ralph Friedman, *A Touch of Oregon* (New York: Ballantine, 1974), pp. 101–7.

47. Boardman to Brogan, 8 Oct. 1938; Boardman to Sawyer, 17 May 1939, 8 June 1940, and 10 Apr. 1943, RSP, 3; Boardman to Conrad Wirth, 25 Jan. 1941, NPSSPP, 601.03.01, Oregon; Boardman, "Brief History," pp. 221–26; Samuel H. Boardman, "The Cove-Palisades State Park: The Grand Canyon of Oregon" (mimeographed; [Salem], 1952), copy in PRDP, Boardman files. Commissioner M. A. Lynch, showing a rare moment of interest in

parks, tried to interest Boardman in the site in 1931, but to no avail. Boardman seems to have forgotten it altogether, for he later wrote that he first visited The Cove in 1937 (or even later). With construction of Round Butte Dam on the Deschutes beginning in 1961, park facilities were moved to higher ground, but scenically and geologically it remains one of the most impressive of the state's parks. See: Boardman, Weekly Reports, 21 July 1931, PRDP, Boardman files; Boardman, "The Cove-Palisades State Park"; Armstrong, *History of Oregon Parks*, pp. 203–5.

48. Samuel H. Boardman, "Owyhee: A Recreational Area of Promise" (mimeographed; [Salem], 1952).

49. J. L. Bossemeyer to Eighth Regional Office, 18 Feb. 1936, NPSSPP, 601.03.01, Oregon; E. Lowell Sumner, "Special Report on Cape Lookout State Park and Netarts Bay, Oregon," submitted 15 July 1941, ibid., 207; Boardman to Baldock, 11 Mar. 1941; Boardman to Sawyer, 28 Oct. 1952, RSP, 3; Boardman, "Brief History," pp. 203–6.

50. Armstrong, *History of Oregon Parks*, p. 115; Boardman to Brogan, 8 Oct. 1938, RSP, 3; W. A. Langille, "The Mitchell Country in Wheeler County" (mimeographed; n.p., n.d.).

51. Armstrong, *History of Oregon Parks*, pp. 108–10; J. A. Hussey, *Champoeg: Place of Transition* (Portland: Oregon Historical Society, 1967), pp. 301–6.

52. Boardman to Sawyer, 10 June 1932, RSP, 3.

53. Boardman to Sawyer, 17 Aug. 1943, 16 Aug. 1944, 19 Feb. 1952; Sawyer to Boardman, 27 Aug. 1943 and 8 May 1952, RSP, 3; Samuel H. Boardman, "Oregon's Waysides of the Future," Portland *Oregon Journal*, 3 Dec. 1943. Cf. Boardman to Douglas McKay, 3 Mar. 1950, PRDP, Boardman files, 1950–51; Chester H. Armstrong to Ben Chandler, 19 July 1951, ibid., general files, corres., 1951.

54. Oregon State Planning Board, *Oregon Looks Ahead* (n.p., 1938), pp. 9, 88–89 and passim; Greider, "Parks, Parkways and Recreation Areas Study"; Boardman to Sawyer, 30 Jan. 1933, RSP, 3; V. B. Stanberg, *Oregon State Planning Board: Accomplishments, Progress and Proposed Future Program* (n.p., 1935); Boardman to Mark Astrup, 21 Dec. 1936, PRDP, Boardman personal files, 1936–38; Boardman to Baldock, 20 Apr. 1937, ibid., 1941–43 (1st quotation); Boardman to Henry F. Cabell, 21 Oct. 1942, ibid. (2nd quotation). Boardman was not alone; Albert Turner complained of cooperative park work in Connecticut: "there has been so much back seat driving, leading to waste and inefficiency, that we are distinctly unhappy." Turner to Harlean James, 3 Mar. 1936, NCSPP.

55. Oregon State Planning Board, *Oregon Looks Ahead*, p. 48. When a separate agency finally was established in 1980, it was a result of disenchantment with the amount of highway money that parks (and the state police) were absorbing. With the change, the source of funds Robert Sawyer had provided for parks at last dried up; biennial appropriations from the state legislature, users' fees, and recreational vehicle taxes were now necessary.

56. Travel Information Division, Oregon State Highway Department,

Budget Survey ([Salem], n.d.); Harold B. Say, "Selling Oregon Scenery and Recreation," *Commonwealth Review of the University of Oregon* New Series, 19 (1937): 209–13.

57. Boardman to Baldock, 10 June 1937, PRDP, Boardman files, 1936–38; Boardman to Drury, 24 Mar. 1941, PRDP, Boardman files, corres., 1937–41.

58. Oregon State Parks Department, *Parks Expenditures 1930–1950, Summarized* ([Salem], n.d.); Armstrong, *History of Oregon Parks,* pp. 262–65; Boardman to Herbert Maier, 14 Apr. 1943, NPSSPP, (quotation) 201, Oregon; *Oregon Blue Book, 1945–1946* (Salem: State Printing Department, [1945]), pp. 198–99.

59. Travel Information Division, *Budget Survey; Oregon Blue Book, 1947–1948* (Salem: State Printing Dept., [1947]), pp. 203–4.

60. Armstrong, *History of Oregon Parks,* pp. 59, 71; Armstrong, speech to NCSP, Crescent Lake, Wash., 16 Sept. 1954, PRDP, speeches file; *Oregon Blue Book, 1951–1952* (Salem: State Printing Dept., [1951]), p. 210. Boardman himself seems to have occasionally wavered on the question of overnight camping. See: Boardman to Baldock, 11 Mar. 1941, RSP, 3.

61. Portland *Oregonian,* 8 Aug. 1950, 27 Feb. 1951, 25 May 1952, 6 May and 21 June 1953, 14 Mar., 13 May, 1 Sept., 11 Dec. 1954, 9 Jan. 1955, 5 June 1956, 14 Aug. 1960; Armstrong, *History of Oregon Parks,* pp. 64–65, 70–71, 75–76; Armstrong, speech to NCSP; Armstrong, interview.

62. Armstrong, *History of Oregon Parks,* p. 75; interview, Kenneth Boardman, 15 June 1969.

7. ROBERT E. SMYLIE AND IDAHO'S STATE PARKS: *A Study in Belated Action*

1. Act of 13 Mar. 1909, *Idaho Session Laws, 1909,* p. 145; Idaho, House of Representatives, *Journal . . . Tenth Session,* pp. 213 and *passim;* Idaho, Senate, *Journal . . . Tenth Session,* pp. 209 and *passim.*

2. Idaho State Land Department, *Seventeenth Biennial Report of the State Land Department of the State of Idaho, 1923–1924* (Boise: State Printer, 1924), p. 13; ibid., *Twentieth Biennial Report . . . 1928–1930* (Boise: State Printer, 1930), pp. 13–15, 25; ibid., *Twenty-eighth Biennial Report . . . 1944–1946* (Boise: State Printer, 1946), p. 14; ibid., *Twenty-ninth Biennial Report . . . 1946–1948* (Boise: State Printer, 1948), p. 24; *Boise Capitol News,* 24 Feb. 1931; Boise *Idaho Daily Statesman,* 10 Feb. 1908; Idaho Department of Public Lands, *Idaho Land Grants: Acquisition, Dedication, Disposition* (Boise: State Printer, 1969), pp. 5–7; Idaho State Parks Department, *Ponderosa State Park* (Boise: State Printer, n.d.); Arthur Wilson to Orville Roberts, 16 Sept. 1955, Robert E. Smylie Papers (Idaho State Archives, Boise), Box 4, part 2; Idaho State Land Board, Minutes of meeting, 26 July 1955, ibid., 4–1; Nelson, *State Recreation,* pp. 67, 315.

3. Idaho State Land Department, *Seventeenth Biennial Report,* p. 13; ibid., *Twentieth Biennial Report,* pp. 13–14; ibid., *Twenty-eighth Biennial Report,* p. 14; *State Parks* 3 (Dec. 1925): 10; Nelson, *State Recreation,* p. 316; "Spalding

Memorial Park" (mimeographed; n.p., n.d.; copy in Idaho State Historical Society Boise, Idaho State Parks files, box 1). In the teens and twenties, conservationists (and others) in Idaho were more interested in establishing game preserves and fish hatcheries than in parks. See: Hiram T. French, *History of Idaho: A Narrative Account if Its Historical Progress, Its People and Its Principal Interests* (3 vols; Chicago: Lewis Publishing Co., 1914), 1:546–50; *State Recreation* 1 (May 1927): 9; Nelson, *State Recreation*, pp. 69–70. Spalding Park was officially classified as a picnic area, but this seems to have been merely an administrative convenience to justify placing it with other picnic areas under the Department of Public Works, where it could draw upon highway funds, personnel, and equipment for maintenance and other routine work. It subsequently was made a part of Nez Perce National Historic Park.

4. Nelson, *State Recreation*, pp. 66–67, 315; Lava Hot Springs, Idaho State Parks file, Idaho State Historical Society, *passim*; Pomeroy, *In Search of the Golden West*, pp. 33, 50, 118–20; Huth, *Nature and the American*, pp. 106–8; U.S. Department of Interior, *Reports, 1909*, pp. 517–31.

5. Idaho State Land Department, *Seventeenth Biennial Report*, p. 13; ibid., *Twentieth Biennial Report*, pp. 13–14; *State Recreation* 1 (Jan. 1927): 4; Carl Kraemer, "Heyburn Park," *Idaho Highways and Public Works* 2 (June 1924): 7, 22; Nelson, *State Recreation*, pp. 297–98, 430–31; CCC information, Heyburn Park 1939, Heyburn Park Papers, folder II.

6. Charles Edwin Winter, *Four Hundred Million Acres: The Public Lands and Resources* (Casper, Wyo.: Overland Publishing Co., [1932]), p. 116. For a discussion of such attitudes, and of counter trends, see: Richardson, *Politics of Conservation*; H. Duane Hampton, "Opposition to National Parks," *JFH* 25 (1981): 36–45.

7. Tilden, *State Parks*, p. 6; Shankland, *Steve Mather*, pp. 188–89; *State Parks* 3 (Dec. 1925): 11; Nelson, *State Recreation*, p. 156; James G. Scrugham, "Possibilities for a State Park System in Nevada," paper presented at 1928 NCSP conference (see: 1928 program, NCSPP). On Scrugham, see: James W. Hulse, *The Nevada Adventure: A History* (revised ed.; Reno: University of Nevada Press, 1959), pp. 245–46, 248.

8. Marion Clawson and Burnell Held, *The Federal Lands: Their Use and Management* (Baltimore: Johns Hopkins Press, 1957), p. 38.

9. Hunt to Mather, 16 Apr. 1928, NCSPP; NCSP, *Proceedings, Fourth Conference*, p. 87. See also: [Mather] to Hunt, 17 May 1928, NCSPP.

10. *State Parks* 3 (Dec. 1925): 11; Tilden, *State Parks*, p. 488; David G. Conklin, "The Long Road to Riches: The Development of Montana's State Park System," *Montana Outdoors* 9, no. 7 [1978?]: 2–8, 37; Conklin, "A History of the Development of the State Park Idea: The Montana Experience," paper presented at Missouri Valley History Conference, Omaha, Nebr., 9 Mar. 1979; Kenneth W. Karsmizki, "The Lewis and Clark Caverns: Politics and the Establishment of Montana's First State Park," *Montana: The Magazine of Western History* 31 (Autumn 1981): 32–45. Like Idaho's, Utah's state parks system has been developed only recently. The only other park activity of note

in the mountain states came in Colorado. The city of Denver created a system of parks in the nearby mountains when the state refused to act. It continues to hold them today. See Wilbur Fish Stone, ed., *History of Colorado* (4 vols.; Chicago: S.J. Clarke Publishing Co., 1918), 1: 569–72.

11. Richardson, "Civilian Conservation Corps and the New Mexico State Park System"; Charles G. Sauers to William Walker, 17 Sept. 1934, NCSPP; Thomas Miller, state parks files, Miller Papers, box 4.

12. John L. Christian, "State Parks for Idaho," Boise *Idaho Sunday Statesman*, 10 July 1938.

13. Warren V. Benedict, "The Fight Against Blister Rust: A Personal Memoir," *Forest History* 17 (1973): 21–28: Elmo R. Richardson, "Was There Politics in the Civilian Conservation Corps?" *Forest History* 16 (1972): 14; Judith Austin, "The CCC in Idaho: An Anniversary View," *Idaho Yesterdays* 27 (Fall 1983): 13–18; Idaho State Land Department, *Twenty-fourth Biennial Report of the State Land Department of the State of Idaho, 1937–1938* (Boise: State Printer, 1938), p. 32; State Land Department, National Park Service, and State Forest Department, *Idaho's Parks, Parkways and Recreational Areas* [Boise: State Printer, c. 1938]; Idaho State Historical Society, *Heyburn State Park*, p. 3; Idaho Department of Parks and Recreation, *Idaho State Comprehensive Outdoor Recreation Plan: Preliminary Plan* (mimeographed; [Boise: State Printer], 1972), p. 5; Michael P. Malone, *C. Ben Ross and the New Deal in Idaho* (Seattle: University of Washington Press, 1970), pp. 61–62. Smylie's explanation for the lack of earlier action ("There was lots of room and not so many people—a different situation than exists today") is inadequate. Oregon, Washington, and various other states were still uncrowded when they began building their systems of state parks. See: J. M. Neil, interview with Robert Smylie, *Idaho Heritage* 7 (1977): 6 (tapes of the full interview of 9 Feb. 1976 are in Oral History Collection [Idaho State Historical Society, Boise]).

14. Idaho State Land Department, *Twenty-ninth Biennial Report*, p. 24. Woozley was Land Commissioner from 1947 until he became head of the Bureau of Land Management in the first Eisenhower administration. He pushed for appropriations for state parks. See: Robert E. Smylie to author, 10 Mar. 1975, Cox correspondence.

15. Idaho State Land Department, *Thirtieth Biennial Report of the State Land Department of the State of Idaho, 1948–1950* (Boise: State Printer, 1950), pp. 31, 34–35; Keith Petersen and Mary E. Reed, "'For All the People, Forever and Ever': Virgil McCroskey and the State Parks Movement," *Idaho Yesterdays* 28 (1984): 5–10.

16. Idaho State Land Department, *Thirty-fifth Biennial Report of the State Land Department of the State of Idaho, 1958–1960* (Boise: State Printer, 1960), p. 22; Smylie to author, 10 Mar. 1975, Cox correspondence.

17. Robert E. Smylie, interview by the author (Boise, Ida., 27 Jan. 1975). On Iowa, see: *State Recreation* 6 (Jan. 1932): 6; National Conference on State Parks, *Proceedings, Fourth Conference*, pp. 80, 93–94; Nelson, *State Recreation*, pp. 84–87, 324–29.

18. Elmo Richardson, *Dams, Parks & Politics: Resource Development &*

Preservation in the Truman-Eisenhower Era (Lexington: University Press of Kentucky, 1973), pp. 71–73, 77–78, quotation from pp. 72–73; Smylie, press release, 24 Aug. 1953, Smylie papers, 4–2; Boise *Idaho State Journal,* 17 Mar. 1954; Boise *Idaho Daily Statesman,* 21 Sept. 1954.

19. Boise *Idaho State Journal,* 17 Mar. 1954; Boise *Idaho Daily Statesman,* 21 Sept. 1954; Keith Petersen and Mary Reed, "Harriman State Park and the Railroad Ranch: A History," report prepared for Idaho Department of Parks and Recreation, [1983?], p. 136 (copy in Harriman State Park Papers, Island Park, Idaho); United States Department of Interior, National Park Service, *State Park Statistics, 1955* ([Washington: GPO], 1956), pp. 6–9. In 1955 Oregon spent $999,376 and Washington $1.3 million on parks.

20. Smylie to Green, 14 Oct. 1955, Smylie Papers, 4–2. See also: Green to Smylie, 17 Apr. 1956, ibid., 10–11; State Land Board, agenda of meeting, 14 June 1956, ibid., 10–10; Green to author, 20 Mar. 1975, Cox correspondence.

21. Cox, Smylie interview; Idaho State Land Department, *Thirty-third Biennial Report of the State Land Department of the State of Idaho, 1954–1956* (Boise: State Printer, 1956), p. 31; ibid., *Thirty-fourth Biennial Report . . . 1956–1958* (Boise: State Printer, 1958), p. 27. For other early developments under Smylie, see: Beal and Wells, *History of Idaho,* 2: 281–82, 384–87.

22. Petersen and Reed, "Virgil McCroskey," 10–11 (quotation p. 11).

23. Cox, Smylie interview; Idaho State Land Department, *Thirty-third Biennial Report,* p. 31; ibid., *Thirty-fourth Biennial Report,* pp. 27–31; *Congressional Record,* 85th Cong., 2nd Sess., pp. 2177, 2383–84; Boise *Idaho Daily Statesman,* 13 Feb. 1958, 18 Apr. 1959; *Spokane Daily Chronicle,* 28 Nov. 1974; Emmert to author, 21 Mar. 1975, Cox correspondence.

24. Idaho, House of Representatives, *Journal, Thirty-fifth Session,* pp. 22–23.

25. Neil, Smylie interview, p. 6.

26. Boise *Idaho Daily Statesman,* 18 and 19 Apr. 1959, quotation from Apr. 19. See also: Emmert to author, 21 Mar. 1975; *Coeur d'Alene Press,* 6 Dec. 1960; Cox, Smylie interview.

27. Minutes, State Land Board meeting of 19 Mar. 1959 (Attorney General's files, State Archives, Boise); Boise *Idaho Daily Statesman,* 20 Mar., 18 and 19 Apr. 1959; *Coeur d'Alene Press,* 6 Dec. 1960; Smylie, Remarks to Salvation Army Annual Fund Drive, Twin Falls, 30 Mar. 1961, Smylie Papers, box 32; Smylie, Remarks to Chamber of Commerce Committee on Natural Resources, Boise, 15 Sept. 1961, ibid.; Cox, Smylie interview.

28. Idaho, House of Representatives, *Journal, Thirty-sixth Session,* pp. 14–15.

29. Cox, Smylie interview; *Coeur d'Alene Press,* 10 Feb. 1961; Boise *Idaho Daily Statesman,* 16 Dec. 1960, 23 Mar. 1961; Judith Austin to author, 21 Feb. 1975, Cox correspondence.

30. Idaho, House of Representatives, *Journal, Thirty-sixth Session,* pp. 396, 496, 550, 570, 598; Idaho, Senate, ibid., pp. 576, 733.

31. Cox, Smylie interview; Idaho, Senate, *Journal, Thirty-seventh Session,* p. 29.

32. Cox, Smylie interview; Emmert to author, 21 Mar. 1975, Cox correspondence; *Idaho Wildlife Review* 13 (Jan.–Feb. 1962): 3–5; *The Leisure Times* 2 (Aug. 1973): 7; Idaho Falls *Post-Register,* 22 Dec. 1961; Boise *Idaho Daily Statesman,* 22 Dec. 1961, 13 July 1975; Boise *Idaho Morning Statesman,* 31 Dec. 1961; Boise *Idaho Evening Statesman,* 10 Mar. 1962, 23 May 1963; V. I. Westerdahl to H. J. Swinney, undated note, State Parks Papers (Idaho State Historical Society, Boise), Railroad Ranch file; Petersen and Reed, "Harriman State Park," pp. 126, 136. The Harrimans earlier had developed the resort facilities at Sun Valley. See: Boise *Idaho Daily Statesman,* 30 Aug., 2 Sept., 10 Nov. 1936, 5 Dec. 1939; *Boise Capitol News,* 19 Dec. 1936, 15 Mar. 1937.

33. Neil, Smylie interview, p. 6; Petersen and Reed, "Harriman State Park," pp. 127–29, 132–36; E. Stagg Whitin, "The Opening of Harriman Park," *Independent* 71 (27 July 1911): 182–85; Whipple, *Natural Resources of the Empire State,* p. 162; E. Roland Harriman, *I Reminisce* (Garden City, N.Y.: Doubleday, 1975), p. 174 (1st quotation); Boise *Idaho Statesman,* 11 July 1982 (2nd quotation).

34. Boise *Idaho Daily Statesman,* 1, 22 (quotation), and 31 Dec. 1961; Neil, Smylie interview, p. 6; Petersen and Reed, "Harriman State Park," pp. 126–27, 136–38; Steve Smylie, "The Harrimans and Idaho's State Parks," unpublished paper, Harriman State Parks Papers, pp. 5–6.

35. Cox, Smylie interview. Other provisions in the agreement called for fly fishing only, payment to Fremont County by the state of money in lieu of taxes, and the continued occupancy of the ranch by E. Roland Harriman and his wife until their deaths. The park was not to be opened to the public until after the Harrimans were deceased. See: Boise *Idaho Daily Statesman,* 22 Dec. 1961, 13 July 1975; Boise *Idaho Evening Statesman,* 10 Mar. 1962; Smylie, "The Harrimans," pp. 9–11; Petersen and Reed, "Harriman State Park," pp. 137–38.

36. Idaho, Senate, *Journal, Thirty-seventh Session,* p. 29.

37. Ibid., pp. 94, 111, 308, 469, 483, 501, 898–99; Idaho, House of Representatives, *Journal, Thirty-seventh Session,* pp. 111–12, 137, 247, 264, 294, 564, 578, 637, 664, 710–11; Neil, Smylie interview, p. 6; Cox, Smylie interview. For earlier Republican concern over patronage, see: Benewah County Republican Central Committee to Arthur Wilson, 3 May 1955, Smylie Papers, 4–2. Cf. *Coeur d'Alene Press,* 17 Nov. 1969.

38. Boise *Idaho Evening Statesman,* 10 Mar. 1962.

39. Cox, Smylie interview; Emmert to author, 21 Mar. 1975, Cox correspondence; *Leisure Times* 2 (Jan. 1973): 2; Idaho State Parks and Recreation Department, *Farragut State Park,* (n.p., n.d.).

40. Idaho State Land Board, *Thirty-seventh Biennial Report of the State Land Department of the State of Idaho, 1962–1964* (Boise: State Printer, 1964), p. 44.

41. Idaho Department of Parks, *First Biennial Report, 1965–1966* (Boise: State Printer, 1966), pp. 8–10; ibid., *Second Biennial Report, 1966–1968* (Boise: State Printer, 1968), p. 11.

42. When Smylie failed of re-election to a fourth term in 1966, his luke-warm support of Barry Goldwater's presidential campaign in 1964, his subsequent leadership in the ouster of Goldwater's choice, Dean Burch, as Republican National Chairman, and his opposition to conservative positions while chairman of the Republican Governor's Conference were among the reasons. See: *Newsweek* 65 (11 Jan. 1965): 27; *Time* 88 (12 Aug. 1966): 12–13; (28 Oct. 1966): 29. On his role in state politics, see: Judith Austin, interview with Robert Smylie, 10 Mar. 1982, Oral History Collection (Idaho State Historical Society, Boise).

43. *Congressional Record,* 88th Cong., 2nd Sess., pp. 16520–26, 19094–19120 and *passim;* Udall to Smylie, 26 Mar. 1963, Smylie Gubernatorial Papers, 24–1; Fred Overly Papers (Suzzallo Library, University of Washington, Seattle), box 4, file 27, *passim.*

44. Idaho, House of Representatives, *Journal, Thirty-eighth Session,* pp. 103, 126, 146, 152, 153, 164, 170, 176, 186; Idaho, Senate, *Journal, Thirty-eighth Session,* pp. 168, 186, 194, 212–13, 226, 227, 241–43; Act of 6 Mar. 1965, *Idaho Session Laws, 1965,* pp. 139–46; Boise *Idaho Daily Statesman,* 5 Mar. 1965; Neil, Smylie interview, p. 6.

45. Boise *Idaho Daily Statesman,* 10 May 1969, 8 Oct. 1979; "He Fights to Save Mountain Beauty," *Beta Theta Pi* 102 (1975): 238; Cox, Smylie interview; Julie Cannon, "The White Clouds—Vulnerable Wilderness," *Sierra Club Bulletin* 54 (May 1969): 9; *Sierra Club Bulletin* 54 (July 1969): 12; Russell Brown, "Park or Pit?" *Sierra Club Bulletin* 55 (May 1970): 8–11.

46. Idaho, Senate, *Journal, Thirty-seventh Session,* pp. 501, 898; ibid., *Journal, Thirty-eighth Session,* pp. 241–42; Cox, Smylie interview; Neil, Smylie interview, p. 7; *Coeur d'Alene Press,* 17 Nov. 1969.

47. See, for examples: Office of the Governor, "Harriman State Park Background Sheet" (Boise, n.d.); Boise *Idaho Statesman,* 2 Dec. 1976; 26 Apr., 11 May, 26 Oct. 1977. Andrus's lukewarm early attitude toward parks seems out of character with his strong environmental record while Secretary of the Interior in the Carter administration. In fact, Andrus had always appreciated nature and from that base his interest in parks grew steadily, especially after he was able to stop viewing them as the partisan program of a Republican opponent. On Andrus, see Glenn Oakley, "The Ideal Candidate," *Northern Lights* 1 (Sept.–Oct. 1985): 13–15.

48. *Park Gems* 7 (1971): 3, gives a brief biographical sketch of Beckert. He was selected for the position only after some maneuvering among candidates. See: Overly to Edward Crafts, 31 Aug. 1965, Overly Papers, 4–39; Cox, Smylie interview. Beckert was followed by Steven Bly in 1971, Dale Christiansen in 1976, and Robert Peterson in 1984.

49. Boise *Idaho Statesman,* 29 May, 9 July 1975. See also: Beckert to R. Robson, 18 May 1970, Department Files—Land, 1970, Idaho State Archives, Boise; Robson to Beckert, 4 Nov. 1970, ibid. For a fuller discussion, see Cox, "Weldon Heyburn, Lake Chatcolet, and the Evolving Concept of Public Parks," esp. pp. 14–15.

50. Smylie's success in building support on this base seems to have been

limited, his popularity resting more on his general image. As he put it in retrospect, conservationists are "more apt to go to meetings than to the polls." Cox, Smylie interview.

51. Lyndon B. Johnson, "Special Messages to the Congress on Conservation and Restoration of Natural Beauty," *Public Papers of the Presidents of the United States: Lyndon B. Johnson, 1965* (Washington: GPO, 1966), 1: 155–65. Johnson uses the terms "new conservation" and "third wave" on p. 156. The latter term, especially, was soon adopted by those wishing to differentiate the conservation activity of the 1960s from what had preceded it. See also, Chapter 9, pp. 135–37.

8. ALL THE GOVERNOR'S MEN: *Parks and Politics in Washington State, 1957–1965*

1. Earl Coe, *Historical Highlights of Washington State* [Olympia, ca. 1950], p. 57; Washington State Parks and Recreation Commission, "The First Fifty Years of Washington State Parks" (mimeographed; n.p., [1967]); W. G. Weigle to Mrs. Alexander McEwan, 3 Jan. 1939, Washington State Conservation Society Papers, 1–28; "W. G. Weigle," *Timber-Lines* 17 (1963): 25–26; Clayton Anderson to N. Meyers, 11 May 1962, Albert D. Rosellini Papers (Washington State Archives, Olympia [hereafter ARP]), Parks and Recreation Commission files [hereafter PRC], 1962; Boardman to Sawyer, 9 Aug. 1943, RSP, 3–8.

2. Ruth E. Peeler, "Will Our State Parks Go to Ruin?" *Seattle Times,* 12 Sept. 1948; F. F. Warren to Albert D. Rosellini, 20 Jan. 1961, ARP, PRC, 1961. See, also: Byron Fish, "State Parks Program Slow in Developing," *Seattle Times,* 10 Nov. 1958; Warren to Rosellini, 20 Jan. 1961, ARP, PRC, 1961; John Vanderzicht to Rosellini, 30 Mar. 1961, ibid.

3. *Seattle Times,* 27 Feb. (quotation), 17 Apr. 1958, 14 Dec. 1960; Samuel O. Long to Rosellini, 5 Sept. 1961, ARP, PRC, 1961.

4. *Seattle Times,* 8, 13, and 27 Feb. 1959; *Bellingham Herald,* 2 July 1959; Rosellini to Warren, 24 Jan. 1961, ARP, PRC, 1961. See, also: Rosellini to K. Bolender, 3 May 1961; Rosellini to M. W. Bezzio, 29 Aug. 1961, ibid.

5. C. E. Johns, "Affairs of State," *Argus* 66 (26 June 1959): 1; *Seattle Times,* 30 June 1958 (Rosellini quotation); *Argus* 66 (2 Jan. 1959): 1; (16 Oct. 1959): 1; (30 Oct. 1959): 2; 67 (8 Jan. 1960): 1; (15 Jan. 1960): 8; (22 Jan. 1960): 1 (quotation); (15 Apr. 1960): 5; (22 Apr. 1960): 3; 69 (19 Jan. 1962): 1, 8; *Seattle Times,* 10, 12, 13, and 15 Apr. 1960; "A Great Governor?" *Marine Digest* (24 Oct. 1964): 38–39; Don Duncan, "The Rosellini Years," *Seattle Times,* 29 Oct. 1972; Clayton E. Anderson, interview, Salem, Oregon, 27 July 1984.

6. *Seattle Times,* 17 Apr. 1958, 14 Dec. 1960; *Ilwaco Tribune,* 30 Sept. 1960; Pasco *Tri-City Herald,* 3 May 1961; Washington State Parks and Recreation Commission, "State Parks Administration and Policy" [Olympia, c. 1967], pp. 1–2.

7. *Seattle Times,* 24 Nov. 1960, 8 Dec. 1960, 11 and 23 Apr., 23 June 1961,

20, 21, and 22 Aug. 1963; Pasco *Tri-City Herald,* 3 May 1961 (quotation); Melvin Voorhees, "One Man's Opinion," *Argus* 67 (18 Mar. 1960): 1, 3; Voorhees, "Rosellini—After a Quarter Century," *Argus* 70 (30 Aug. 1963): 1, 3; "No Tampering with Civil Service," *Washington Public Employee* 7 (Dec. 1960): 1, 3. See, also: *Argus* 67 (23 Dec. 1960): 4.

    8. *Seattle Times,* 14 Dec. 1960; Pasco *Tri-City Herald,* 3 May 1961; Mrs. W. K. Osborn to Rosellini, 16 Mar. 1961; Rosellini to Osborn, 17 Mar. 1961; memo, Rosellini to Bob Reed, 5 Dec. 1961; memo, dated 1 Jan. 1961, ARP, PRC, 1961. See, also: *Seattle Times,* 18 June 1961.

    9. *Seattle Times,* 18 (Vanderzicht quotation) and 20 June, 7 July 1961; *Bremerton Sun,* 21 Sept. 1961; Pasco *Tri-City Herald,* 21 June 1961; Vera Gault to Rosellini, 23 Mar. 1961; Rosellini to Ivan R. Smith, 17 Apr. 1961; Rosellini to Ralph Pinkerton, 4 May 1961 (quotation), ARP, PRC, 1961; Rosellini to Hubert Humphrey, telegram, [Feb. 1963]; Rosellini to Harold Ford, 14 March 1963, ibid., 1963.

    10. *Seattle Times,* 20 June, 7 July, 1 Aug., 31 Sept. 1961; *Wenatchee Daily World,* 23 June 1961; Dwight Baird to Rosellini, 28 June 1961, Richard Bowe to Rosellini, 30 June 1961, ARP, PRC, 1961. There are numerous other letters regarding Vanderzicht's removal, mostly protests, in ibid.

    11. *Seattle Times,* 20 June 1961 (Greeley quotation); Rosellini to Baird, 7 July 1961; Rosellini to Greeley, 13 July 1961, ARP, PRC, 1961; Charles H. Odegaard, interview, Seattle, 2 June 1982.

    12. *Seattle Times,* 1 Aug. 1961; James B. Hovis to Greeley, 27 July 1961; Rosellini to Putnam, 15 Sept. 1961, PRC papers (Washington State Archives, Olympia [hereafter PRCP]), box 2, Governor's office file, 1957–61. See, also: Long to Rosellini, 5 Sept. 1961, ARP, PRC, 1961.

    13. *Seattle Times,* 21, 22, and 24 Sept. 1961; *Bremerton Sun,* 21 Sept. 1961; Mrs. W. K. Osborn to Robert Schaefer, 17 Nov. 1961 (quotation), ARP, PRC, 1961.

    14. *Seattle Times,* 4 Oct., 8 Nov. 1961.

    15. Ibid., 22 Nov. 1961 (first quotation); Long to Putnam, 21 Nov. 1961 (second quotation); Putnam to Long, 22 Nov. 1961, ARP, PRC, 1961. Washington's experimental youth corps, the first in the nation, was made permanent by the legislature in 1961. At the federal level, where a good portion of the financial support came from, Senator Henry Jackson of Washington was a major author of the program.

    16. *Seattle Times,* 19 and 22 Dec. 1961; memo, Bob Reed to Rosellini, 15 Nov. 1961, ARP, PRC, 1961; Duncan, "Rosellini Years".

    17. *Seattle Times,* 22 Dec. 1961, 22 Jan. 1962; *Argus* 68 (29 Dec. 1961): 2.

    18. *Seattle Times,* 22 Dec. 1961 (Putnam quotation) and 25 Jan. 1962.

    19. Ibid., 19 and 22 Dec. 1961; Whipple to Rosellini, 21 Dec. 1961; Rosellini to Whipple, 26 Dec. 1961, ARP, PRC, 1961; P. R. Chadbourne to Anderson, 3 Jan. 1962, ibid., 1962; Anderson, interview; Odegaard, interview.

    20. Anderson, interview. There is no corroborating evidence for Anderson's recollections, but they do fit the known facts of the case.

21. Anderson to Warren Bishop, 7 Feb. 1962, ARP, PRC, 1962 (quotation); Anderson, interview; Odegaard, interview.

22. *Seattle Times,* 22 Dec. 1961, 27 (quotation) and 28 Feb. 1962.

23. Ibid., 28 Feb. 1962; C. E. Johns, "Park Comm., New Director Say Press Unfair," *Argus* 69 (16 Mar. 1962): 1, 6. In retrospect, Anderson also noted that he was "young and probably somewhat politically naive" when he was Washington's director of parks. Anderson, interview.

24. *Seattle Times,* 28 Feb., 1 Mar. (both quotations) 1962; Rosellini to Park Commissioners, telegram, 1 Mar. 1962, ARP, PRC, 1962.

25. *Seattle Times,* 6 Mar. 1962; Long, press release, 6 Mar. 1962 (quotation), ARP, PRC, 1962. Anderson subsequently tried to appoint John Pinkerton, a forester in the department, to head YDCC, but was informed he had to go through regular recruiting procedures, present a list of three names to the governor, and then confer with him on the final selection. See: Warren Bishop to Anderson, 27 Mar. 1962, ARP, PRC, 1962. According to Anderson, Long was embittered by the events that led to his withdrawal, believing himself betrayed by the governor. Anderson, interview.

26. *Seattle Times,* 8 Mar. 1962; Rosellini to Anderson, 14 Mar. 1962; Anderson to Bishop, 21 July 1962; Horchler to Bishop, 3 Aug. 1962, and attachments; Inter-Agency Outdoor Recreation Commission, minutes of meeting, 24 April 1962, ARP, Inter-Agency Outdoor Recreation Commission file [hereafter IORC], 1963 [sic]; Rosellini, statement in support of SB 3117, 10 May 1962, ARP, PRC, 1962. The study carried out under the interagency commission reflected an approach favored by Rosellini. As the *Argus* observed, no governor of Washington "has moved more toward the policy of encouraging study of problems and major areas of governmental responsibility. . . . There are boards for parks and recreation, for game and fish, for natural resources, and for institutions. There is one for the arts, and one for sports." See: *Argus* 67 (18 Nov. 1960): 4.

27. Anderson to Rosellini, 24 Apr. 1962; Rosellini to Gaylord Nelson, 7 Aug. 1962; John A. Biggs to Rosellini, 13 Aug. 1962; memo, Rosellini to Judge Rosellini et al., 24 Aug. 1962, ARP, IORC, 1963; Washington Outdoor Recreation Study, progress report, 19 Sept. 1962; Rosellini to Tom Wimmer, 8 Nov. 1962, ARP, New Outdoor Recreation Study file [hereafter · ORS]; Rosellini, special message to the legislature, 7 Feb. 1963, ARP, PRC, 1963; Rosellini to Mark Hatfield, 7 Mar. 1963, ibid.; *Seattle Post-Intelligencer,* 12 Sept. 1965; Duncan, "Rosellini Years." Considerable additional material is in ARP, ORS (including a copy of the completed study) and in ARP, Governor's Outdoor Recreation Proposal file, 1963. Apparently Anderson first proposed that at least a portion of unreclaimed pleasure boat fuel taxes be used for marine parks, even though he recognized that such a change would be opposed by the highway department and the cities and counties which up to that time had received the money.

28. *Seattle Times,* 10 Feb. 1963; Jack Robertson to Rosellini, 31 July 1962, ARP, PRC, 1962; Rosellini to Brian Sexson, 6 Feb. 1963; Rosellini to C. C. Beery, 21 Mar. 1963, ibid., 1963; memo dated 12 Nov. 1963, ARP, ORS, 1963;

Anderson to Rosellini, 15 and 21 Aug. 1963; Rosellini, statement, 21 Sept. 1962, ARP, IORC, 1963; *Washington Public Employee* 10 (July 1963): 4; C. E. Johns, "Gov. Rosellini: Hard Look at an Old Pro," *Argus* 70 (17 May 1963): 1; Duncan, "Rosellini Years." Considerable additional material is in ARP, PRC and ORS files, including information on an outdoor recreation conference that Rosellini arranged through the University of Washington and the work of the Citizens for Outdoor Recreation, which worked to gain passage by the voters of the bond issue.

29. *Seattle Times*, 8 July, 15 and 22 Aug., 20 Nov. 1962; Washington State Parks and Recreation Commission, minutes of meeting, 22 Oct. 1962, ARP, PRC, 1962; Anderson, interview. For summaries of his activities, see: Anderson, "Progress Report to Governor, Legislators, and State Parks & Recreation Commission," 21 Nov. 1963; Anderson, "Report to the Legislature," n.d. [c. July 1963], ARP, PRC, 1963.

30. On logging: Emily Haig to Rosellini, 26 Mar. 1962; Rosellini to Haig, 9 Apr. 1962; Washington State Parks and Recreation Commission, agenda for meeting of 16 Apr. 1962; Robert Latz to Rosellini, 10 May 1962, ARP, PRC, 1962. On Fort Ward: *Seattle Times*, 21 July 1963; Winslow *Bainbridge Review*, 24 July 1963. On appointments: Dick Murfin to Anderson, 10 July 1963, PRCP, 11, Director's file. On expenses: Rosellini to James B. Hovis, 24 Jan. 1963; Hovis to Rosellini, 28 Jan. 1963, ARP, PRC, 1963. On comparisons with Oregon: *Seattle Times*, 19 and 29 June, 8 July 1962; Salem (Oregon) *Capital-Journal*, c. 15 June 1962, reprinted in *Seattle Times*, 29 June 1962. On Culverwell and abolishing commission: *Seattle Times*, 13, 21, and 23 July 1962, 26 Feb. 1963; Roald Tryxell to Rosellini, 16 July 1962; R. D. Daugherty to Rosellini, 16 July 1962, ARP, PRC, 1962. See, also: Federal Way *News Advertiser*, 18 July 1962; C. E. Johns, "State Parks Suffer as Board Meddles in Admin." *Argus* 69 (6 July 1962): 1, 8; Jack Pierce to Rosellini, 23 May 1962, ARP, PRC, 1962. The *Seattle Times*, 8 July 1962, observed correctly that invidious comparisons with Oregon's parks tended to overlook the fact that Washington's system was broader, including historic, geologic, and archeological sites, marine parks, a youth development and conservation corps, and five ski areas, while Oregon's system "concerned itself with parks alone." See, also: Anderson to Rosellini, "Six Months Progress Report," 26 July 1962, ARP, PRC, 1962; Albert Culverwell, "State Parks are Rich in History," *PNQ* 45 (1954): 85–90.

31. Anderson, "Six Months Progress Report," ARP, PRC, 1962; Rosellini to Howard Martin, 22 Feb. 1963, ibid., 1963; Anderson to Dana, 11 Apr. 1963, PRCP, 11, Director's file.

32. Memo, Kay [MacDonald] to Rosellini and W. Bishop, 30 July 1962, ARP, PRC, 1962; [MacDonald] to G. Prescott, 11 Feb. 1963 (quotation); memo, Rosellini to "Certain Directors," 7 Feb. 1963, ibid., 1963.

33. *Seattle Post-Intelligencer*, 3 Aug. 1963; *Seattle Times*, 14 Aug. 1963; E. Anderson to C. Anderson, 30 July 1963, ARP, PRC, 1963; Anderson, interview.

34. C. Anderson to Park Commissioners, 8 Aug. 1963, PRCP, 11, C. Anderson file; Rosellini to E. Anderson, 16 Aug. 1963; Rosellini, memo to Kay McDonald, 16 Aug. 1963, ARP, PRC, 1963.

35. Anderson, interview. This is Anderson's reading of the situation; there is no corroborating evidence, but he is no doubt correct.

36. *Seattle Times*, 14 (quotation) and 15 Aug. 1963; *Bremerton Sun*, 14 Aug. 1963. The *Kitsap County Herald*, 22 Aug. 1963, agreed that Anderson's problems primarily originated with politics, but felt that this was exacerbated by Anderson's inability to keep the department from getting a steady and unfavorable press.

37. *Seattle Times*, 15 Aug. 1963; *Eugene Register-Guard*, 15 Aug. 1963; Anderson, interview.

38. Carey to Rosellini, 15 Aug. 1963; PRCP, 11, Director's file; Anderson to Rosellini, 15 Aug. 1963, ibid., Personnel file; Odegaard, interview; David G. Talbot, interview, Salem, Oregon, 21 Oct. 1983. See also: *Seattle Times*, 20 Aug. 1963; Carey to Anderson, 29 Aug. 1963, PRCP, 11, Director's file.

39. *Seattle Times*, 17 Aug. 1963 (quotation); *Kitsap County Herald*, 22 Aug. 1963; Duncan, "Rosellini Years"; Washington State Parks and Recreation Commission, minutes of meeting, 19 Aug. 1963, PRCP, 11, Director's file.

40. Tuttle to Rosellini, 21 Sept. 1963, ARP, PRC, 1963; *Seattle Times*, 21 Sept. 1963 (Whiting quotation); *Kitsap County Herald*, 22 Aug. 1963. ARP contain only one letter (Carey's) and one telegram protesting Anderson's ouster, perhaps because, as Don Duncan put it, "the governor . . . eventually fired Anderson with what most observers felt was good cause." However, there are letters by Anderson in PRCP, 11, personal file, suggesting that others expressed support for him; Howard Martin found support for Anderson in the departmental field staff; and Robert Straub, later a Democratic governor of Oregon, was so critical of Rosellini as to suggest that being fired by him was to Anderson's credit. See: Duncan, "Rosellini Years"; Martin to Anderson, 4 Sept. 1963, PRCP, 11, Director's file; Straub, interview, Salem, Oregon, 21 Oct. 1983.

41. *Seattle Times*, 6 and 26 Nov. 1963; *Bellingham Herald*, 6 Nov. 1963; Rosellini to Odegaard, 22 Aug. 1963, ARP, PRC, 1963; C. E. Johns, "Rosellini Battens Down Hatches," *Argus* 71 (24 Apr. 1964): 1; Washington State Parks and Recreation Commission, *A Decade of Conservation and Service, 1960–1970* (Olympia: State Printer, 1970), pp. 1–3, 6, 11; Odegaard, interview; Talbot, interview; Charles H. Odegaard, "Million-Dollar Ideas for Park and Recreation Departments," *Parks & Recreation* 3 (Oct. 1968): 21, 46. Odegaard's survival under Governor Evans may have been helped by his wife's activity in support of the new governor, although Evans was certainly a politician of a very different stripe than Rosellini.

42. Anderson to Ethel Aldrich, 22 Aug. 1963, PRCP, 11, Personal; Rosellini to Tuttle, 24 Sept. 1963; Anderson to Odegaard, 20 Nov. 1963, Anderson to Rosellini, 21 Nov. 1963, ARP, PRC, 1963; Odegaard, interview. On Anderson's legacy, see Anderson, "Progress Report," 21 Nov. 1963, and Anderson, "Report to the Legislature" [1963], ARP, PRC, 1963.

43. *Seattle Times*, 8 and 17 Jan., 8 and 23 Feb. 1967, 3 June 1968, 19 Jan., 29, 30, and 31 Mar., 3, 5, 7, and 10 Apr. 1977, 13 Jan., 28 June, 15 and 19 July 1979; *Seattle Post-Intelligencer*, 20 Jan., 11 Feb., 24, 29, and 31 Mar., 1, 2, 3, 6,

and 13 Apr. 1977, 26 June 1979; *Tacoma News-Tribune*, 11 Feb., 25 Mar. 1977, 26 Aug. 1979; *Bremerton Sun*, 22 Dec. 1978; Anderson, interview; Talbot, interview.

9.   TO SAVE A RIVER: *Robert Straub, Karl Onthank, Tom McCall, and the Willamette Greenway*

1. *Eugene Register-Guard*, 20 July 1966; *Oregonian*, 20 July 1966; Robert W. Straub, "Willamette River Rediscovered: Conservation and Utilization of the Scenic and Recreation Resources of the Willamette River," mimeographed proposal with map, n.d., Karl W. Onthank Papers [hereafter KOP] (University of Oregon Library, Eugene), box 15, Willamette Greenway [hereafter WRG] files. Quotations from *Register-Guard*.

2. *Eugene Register-Guard*, 21 and 22 July 1966; *Oregonian*, 22 July 1966; Tom McCall with Steve Neal, *Tom McCall: Maverick* (Portland: Binfords & Mort, 1977), pp. 68–70. See, also: *Eugene Register-Guard*, 24 July 1966; Straub to editor, *Oregonian*, 28 July 1966. As the newspapers show, McCall's account oversimplifies the sequence of events. He was not simply being self-serving, however. Long before Straub's speech, McCall had gone on record with proposals to control air and water pollution and preserve the "livability" of Oregon. His environmental concern was certainly genuine. See: *Oregonian*, 13 May 1966, 22 Dec. 1974.

3. Donald Fleming, "Roots of the New Conservation Movement," *Perspectives in American History* 6 (1972): 7–91; United States, Department of the Interior, *The Third Wave: America's New Conservation*, Conservation Yearbook No. 3 (Washington: GPO, 1966); Stewart L. Udall, *The Quiet Crisis* (New York: Holt, Rinehart & Winston, 1963), p. 83 ff; Cox et al., *This Well-Wooded Land*, pp. 247–53; Samuel P. Hays, "From Conservation to Environment: Environmental Politics in the United States since World War II," *Environmental Review* 6 (Fall 1982): 14–41; Richard A. Baker, "The Conservation Congress of Anderson and Aspinall, 1963–64," *JFH* 29 (1985): 104–19. These sources emphasize ecological aspects of the new conservation and largely overlook the rising interest in parks and recreation.

4. U.S. Congress, Senate Select Committee on National Water Resources, "Water Recreation Needs in the United States, 1960–2000," *Water Resources Activities in the United States* (Washington: GPO, 1960), esp. p. 2; Outdoor Recreation Resources Review Committee, *Outdoor Recreation for America: A Report to the President and to the Congress* (Washington: GPO, 1962), pp. iii–iv, 1–2, 8, 178; Terry Michael DiMattio, "The Wild and Scenic Rivers Act of 1968" (M.A. thesis, San Diego State University, 1976), pp. 31–34.

5. DiMattio, "Wild and Scenic Rivers Act," pp. 9–29, provides a convenient overview of these efforts. There is an extensive literature of article-length material, but very little is even-handed and scholarly and almost none deals with more than a single stream or watershed.

6. Richardson, *Dams, Parks, & Politics,* pp. 116–27; Bert E. Swanson and Deborah Rosenfield, "The Coon-Neuberger Debates of 1955: 'Ten Dam Nights in Oregon'", *PNQ* 55 (1964): 55–66; Franklyn D. Mahar, "The Politics of Power: The Oregon Test for Partnership," ibid. 65 (1974): 29–37.

7. *New York Times,* 6 Mar. 1949; Richard L. Neuberger, "Fish and Concrete," *The Nation* 175 (8 Aug. 1952): i; "McKenzie River Victory at Polls," *Sierra Club Bulletin* 41 (June 1956): 6; William O. Douglas, *My Wilderness: The Pacific West* (Garden City, N.Y.: Doubleday & Co., 1960), pp. 196–201; "Minam River Public Hearing," *Living Wilderness* 77 (Summer–Fall 1961): 29–31. KOP, box 1, contains much material on the Beaver Marsh controversy. Additional material is scattered elsewhere in the collection; it includes a letter to Onthank from Robert W. Sawyer (by then retired from his editorship of the *Bend Bulletin)* on 30 Mar. 1956, applauding the outcome of the Beaver Marsh issue (KOP, 16, incoming corres.).

8. McCall, *Tom McCall,* pp. 59–61, 178–80; William Robbins, *The Oregon Environment: Development vs. Preservation, 1905–1950* ([Corvallis]: Oregon State University, 1975), pp. 20–31; William D. Honey, Jr., *The Willamette River Greenway: Cultural and Environmental Interplay* (Corvallis: Oregon State University, Water Resources Institute, 1975), pp. 20–27; City of Portland, "Willamette Greenway Historic Chronology, 1805–1978" (mimeographed, n.d.), Transportation Planning Files, 1951–1979 (Portland City Archives and Record Center, Portland), 7602-26, 7/6; Webb Sterling Bauer, "A Case Analysis of Oregon's Willamette River Greenway Program" (Ph.D. diss., Oregon State University, 1980), pp. 42–51; C. V. Langton and H. S. Rogers, "Preliminary Report on the Control of Stream Pollution in Oregon," Engineering Experiment Station, Bulletin No. 1 (Corvallis: Oregon State College, 1929); Fred Merryfield and W. G. Wilmont, "1945 Progress Report on Pollution of Oregon Streams," ibid., Bulletin No. 12 (1945). See also: Stewart L. Udall, "Comeback for the Willamette River," *National Parks and Recreation Magazine* 42 (Mar. 1968): 4–8; Anthony Netboy, "Cleaning up the Willamette," *American Forests* 78 (May 1972): 12–15, 57; Thomas A. Weller, "The Saving of the Willamette," *Oregon Stater* 18 (November 1984): 2–3.

9. *Oregonian,* 18 Sept. 1964; U.S., President, *Public Papers, 1963–1964,* 2: 1567; ibid., *1965,* 1: 8.

10. Robert W. Straub, interview, Salem, Ore., 21 Oct. 1983. At the time, Straub listed California's American River, as well as the Potomac, as a source of inspiration: *Eugene Register-Guard,* 20 July 1966. See, also: [Karl Onthank], "Notes on Bob Straub at Eugene Rotary," 23 Aug. 1966, KOP, 15, WRG file; *Eugene Register-Guard,* 20, 24, and 26 July 1966.

11. McCall, *Tom McCall,* p. 68; McCall to Onthank, 2 July 1965, KOP, 15, WRG files; Honey, *Willamette River Greenway,* pp. 53–54. Ken Johnson, a one-time aide to Straub, later claimed that Straub not only got the idea from Udall and *The Way West,* but also that he then interested Onthank in it and Onthank recruited others, including McCall. See: Salem *Oregon Statesman,* 14 Aug. 1977; Bauer, "A Case Analysis," pp. 52, 176, 205–6.

12. Talbot, interview, 21 Oct. 1983. The title of the head of Oregon's

state parks was changed from Superintendent to Administrator during reorganization in 1969. Talbot has claimed that he was the one who planted the seed both with Onthank and Jackson. See: Bauer, "A Case Analysis," pp. 205–6. On Talbot, see: *Oregon Recreation Views* 5 (May 1962): 1; 15 (May 1965): 1; Portland *Oregonian,* 29 Dec. 1982. In separate interviews, Straub, Talbot, and Charles Odegaard all volunteered comments on Jackson's great influence. On Jackson, see: *Oregonian,* 21 June 1980, 25 Sept. 1983; Bauer, "A Case Analysis," p. 177.

13. Edwin R. Bingham, interview, Eugene, Ore., 16 Apr. 1980.

14. McCloskey to author, 18 Mar. 1980, Cox correspondence; McCloskey, "Karl Onthank, 1890–1967" *Sierra Club Bulletin* 53 (Jan. 1968): 27.

15. Onthank to Mary C. Brown, 13 Dec. 1958 (quotation), 10 Jan. 1959; Brown to Onthank, 11 Dec. 1958, 8 Jan. 1959, KOP, 14, Smith Rocks file; Onthank to Armstrong, 9 Sept. 1959, KOP, 13, Oregon State Parks file; Onthank to Oregon State Highway Commission, 13 Feb. 1959, KOP, 14, Oregon State Highway Comm. file. For Onthank's championing of early acquisition, see also: Onthank to Mimi Bell, 25 Aug. 1966, KOP, 16, outgoing corres.; Onthank to Glenn Jackson, 3 Jan. 1967; Onthank to Talbot, 12 Apr. 1967, KOP, 15, WRG files. His work with the Oregon Roadside Council is revealed in three thick files in KOP, 13.

16. On Onthank and the Minam, see KOP, 14, Save the Minam file, esp. David R. Brower to William O. Douglas, 23 Dec. 1960. Material on Onthank's work to protect the McKenzie is primarily in KOP, box 1, Beaver Marsh files; on the Lane County Parks and Recreation Commission [hereafter LCPRC], box 3; on the Columbia Basin Inter-Agency Commission, boxes 2 and 15; and on the Upper Willamette Resource and Conservation Development Project, box 15.

17. Onthank to C. H. Armstrong, 14 Dec. 1956, KOP, 13, State Parks file; Harold G. Schick to Onthank, 12 July 1961, KOP, 16, incoming corres.; *Eugene Register-Guard,* 3 Aug. 1961; [Onthank], "Brief History and Current Status of North Bank Park Project," typescript draft (n.p., [1965]), KOP, 13, North Bank Park file; Bauer, "A Case Analysis," pp. 205–6.

18. See, KOP, 2, Columbia Basin Inter-Agency Committee files. See, also: Onthank to Elmer Aldrich, 14 Dec. 1964; "Recreation Resources Study Team: Specific Goals of Study," n.d., KOP, 15, Willamette River Basin Survey [hereafter WRBS] files. Related work was being done by the Upper Willamette Resource and Conservation Development Project. On the project's interest in the greenway, see: Dale Munk to Darrell Jones, 10 Oct. 1967, Willamette River Greenway Papers [hereafter WRGP] (Oregon Parks and Recreation Department), box 1, old Greenway committee files [hereafter OGC], general corres., 1967–69.

19. Superintendent's report, 26 Jan. 1965, KOP, 3, LCPRC files; Onthank to Andrew Sherwood, 4 Oct. 1965, KOP, 16, outgoing corres.

20. *Sunset: The Pacific Monthly* 133 (Oct. 1964): 30–39. There is no indication that Onthank knew of this greenstrip earlier.

21. Onthank to Elmer Aldrich, 14 Dec. 1964, KOP, 15, WRBS file; Mervyn L. Filipponi, "The American River Greenstrip: Parkway Achievement through Coordinated Action," paper presented at University of Oregon, 22–23 July 1965; "Saving a River: A Brief History of the American River Parkway," (n.p., n.d.), KOP, 15, WRBS files; Onthank to Catherine Evenson et al., 14 Oct. 1965, KOP, 16, outgoing corres; McCall, *Tom McCall*, p. 68; *New York Times*, 28 March 1967.

22. McCall to Onthank, 2 July 1965, KOP, 15, WRG files; McCall, *Tom McCall*, p. 68; Straub, interview, 21 Oct. 1983. Biographical material on Straub is limited. However, see: *Oregonian*, 15 Dec. 1974; Larry Leonard, "Straub: Endings & Beginnings," *Northwest Magazine*, pp. 6–10, in *Oregonian* 15 Jan. 1984.

23. WRBS, Recreation Subcommittee, minutes, 13 Dec. 1965, KOP, 15, WRBS files; Oregon Outdoor Recreation Council, minutes, 22 Apr. 1966, KOP, 12, Oregon Outdoor Recreation Council files; LCPRC, minutes, 26 May 1966, KOP, 3; Filipponi, "American River Greenstrip," p. 10.

24. Onthank to Don McKinley, 25 July 1966, KOP, 16, outgoing corres.; Onthank to Mark J. Pike, 8 Aug. 1966, KOP, 15, WRBS files.

25. Onthank to Pike, 8 Aug. 1966, KOP, 15, WRBS files; "Random Notes on Willamette River Boat Trip, August 9 and 10, 1966" WRGP, 1, OGC, corres., 1967 boat trip file (quotation, unidentified participant). The trips became annual events, but none received the attention of the one that followed McCall's election. See: WRGP, 1, OGC, corres., boat trips files.

26. [Onthank], "Notes on Bob Straub at Eugene Rotary," 23 Aug. 1966; Straub, Statement to Portland City Council, 24 Aug. 1966; Straub to J. Herbert Stone, 24 Oct. 1966, KOP, 15, WRBS files; Onthank to Straub, 12 and 29 Aug. 1966, ibid., WRG files; Newman to Straub, 6 Oct. 1966, ibid.; Bauer, "A Case Analysis," pp. 53–55.

27. Onthank to McKinley, 25 July 1966, KOP, 16, outgoing corres.; Onthank to Rod Pegues, 10 Aug. 1966; Frederick A. Cuthbert to Onthank, 24 Aug. 1966; Onthank, "For an Oregon Coast Parkway," [Sept. 1966], KOP, 13, Oregon Coast Highway file; Onthank to Jackson, 3 Jan. 1967, KOP, 15, WRG files; Straub, interview, 21 Oct. 1983; Robert A. Elliott to Onthank, 18 July 1966, KOP, 15, incoming corres.; Onthank to Springer, 7 Oct. 1966, KOP, 3, Oregon County Parks Association, corres. files. On the coast highway issue, see also: Fred Overly to [Lawrence Stevens], 17 June 1966, Overly Papers, box 4, file 39; Stewart Udall to McCall, 24 Aug. 1967, ibid., 4: 44; McCall to Udall, 28 Aug. 1967, ibid., 4: 17; Straub to Udall, 1 Sept. 1967, ibid., 4: 18; Darrell Jones, memo to files, 13 Mar. 1968, WRGP, 1, OGC, general, 1968; *Oregonian*, 21 and 22 July 1966, 1 Aug., 22, 23, and 24 Sept., 2 and 11 Oct. 1967; *Eugene Register-Guard*, 21 July 1966; *Sierra Club Bulletin* 53 (Sept. 1968): 25.

28. Straub, interview, 21 Oct. 1983.

29. Burton W. Onstine, *Oregon Votes: 1858–1972* (Portland: Oregon Historical Society, 1973), pp. 89, 167, and passim; McCall, *Tom McCall*, pp. 70–75; *Oregonian*, 24 June 1967; WRGP, 1, OGC, 1967 boat trip, passim;

Straub, "Willamette River Rediscovered," KOP, 15, WRG files; Bauer, "A Case Analysis," pp. 55–56, 177. Mark Hatfield, unable under Oregon law to continue as governor for a third term, went on to the United States Senate.

30. Onthank to [committee], [1 Dec. 1966]; Onthank to Overly, 5 Dec. 1966; [Beistel], "The Willamette Recreational Waterway Concept," n.d.; Onthank, "Future Recreation Problems which Parks in the Willamette Basin Face" (n.p., n.d.), KOP, 15, WRBS files; Onthank to McCall, 12 Dec. 1966; Onthank to Straub, 12 Dec. 1966, KOP, 15, WRG files; [Onthank], "The Role of County Parks in the Future Development of the Recreational Resources of the Willamette Basin," report to Willamette Basin Survey committee (mimeographed; [c. 1 Aug. 1966]), WRGP, active files, drawer 1, beginnings file; Mark J. Pike to committee, [c. 13 Dec. 1966], ibid. (copies of related documents, including the Onthank and Beistel reports, are also in this file).

31. Onthank to [committee], [1 Dec. 1966], KOP, 15, WRBS files; Onthank to McCall, 12 Dec. 1966; [Onthank], notes on Willamette Recreational Waterway Advisory Committee, n.d., KOP, 15, WRG files. See also: Bauer, "A Case Analysis," pp. 55–57.

32. Onthank to Overly, 5 Dec. 1966, KOP, 15, WRBS files. Compare: Overly to Edward C. Crafts, 6 Aug. 1965, Overly Papers, 4:39.

33. Onthank to Overly, 5 Dec. 1966, KOP, 15, WRBS files. See, also: Robert L. McNeil to Onthank, 13 Dec. 1966, ibid.; *New York Times*, 28 Mar. 1967.

34. Onthank to McCall, n.d.; Onthank to Jackson, 3 Jan. 1967, KOP, 15, WRG files. In all likelihood, Duncan and Beistel would have been invited even if Onthank had not suggested them, for they were the very type of people McCall was interested in including and neither was unknown.

35. Charles S. Collins, Natural Resource Coordinator for Douglas County and immediate past president of the Oregon County Parks Association, was named chairman, but Beistel was responsible for conducting the group's study. Other members of the task force were Laurence V. Espey of Medford, a recreation specialist for Pacific Power & Light Company; Tony N. Kom, assistant professor of landscape architecture at the University of Oregon; Mervyn L. Filipponi, by then an outdoor recreation specialist at Oregon State University: and Orval Etter of Eugene, an attorney. See: *Governor Tom McCall's Willamette River Proposal* ([Salem] 1967), p. [1]; Superintendent's report, 23 Dec. 1966, KOP, 3, LCPRC files; Bauer, "A Case Analysis," p. 217.

36. Superintendent's report, 23 Dec. 1966, 9 Jan. 1967, KOP, 3, LCPRC files; Willamette River Greenway Association, Bulletin #1 (mimeographed; 1 May 1967): 1; "Notes on the Presentation of the Willamette Greenway Plan," 3 Feb. 1967, KOP, 15, WRG files.

37. Superintendent's report, 9 Jan. 1967; LCPRC, minutes, 12 Jan. 1967, KOP, 3, LCPRC files; McCall, *Tom McCall*, p. 77.

38. "Notes on the Presentation of the Willamette Greenway Plan," 3 Feb. 1967, KOP, 15, WRG files; Bauer, "A Case Analysis," pp. 59–62. When

the eleven members of the new committee were announced, Onthank was among their number. See: "Governor McCall's Willamette River Proposal," p. [2].

39. Willamette River Recreational Greenway Committee, minutes, 16 Feb. 1967, WRGP, 1, OGC, minutes, 1967–1975 (copies of minutes for early meetings are also found in KOP, 15, WRG files); Talbot to Keith Burns, 18 Feb. 1975, WRGP, active, drawer 1, history file (quotation).

40. WRG Committee, minutes, 22 Feb. 1967; Talbot to Burns, 18 Feb. 1975, WRGP, active, drawer 1, history file; *Oregonian,* 26 Feb. 1967; Talbot, interview, Salem, Oregon, 27 July 1984.

41. "Governor McCall's Willamette River Proposal," pp. [7–11] (quotation p. 7).

42. Portland *Oregon Journal,* 1 March. 1967; *Oregonian,* 2 Mar. 1967; Salem *Oregon Statesman,* 2 Mar. 1967.

43. *Oregon City Enterprise-Courier,* 2 Mar. 1967; Portland *Oregon Journal,* 3 Mar. 1967; Willamette River Greenway Association, Bulletin #1 (1 May 1967): 1.

44. WRG Committee, minutes, 27 Mar. 1967.

45. WRG Committee, minutes, 27 Mar. 1967; WRG Association, Bulletin #1 (1 May 1967): 1–2.

46. Talbot, interview, 21 Oct. 1983; WRG Committee, minutes, 19 June 1967; McCall, *Tom McCall,* p. 186; *New York Times,* 28 Mar. 1967; McCall to Fred Brenne, 19 May 1967, WRGP, 1, OGC, general corres., 1967–69; Howard Fujii, "Who Will Pay for Willamette Greenway?" *Oregon Agriculture* 25 (25 Mar. 1967): 2; Bauer, "A Case Analysis," pp. 64–65; Brent LaGrand Lake, "The Reaction of Agricultural Landowners to the Willamette River Park and Recreation System" (M.S. thesis, Oregon State University, 1973).

47. WRG Association, Bulletin #1 (1 May 1967): 1; WRG Committee, minutes, 19 June 1967; *New York Times,* 28 Mar. 1967.

48. George Churchill to Erik East, 24 Feb. 1969, WRGP, 1, Willamette River Park System, misc., 1969; WRG Committee, minutes, 19 June 1967; McCall, *Tom McCall,* p. 186; *Oregonian,* 25 May, 1, 3, and 7 June, 25 Nov. 1967; Honey, *Willamette River Greenway,* pp. 54–55; George Churchill, "The Story of a Great River," *Parks and Recreation* 7 (1972): 103–4.

49. WRG Committee, minutes, 19 June 1967. Copies of the various bills and proferred amendments are with WRG Committee, minutes, 27 Mar. 1967.

50. McCall, *Tom McCall,* p. 186; Talbot, interview, 21 Oct. 1983; WRG Committee, minutes, 19 June 1967; *Oregon Journal,* 11 Dec. 1968; *Oregonian,* 11 Dec. 1968; Bauer, "A Case Analysis," pp. 69, 76, 81–82.

51. [Springer] to Onthank, 29 June 1967, KOP, 15, WRG files; *Oregonian,* 17 July 1969. See, also: LCPRC, minutes, 10 Aug. 1967; Onthank to Talbot, 19 Sept. 1967, WRGP, 1, OGC, general corres., 1967–69.

52. WRG Committee, minutes, 5 May 1967, 2 Feb. and 16 July 1968, 5 Aug. 1969, 19 Aug. 1971; Talbot, memo to files, 9 Oct. 1967 (Jackson quote),

WRGP, 1, OGC, general corres., 1967; Michael Starr, memo to files, 26 July 1968, ibid., 1968; *Oregonian,* 10 Nov. 1967; Honey, *Willamette River Greenway,* pp. 55–56; Churchill, "Story of a Great River," p. 105.

53. WRG Committee, minutes, 30 Aug. 1968, 10 Feb. 1969, 29 July 1970, 12 Jan. and 9 Aug. 1971, 31 Jan. 1973; Churchill to committee, 8 July and 14 Oct. 1969, WRGP, 1, OGC, WRG Committee, misc., 1969; Bauer, "A Case Analysis," pp. 68–78. Federal funds did bring some problems with them, however. The greenway was a long-range plan; state authorities wished to concentrate their efforts—and funds—on acquiring land, but BOR officials pushed for early development and were unhappy with some of the uses Oregon allowed on some of the land while it awaited eventual development. See: Walter J. McCallum to Lloyd Shaw, 27 Feb. 1970, WRGP, 1, general corres., 1970; Forrest Cooper to Overly, 3 Mar. 1970, ibid.; Overly to R. L. Porter, 21 Dec. 1970, ibid.; Porter to participants in Willamette River Parks System, 3 Feb. 1971, ibid.; Porter to Overly, 18 Feb. 1971, ibid.; Churchill to C. Howard Lane, 3 May 1970, ibid., misc. corres.; WRG Committee, minutes, 29 July 1970; Talbot, interview, 27 July 1984.

54. *Oregonian,* 11 Dec. 1968; WRG Committee, minutes, 10 Feb. 1969 (McCall quote); ibid., 21 Apr. 1969 (aide's quote [Kessler Cannon]); Darrell Jones, memos to files, 25 and 31 Jan. 1968, WRGP, 1, OGC, general corres., 1968; Bauer, "A Case Analysis," pp. 73–74, 76, 81–82. See also: Betty C. Allman to Martin Davis, 19 Oct. 1970, Oregon Environmental Council Papers (Oregon Historical Society, Portland), box 3, file 1.

55. WRG Committee, minutes, 10 Feb. and 13 Mar. (Jackson quote) 1969, 29 July 1970 (second quote); Talbot, memo to files, 17 Mar. 1969, WRGP, 1, OGC, corres., 1969; Churchill to Talbot, 24 Apr. 1969, ibid.; *Oregon Recreation Briefs* 4 (Feb. 1974): 2; Bauer, "A Case Analysis," pp. 82–87. The five parks were at Lone Tree Bar, Lower Kiger Island, Mollala–Pudding River, Norwood Island, and Dexter Dam.

56. WRG Committee, minutes, 12 Jan. 1971 (first quote [Lloyd Shaw]); Churchill to George Kovatch, 16 Oct. 1969, WRGP, 1, OGC, misc., 1969; Honey, *Willamette River Greenway,* p. 56.

57. WRG Committee, minutes, 30 Aug. 1968, WRGP, 1, OGC, corres., 1969; Salem *Oregon Statesman,* 7 Oct. 1970; *Oregonian,* 26 Oct. 1970 (Straub quote); Bauer, "A Case Analysis," pp. 77–78. The 1969 legislature also passed a reorganization bill. The old Highway Commission was replaced by a Transportation Commission with four administrative divisions under it. State parks became the Parks and Recreation Branch of the Highway Division. Glenn Jackson had been chairman of the old commission and stayed on to chair the new one.

58. WRG Committee, minutes, 13 Apr. 1971; Churchill to Eugene Peterson, 11 Feb. 1971, WRGP, 1, general corres., 1971; Churchill to Talbot, 25 March 1971, ibid.; report, "Willamette River Sections proposed for Scenic Waterway Designation," n.d., ibid.; Churchill to Committee, 2 March 1971, ibid., Willamette River Parks System legislation, 1971; Churchill to Charles S.

Collins, 9 Mar. 1971, ibid.; Churchill to L. L. Smelser, 15 Apr. 1971, ibid. See also: WRGP, 4, scenic waterways, general corres., 1974–76.

59. WRG Committee, minutes, 12 Jan. 1971; Bauer, "A Case Analysis," pp. 88–95.

60. WRG Committee, minutes, 29 July 1970, 12 Jan., 13 Apr., 19 Aug., 13–14 Dec. 1971; Churchill to committee, 26 May and 14 June 1971, WRGP, 1, OGC, legislation, 1971; G. Douglas Hofe to R. L. Porter, 31 Jan. 1972, ibid. See also: McCall to Rogers C. B. Morton, 27 Aug. 1971; "A Unique Opportunity to Preserve a Wilderness Setting in the Midst of a Growing Region" (grant application), WRGP, 1, OGC, corres., $10 million program file; "Brief History of the Willamette River Greenway" (mimeographed; n.p., n.d.), WRGP, active, drawer 1, history; Bauer, "A Case Analysis," pp. 91–92.

61. WRG Committee, minutes, 19 Aug. 1971 (Jackson quotes); 18 Apr. and 18 July 1972, 31 Jan. and 15 Oct. 1973; State Land Board Advisory Committee, minutes, 13–14 Dec. 1971, WRGP, 1, general, 1971; Talbot to Burns, 18 Feb. 1975, WRGP, active, drawer 1, history; "Brief History of Greenway," ibid. In July 1972 the committee directed Talbot to use condemnation when necessary. WRG Committee, minutes, 18 July 1972, 31 Jan. and 15 Oct. 1973; Churchill to Mount, 21 July 1972, WRGP, 1, OGC, WRG committee, corres., 1972; Churchill to committee, 18 Aug. 1971, in WRG Committee, minutes, 19 Aug. 1971; Churchill to committee, 13 July 1972, in ibid., 18 July 1972.

62. Robert G. Davis, testimony to House Transportation Committee, 25 Jan. 1973 (filed with WRG Committee, minutes, 31 Jan. 1973); Churchill to D. M. Uman, 9 Sept. 1974, WRGP, 4, outgoing corres., 1974; Talbot to Burns, 18 Feb. 1975, WRGP, active, drawer 1, history; Talbot, interview, 21 Oct. 1983; *Oregonian*, 2 Mar., 12 June 1973, 7 Feb. (Straub quote), 25 and 27 July 1974; *Oregon Recreational Briefs* 4 (Sept. 1974): 2; Lake, "The Reaction of Agricultural Landowners," p. 28; Bauer, "A Case Analysis," pp. 103–9; George Churchill, "Willamette River Parks System," in *Land and Water Uses in Oregon* (Corvallis: Oregon State University, Water Resources Research Institute, 1974), pp. 60–61; Honey, *Willamette River Greenway*, pp. 56–59. See also: Talbot to Warren Gaskill, 20 Jan. 1976, WRGP, active, drawer 1, history; Talbot to Walter Brown, 9 Mar. 1983, ibid.

63. WRG Committee, minutes, 15 Oct. 1973; Churchill to Larry McKay, 20 Feb. 1974, WRGP, 4, outgoing corres., 1974; Talbot, interview, 21 Oct. 1983; *Oregon Recreation Briefs* 4 (Feb. 1974): 1, 2; ibid. (Sept. 1974): 1; Harold F. Brauner to mayors and county commissioners, 14 Oct. 1975, Don Clark Papers (Oregon Historical Society, Portland), box 45, file 14; R. L. Porter to Davis, 20 Apr. 1971, Oregon Environmental Council Papers, 20: 28; Larry Williams to Karen Angel, 17 Aug. 1973, ibid., 46: 1; "Analysis of Environmental Issues for Oregon Legislature, 1973" (mimeographed; n.p., n.d.), ibid., 30: 18; Bauer, "A Case Analysis," pp. 109–16.

64. Churchill, undated memo, [c. 7–13 Aug. 1974] (quote), WRGP, 4, outgoing corres., 1974; Churchill to D. J. Doubleday, 10 Apr. 1974, ibid.;

Churchill to L. B. Day, 25 Aug. 1974, ibid.; McCall, *Tom McCall,* pp. 199–201; Bauer, "A Case Analysis," pp. 102, 116–19, 132; Honey, *Willamette River Greenway,* pp. 59, 68–71. On SB 100, see: Oregon Environmental Council Papers, 31: 18; Larry Williams to McCall, 9 May 1973, 46: 1; McCall to Williams, 29 May 1973, ibid.; Williams to Karen Angel, 17 Aug. 1973, ibid.; Charles E. Little, *Oregon Environmental Council Legislative Alert,* 23 Feb., 23 Mar., 19 Apr., 18 May 1973; "The Legacy of Tom McCall," *American Land Forum* 4 (Spring 1983): 3–5. In the midst of all this, the state was also engaged in reviewing a controversial proposal for an addition to the greenway in Portland. Many thought the proposal favored real estate developers more than the public. See: WRG Committee, minutes, 17 Sept. 1974; Churchill to Neil Goldschmidt, 18 Sept. 1974, WRGP, 4, outgoing corres., 1974; Churchill to Committee, 27 Sept. 1974, ibid., 1, OGC, corres. Additional materials on this subject are in Transportation Planning Files, boxes 5–8, Park Superintendent's Correspondence, 1949–1973 (Portland City Archives and Records Center, Portland), box 20; and in Don Clark Papers, 41: 34.

65. McCall, *Tom McCall,* p. 200 (Day quote); Churchill to D. M. Uman, 9 Sept. 1974, WRGP, 4, outgoing corres., 1974; Talbot, interview, 21 Oct. 1983; Bauer, "A Case Analysis," pp. 117–19.

66. Talbot to State Parks and Recreation Advisory Committee, 7 Nov. 1974, WRGP, 4, outgoing corres., 1974; Churchill to Jackson, 26 Dec. 1974, ibid.; Churchill to WRG Committee, 13 Feb. 1975, ibid.; *Oregonian,* 7 Feb. 1974 (Straub quote); Royston, Hanamoto, Beck & Abey, *Preliminary Willamette River Greenway: A Plan for the Conservation and Management of the Willamette River Greenway* (Salem: Oregon Department of Transportation, 1974); Straub, "Special Message to the Fifty-Eighth Legislative Assemby," 7 Mar. 1975, copy in WRGP, active, drawer 1, history; Bauer, "A Case Analysis," pp. 120–24, 219, 220. Straub's criticism of easements was sound. Appraisals ran from 80 to 90 percent of the full market value of the land. As Honey's research has shown, Straub was also correct in believing there was widespread public support for the greenway. See: WRG Committee, minutes, 15 Oct. 1973; Honey, *Willamette River Greenway,* pp. 68–111, 116–17.

67. Talbot to Oregon Transportation Commission, 24 Mar. and 27 May 1975, WRGP, 4, outgoing corres., 1975; Potter to Ronald Blodgett, 13 May 1975, ibid.; Potter to Hal Brauner, [c. 1 July 1975], ibid.; Wallace Hibbard, memo to files, 15 Sept. and 12 Dec. 1975, ibid.; Potter to Talbot, 13 Nov. 1975, ibid.; Hibbard and Potter, memos to files, 21 Nov. 1975, ibid.; Hibbard to Talbot, 31 Oct. 1975, ibid., LCDC; Talbot, interview, 21 Oct. 1983; Bauer, "A Case Analysis," pp. 124–25, 177–78. On Day's removal, cf. McCall, *Tom McCall,* p. 201.

68. Potter, memo to files, 5 Apr. 1976, WRGP, 4, outgoing corres., Jan.–June 1976; Talbot to Transportation Commission, 13 Apr. 1976, ibid.; Potter to Day, 22 Apr. 1976, ibid.; Jim Britton to Potter, 7 Sept. 1976, ibid., Jul.–Dec. 1976; Potter to Mrs. Walter Mason, 16 Sept. 1976, ibid.; Potter to Mark Hatfield, 18 Oct. 1976 (quote), ibid.; Potter to WRG Committee, 31 Aug. 1976, ibid.; Talbot, memo to files, 26 Aug. 1976, ibid., misc. corres.; Williams

to Oregon Environmental Council members, 31 Aug. 1976, ibid.; final draft, WRG statewide planning goal and implementing orders, 22 Nov. 1975, WRGP, active, drawer 1, LCDC greenway file; Janet McLennan to Talbot, 29 Apr. 1976, ibid., history; Talbot to W. Brown, 9 Mar. 1983, ibid.; Portland *Oregon Journal*, 8 Dec. 1975; Oregon Land Conservation and Development Commission, *Willamette River Greenway Program* (Salem: LCDC, 1975); Mc-Call, *Tom McCall*, p. 186; Talbot, interview, 21 Oct. 1983; Oregon Environmental Council, *Legislative Bulletin*, 2, 9, 23, and 30 Mar. 1975 (copies in Oregon Environmental Council Papers); Bauer, "A Case Analysis," pp. 125–27, 132–53, 176–77. To dramatize his support of the greenway, Straub stole a page from McCall's script by joining the 1975 boat trip. He also reinstituted the Willamette Greenway Committee and lobbied vigorously for his greenway proposals. However, none of this won sufficient support to get his proposals through the legislature.

69. Churchill to WRG Committee, 5 Mar. 1974, WRGP, 1, OGC, corres., 1974; Talbot to State Parks and Recreation Advisory Committee, 7 Nov. 1974, WRGP, 4, outgoing corres., 1974; Churchill, memo, 10 Jan. 1975, ibid., 1975; Straub to W. G. Pearcy (draft), 17 Apr. 1975, ibid.; Talbot to State Parks and Recreation Advisory Committee, 17 Nov. 1979, WRGP, active, drawer 1, corres.; Talbot, interview, 21 Oct. 1973. By giving state parks higher public visibility than ever before, the controversies over the greenway probably helped to bring on the loss of highway funds.

70. President's Council quoted in McCall, *Tom McCall*, p. 187; Talbot, interview, 27 July 1984. As of 31 Dec. 1978 there had been 252 acquisitions by state and local governmental authorities for the greenway (all but four in fee-simple) totalling 65.5 riverbank miles; of these sites 70 were programmed for or in development. Revised preliminary plans had been adopted by all jurisdictions along the mainstem of the river except Portland and a part of Benton County; altogether 49,982 acres had been brought under greenway planning. See: Bauer, "A Case Analysis," pp. 155–65.

10. PARKS AND THEIR BUILDERS IN PERSPECTIVE

1. See Ch. 1, n. 28. Every major parks activist covered in this volume fits the standard progressive profile, and every major citizen's group through which they worked was made up largely of people who fit it too. Some, however—such as Madison Grant and Weldon Heyburn—were certainly not progressives in most of their views, and many recent figures—such as Albert Rosellini—were primarily shaped by post-progressive forces.

2. Schmitt, *Back to Nature*, esp. pp. 154–66; Swain, *Federal Conservation Policy*, pp. 130–32. For examples of the concern among outdoor champions with advertising scenery and making it accessible to the public, see: *Mazama* 1 (May 1896): 21–22; (Oct. 1897): 280; 4 (Dec. 1914): 116; (Dec. 1915): 86; 5 (Dec. 1916): 70–75; 6 (Dec. 1923): 77.

3. For examples, see: NCSP, *Proceedings, Second Conference*, pp. 68–69, 83. Bureaucratization and class conflicts over nature and parks are discussed

in: McDonald, "'Holy Retreat' or 'Practical Breathing Spot'?" esp. pp. 127–28, 137–42; Samuel P. Hays, "The Structure of Environmental Politics Since World War II," *Journal of Social History* 14 (1981): 719–38; Hays, "From Conservation to Environment"; Paul J. Culhane, *Public Lands Politics: Interest Group Influence on the Forest Service and the Bureau of Land Management* (Baltimore: Johns Hopkins University Press, 1981). At the Des Moines meeting of the NCSP, Arthur H. Carhart's charge that the national parks were retreats for the wealthy, while the national forests were more accessible to the poor drew a heated rebuttal from Stephen Mather. See: *Des Moines Register,* 11 Jan. 1921.

4. The classic analysis of the influence of science, planning, and technocracy on the conservation movement is Hays, *Conservation and the Gospel of Efficiency.* See also: Swain, *Federal Conservation Policy,* pp. 161–69. Preventing despoliation of natural wonders and "curiosities" was a theme that appeared again and again in pro-parks discussions. Not until Everglades National Park, established in 1934, was there a significant departure from this approach among national parks. State parks showed rather more diversity from the first, but followed a similar course. See: Runte, *National Parks,* pp. 128–37.

5. Pomeroy, *Pacific Slope,* pp. 195–200, 327–28; Gordon B. Dodds, *Oregon: A Bicentennial History* (New York and Nashville: W. W. Norton & Co. and American Association for State and Local History, 1977), pp. 161–84; "The Governor They Call *Tom,*" *Northwest Magazine,* Portland *Oregonian,* 4 Nov. 1973; *Oregonian,* 15 Jan. 1970, 22 Dec. 1974; McCall, *Tom McCall,* pp. 169 and passim. McCall himself traced his progressivism to the influence of his grandfather, Governor Samuel W. McCall of Massachusetts, rather than to precedents in Oregon. His sources of inspiration were in fact probably broader than he recognized.

6. Pomeroy, *Pacific Slope,* pp. 206–7; F. Ross Peterson, *Idaho: A Bicentennial History* (New York and Nashville: W. W. Norton & Co. and American Association of State and Local History, 1976), pp. 92–97, 160–68.

7. On the weakness of the state parks movement in the Mountain and Inter-Mountain Basin states, see Chapter 7. As noted, in Colorado the absence of state parks was partially made up by city parks in the mountains west of Denver. Class and economic overtones colored debates over parks in Colorado. Rural forces in the legislature repeatedly blocked efforts in behalf of state parks, seeing them as benefitting only affluent urban automobilists. Similar attitudes could be detected in opposition that surfaced in Idaho to the creation of Harriman State Park. See: NCSP, *Proceedings, Second Conference,* pp. 89–92, 160; Stone, *History of Colorado,* 1: 569–72; Burnham, "Gasoline Tax and the Automobile Revolution," p. 441; Peterson and Reed, "Harriman State Park," pp. 138–39.

8. For background and a related assessment, albeit one that does not focus on parks, see: Norman H. Clark, *Washington: A Bicentennial History* (New York and Nashville: W. W. Norton & Co. and American Association of State and Local History, 1976), pp. 99–144, 170–85.

9. Evison to Albright, 31 Oct. 1929; Albright to Evison, 2 Feb. 1933 [filed under 1923]; M. L. Hutton to Evison, 16 Oct. 1934; NCSP, minutes of board meeting, 26 May 1943; Harlean James to board members, 8 Aug. 1944; O. A. Tomlinson, memorandum for the director [NPS], 23 Nov. 1945, NCSPP; Talbot to author, 20 Feb. 1980, Cox correspondence; *Recreation* 58 (1965): 15–17.

10. Pomeroy, *In Search of the Golden West*, pp. 125–30, 146–51, 155–58, 205–17; Craig W. Allin, *The Politics of Wilderness Preservation* (Westport, Conn., 1982), pp. 111–12 and passim. The democratizing effects of the automobile revolution on parks was recognized at an early date. See: NCSP, *Proceedings, Second Conference*, pp. 103–6; Robert Sterling Yard, "The People and the National Parks," *Survey* 48 (1922): 547–53, 583; James, *Land Planning*, pp. 197–98.

11. Talbot, interview, 21 Oct. 1983; *Oakridge* (Oregon) *Telegram*, 3 Dec. 1968. See also: Churchill to J. Keith West, 5 Feb. 1969, WRGP, 1, general corres., 1967–69.

12. However, more typical projects still managed to gain the limelight from time to time. In 1982 3,300 acres of riverfront land near the mouth of the Deschutes River, one of the nation's premier fishing streams, came up for sale. Private purchasers were eager to obtain the land for a fishing club, which would have closed twelve miles of the river to the public; the state moved quickly to obtain the site and thereby maintain public access. Lacking sufficient discretionary funds in the parks budget to purchase an option, David Talbot and Governor Victor Atiyeh turned to the public for help. The campaign that followed resulted not only in keeping access to the river open, but also in the addition of a spectacular canyonland site to the state park system. Talbot, interview, 27 Aug. 1984; *Salem Statesman-Journal*, 14 Nov. 1982; Oregon State Parks and Recreation Division, *Deschutes River Scenic Waterway Recreation Use Management Program: Status Report, 1982 to 1984* ([Salem], 1985), pp. 7, 10; "The Deschutes: An Oregon Heritage" (Portland: Oregon Wildlife Heritage Foundation, [1983?]).

13. Boise *Idaho Statesman*, 13 July 1975, 2 Dec. 1976, 11 Jan. 1979, 11 and 18 July 1982; Office of the Governor, "Harriman State Park Background Sheet"; Idaho State Parks and Recreation Department, "Harriman State Park of Idaho: Dedication, July 17, 1982" (n.p. [1982]); Idaho State Parks and Recreation Department, "Harriman State Park of Idaho, A Special Place" (n.p., n.d.).

14. NCSP, *Proceedings, Second Conference*, pp. 13–20, 155.

15. Swain, *Federal Conservation Policy*, esp. pp. 27–29, 49–52, 142–43, 158–59, 161–70.

16. Progressivism perserverd in politics too, at least in the West. See: Richard T. Ruetten, "Senator Burton K. Wheeler and Insurgency in the 1920's" in Gene M. Gressley, ed., *The American West: A Reorientation* (Laramie: University of Wyoming, 1966), pp. 111–31.

17. J. Huizinga, "The Idea of History," trans. by Rosalie Colie, in Fritz Stern, ed., *The Varieties of History: From Voltaire to the Present* (New York: Meridian Books, 1956), pp. 290–303.

Bibliographic Essay

There is a wealth of background material for the student of the parks movement. Among the more important works are Hans Huth, *Nature and the American: Three Centuries of Changing Attitudes* (Berkeley: University of California Press, 1957; reprint, Lincoln: University of Nebraska Press, 1972); Roderick Nash, *Wilderness and the American Mind* (3rd. ed.; New Haven, Conn.: Yale University Press, 1982); Samuel P. Hays, *Conservation and the Gospel of Efficiency: The Progressive Conservation Movement, 1890–1920* (Cambridge, Mass.: Harvard University Press, 1959; New York, Atheneum, 1969); Donald C. Swain, *Federal Conservation Policy, 1921–1933* (Berkeley: University of California Press, 1963); Peter J. Schmitt, *Back to Nature: The Arcadian Myth in Urban America* (New York: Oxford University Press, 1969); John A. Jakle, *The Tourist: Travel in Twentieth Century North America* (Lincoln: University of Nebraska Press, 1985); William H. Wilson, "J. Horace McFarland and the City Beautiful Movement," *Journal of Urban History* 7 (1981): 320–30; and Donald Fleming, "Roots of the New Conservation Movement," *Perspectives in American History* 6 (1972): 7–91.

Among regionally focused works, Earl Pomeroy, *In Search of the Golden West: The Tourist in Western America* (New York: Alfred A. Knopf, 1957), Susan Schrepfer, *The Fight to Save the Redwoods: A History of Environmental Reform, 1917–1978* (Madison: University of Wisconsin Press, 1983), and Lawrence Rakestraw, "Before McNary: The Northwest Conservationist, 1889–1913," *Pacific Northwest Quarterly* 51 (1960): 49–56, provide invaluable insights into developments in the Pacific Northwest. Peter Wild, *Pioneer Conservationists of Western America* (Missoula, Mont.: Mountain Press Publishing Co., 1979) is less original, balanced, and thorough, but still worth consulting.

There are also numerous works focusing more explicitly on parks. Especially useful are Robert Shankland, *Steve Mather of the National Parks* (3rd ed.; New York: Alfred A. Knopf, 1970); Donald C. Swain, *Wilderness Defender: Horace M. Albright and Conservation* (Chicago: University of Chicago Press, 1970); Laura Wood Roper, *FLO: A Biography of Frederick Law Olmsted* (Baltimore: Johns Hopkins University Press, 1973); Alfred Runte, *National Parks: The American Experience* (Lincoln: University of Nebraska Press, 1979); Galen Cranz, *The Politics of Park Design: A History of Urban Parks in America* (Cambridge, Mass.: Harvard University Press, 1982); and J. William Futtrell, "Parks to the People: New Directions for the National Park System," *Emory*

234

Law Journal 25 (1976): 255–316. Numerous studies of individual national, state, and city parks also exist. Ronald J. Fahl, *North American Forest and Conservation History: A Bibliography* (Santa Barbara, Calif.: A.B.C.-Clio Press, 1977) and, for later years, the Biblioscope section of the *Journal of Forest History* are the essential guides to these.

Much though there is on individual parks, the state parks movement as a whole has been little studied. Robert A. Frederick, "Colonel Richard Lieber, Conservationist and Park Builder: The Indiana Years" (Ph.D. diss., Indiana University, 1960) evaluates one of the movement's key leaders. Michael P. McCarthy, "Politics and Parks: Chicago Businessmen and the State Recreation Movement," *Journal of the Illinois State Historical Society* 65 (1972): 158–72, and Joseph H. Engbeck, Jr., *State Parks of California from 1864 to the Present* (Portland, Ore.: Charles H. Belding and Graphic Arts Publishing Co., 1980) have implications beyond their areas of geographic focus. Beatrice Ward Nelson, *State Recreation: Parks, Forests, and Game Preserves* (Washington, D.C.: National Conference on State Parks, 1928), Herbert Evison, ed., *A State Park Anthology* (Washington, D.C.: National Conference on State Parks, 1930), and the published proceedings of the National Conference on State Parks— covering the conferences of 1922, 1923, and 1924—all supply important first-hand information. Freeman Tilden, *The State Parks: Their Meaning in American Life* (New York: Alfred A. Knopf, 1962), is only partly historical and aimed at a popular audience, but useful nonetheless.

Little scholarly attention has been given to state parks of the Pacific Northwest. Two former superintendents of Oregon's parks have left "histories." Samuel H. Boardman, "Oregon State Park System: A Brief History," *Oregon Historical Quarterly* 55 (1954): 179–233, is anecdotal reminiscences; Chester H. Armstrong, *History of Oregon State Parks, 1917–1963* (Salem: Oregon State Highway Dept., 1965), is broader, but uneven and incomplete. Ronald J. Fahl, "S. C. Lancaster and the Columbia River Highway: Engineer as Conservationist," *Oregon Historical Quarterly* 74 (1973): 101–44, and Hugh Myron Hoyt, "The Good Roads Movement in Oregon, 1900–1920" (Ph.D. diss., University of Oregon, 1970) provide useful insights into the milieu from which Oregon's first parks sprang. Webb Sterling Bauer, "A Case Analysis of Oregon's Willamette River Greenway Program" (Ph.D. diss., Oregon State University, 1980) is a good study of later events.

Aspects of the history of Idaho's parks are well covered in Keith Peterson and Mary E. Reed, "'For All the People, Forever and Ever': Virgil McCroskey and the State Parks Movement," *Idaho Yesterdays* 28 (1984): 2–15, and in their "Harriman State Park and Railroad Ranch: A History" (typescript; copy in Harriman State Park files, Island Park, Idaho).

Washington's state parks are largely unstudied, but a number of works provide valuable background. Among these are Richard White, *Land Use, Environment, and Social Change: The Shaping of Island County, Washington* (Seattle: University of Washington Press, 1980); Arthur D. Martinson, "Mountain in the Sky: A History of Mount Rainier National Park" (Ph.D. diss., Washington State University, 1966); Elmo R. Richardson, "Olympic

National Park: Twenty Years of Controversy," *Forest History* 12 (1968): 6–15; and John Fahey, "A. L. White, Champion of Urban Beauty," *Pacific Northwest Quarterly* 72 (1981): 170–79.

Although there is a wealth of background material, serious study of the region's state parks must still be carried out largely in manuscript materials. There is no dearth of these. The records of the three state parks departments—located in Boise, Salem, and Olympia—are invaluable. They are especially useful for the Boardman era in Oregon and the Rosellini years in Washington. Private papers are even more important. The key collections are the Robert Smylie papers in the Idaho State Historical Society, Boise; the Robert W. Sawyer papers (two separate collections) and the Karl Onthank and Ben W. Olcott papers in the University of Oregon library, Eugene; the papers of the Oregon Environmental Council in the Oregon Historical Society library, Portland; and the Asahel Curtis, Edmond Meany, and Robert Moran papers in the Henry Suzzallo Library of the University of Washington, Seattle. Records of the National Parks Service are also important. The historical records in the Mount Rainier National Park headquarters in Longmire tell much of the story of the Mather Memorial Parkway and other activities of Asahel Curtis, while NPS records in the National Archives (Record Group 79) are important for the Depression years, when much cooperative work was done with state parks authorities, and for the records of the National Conference on State Parks, whose records the NPS maintained from the founding of the conference in 1921 until 1949.

Printed materials provide important supplementary materials. Local newspapers have been remarkably constant in their interest in state parks; publications like *Parks & Recreation* (and predecessor journals) also contain useful, but fugitive information. More valuable are mimeographed newsletters of special interest groups, such as *State Recreation,* put out by the National Conference on State Parks; *Natural Parks Bulletin,* put out by the Natural Parks Association of Washington State; and the *Bulletin* of the Willamette River Greenway Association in Oregon. Unfortunately, these are scattered in manuscript collections, but do not seem to exist as separate runs. State agencies have published reports, newsletters, and the like, but with less consistency than one would expect. Valuable studies were done in cooperation with federal agencies during the Depression, but for most periods there is little published by the states that has either breadth or depth. In the end, one must rely overwhelmingly on manuscript sources, newspapers, and reminiscences of principals in order to get the complete story or anything close to it.

Index